Sudan, Civil War and Terrorism, 1956–99

Sudan, Civil War and Terrorism, 1956–99

Edgar O'Ballance

First published in Great Britain 2000 by
MACMILLAN PRESS LTD
Houndmills, Basingstoke, Hampshire RG21 6XS and London
Companies and representatives throughout the world

A catalogue record for this book is available from the British Library.

ISBN 0–333–80147–4

 First published in the United States of America 2000 by
ST. MARTIN'S PRESS, LLC,
Scholarly and Reference Division,
175 Fifth Avenue, New York, N.Y. 10010

ISBN 0–312–23360–4

Library of Congress Cataloging-in-Publication Data
O'Ballance, Edgar.
Sudan, civil war and terrorism, 1956–99 / Edgar O'Ballance.
    p.   cm.
Includes bibliographical references and index.
ISBN 0–312–23360–4 (cloth)
1. Sudan—Politics and government—1956–1985. 2. Sudan—Politics and
government—1985– I. Title.

DT157.3 O2   2000
962.404—dc21
                                                        00–022312

This book is printed on paper suitable for recycling and made from fully managed and sustained forest sources.

10   9   8   7   6   5   4   3   2   1
09   08   07   06   05   04   03   02   01   00

Printed and bound in Great Britain by
Antony Rowe Ltd, Chippenham, Wiltshire

Contents

v

List of Maps

Preface

Until the nineteenth century the country we now know as Sudan, the largest country in Africa, had no political entity or defined frontiers. It is thought that in ancient times the Kingdom of Kush occupied an area on either side of the Nile river between Khartoum and Wadi Halfa, until it was eclipsed in the third century AD by early Christian kingdoms, which were eventually submerged by small Arab migrations, bringing Islam with them. The extreme south of the country reached into unknown Black Africa and was referred to as Bilad al-Sudan, loosely translated as the Land of the Blacks, the mystery of the source of the Nile remaining tantalisingly unsolved until the nineteenth century.

Early that century Mohammed Ali, an Albanian soldier of fortune, was proclaimed Pasha of Egypt, then nominally part of the Ottoman Empire. Mohammed Ali began a military expansion into Sudan in search of fabled riches of gold and ivory, subduing in 1824 the once powerful Funj kingdom at Sennar, a notorious slave market town. Realising there were in fact no riches at the end of the rainbow, he established a fort near the confluence of the White Nile and the Blue Nile. He named the site Khartoum, said to mean 'elephant's trunk', and took over the slave trading monopoly. His troops penetrated southwards, establishing a chain of forts along the riverside. The Congress of Berlin in 1886, which defined the spheres of influence of the colonising European powers in Africa, outlined Sudan's modern boundaries.

The British remember Sudan for its colonial defeats and victory, the death of General Gordon and the sacking of Khartoum (1885), and the Battle of Omdurman (1898), when a small Anglo-Egyptian force, armed with rifles and machine guns, defeated the Mahdi's primitively armed Ansar hordes. The Anglo-Egyptian Condominium followed, with the British in the driving seat, which brought Sudan under its colonial administration. The British practised their 'divide and administer policy', separating the smaller black south, from the larger Muslim north and centre. In the completely undeveloped and neglected black south, Christian missionaries were encouraged to establish schools, convert animists and spread the English language as a barrier against encroaching Arabic-speaking Muslims.

In January 1956 Sudan gained its independence by peaceful means, the British passing on its multiparty system of democratic government, which staggered along briefly under corrupt and changing governments, bluntly neglecting the south and brushing aside its call for federalism. The first census, in 1956, showed the population to be just over ten million, about a quarter of whom lived in the south. There were some 572 tribes and 114 recognised languages. Discontent in the south developed into guerrilla warfare, waged by the Land Freedom Army, known as the Anya-Nya ('snake bite'). The war became known as the 'grass curtain war' because news of it was smothered by censorship, and sometimes as the first civil war. President Numeiry came to power in Khartoum by means of a military coup in 1969. Numeiry, realising the guerrilla war was unwinable – it had already cost some 50 000 lives, no one knows the exact figure – ended it in 1973 by granting autonomy to the South. Peace lasted until 1983, the intervening ten years being a disastrous period of northern neglect and southern mismanagement.

In 1983 Numeiry introduced Sharia law, which included punishment by amputation. That year the second civil war began in the south, this time fought by the Sudan People's Liberation Army (SPLA). The war is still in progress and has probably resulted in some 150 000 deaths, but again no one knows exactly how many. Numeiry was ousted by a bloodless coup in 1985. These followed a brief spell of partial democracy, which ended with a military takeover by General Bashir. The saga of Sudan has been one of continual coups, attempted coups, plots and government quarrels with adjoining countries, to the detriment of national development and ending Sudan's dream of becoming the granary of that part of the world. Meanwhile the ongoing civil war devasted the south, which was also periodically afflicted with drought and famine, its development hindered by SPLA action and blackmail. The unwinnable second civil war has reached a rigid impasse, with peace still unable to break through The government has been involved in terrorist activity, and was placed on the US list of states assisting international terrorism, thus blocking the road to Western respectability.

I first became familiar with Sudan during the Second World War, and I have visited it many times since as a journalist and author, charting its misfortunes. During the course of these visits I travelled widely, including in the south, and interviewed presidents and politicians, army commanders and soldiers, and countless other Sudanese. I admire the patient fortitude of the Sudanese of all classes and tribes, and hope that the new millennium will bring the prosperity, peace and good government they have been denied for so long.

EDGAR O'BALLANCE

Acknowledgements

The information contained in this book was mainly gathered during my visits to Sudan over the years. I attended numerous press conferences and briefings and interviewed several Sudanese leaders and many middlemen, official and unofficial, and countless ordinary people, as well as accumulating sheaves of handouts from many sources. Where material was obtained from other sources, due credit is given in the text.

All comments, deductions and opinions are my own, and at times may differ from the current perceived wisdom.

Map sources are mainly Sudanese government publications and *The Times Atlas*. Copy from the following television and radio broadcasters, periodicals and news agencies was consulted, sometimes in translation.

UK: BBC TV and Radio, Channel Four, ITN, ITV, *Daily Telegraph, Financial Times, Guardian, Middle East, New African, The Sunday Times, The Times,* Reuters.

USA: CBS, CNN, *Africa Watch, International Herald Tribune, News Week, New York Times, Time Magazine, Washington Post, USA Today.*

France: *Le Monde.*

USSR: *Pravda.*

Sudan: Radio Khartoum, Radio Omdurman, Radio SPLA, Radio Sudan, *al-Sahafa, Grass Curtain, Nile Mirror, Vigilant,* SUNA.

Egypt: *Al-Ahram.*

Libya: Radio Tripoli.

Abbreviations

ALF	Azania Liberation Army
ANAF	Anya-Nya Armed Forces
BSO	Black September Organisation
CCI	Compagnie de Construction Internationale
CIA	Central Intelligence Agency (USA)
CUSS	Council for the Unity of South Sudan
DUP	Democratic Unionist Party
FBI	Federal Bureau of Investigation (USA)
GUN	General Union of Nubas
HEC	Higher Executive Council
ICRC	International Committee of the Red Cross
IGADD	Inter-Government Authority on Drought and Development
IMF	International Monetary Fund
LFA	Land Freedom Army
NDF	National Democratic Federation
NIF	National Islamic Front/NTA National Transitional Assembly
NUP	National Unionist Party
OAS	Organisation of African States
OAU	Organisation of African Unity
OPEC	Organisation of Petroleum Exporting Countries
PASH	People's Armed Forces for the Salvation of the Homeland
PDP	People's Democratic Party
RCC	Revolutionary Command Council
SALF	Sudan African Liberation Front
SANU	Sudan-African National Union
SDF	Sudan Defence Force
SHRO	Sudan Human Rights Organisation
SPLA	Sudan People's Liberation Army
SPLM	Sudan People's Liberation Movement
SRRA	Sudan Relief and Rehabilitation Association
SSLM	Southern Sudan Liberation Movement
SSPF	Sudanese People's Socialist Front
SSPG	Southern Sudan Provisional Government
SSU	Sudanese Socialist Union
SUNA	Sudanese News Agency
SUP	Sudan Unity Party

UDP	Unionist Democratic Party
UK	United Kingdom
UN	United Nations
UNESCO	UN Education, Scientific and Cultural Organisation
USSR	Union of the Soviet Socialist Republics

Chronology

1929	Nile Waters Agreement
1936	Graduates' General Congress formed
1943	Ansar and Khatmia sects formed
1951	NUP formed
1955	Torit mutiny
1956	
January	Republic of Sudan established
February	Azhari government formed; the Kosti incident; PDP formed
July	Khalil government formed
August	Beja conference
1957	
December	Federalism for the south abandoned
1958	
November	Abboud military coup
1959	
March	Generals' mutiny
1963	
February	SANU formed
September	Land Freedom Army formed; first Anya-Nya attacks
1964	
January	Failed Wau attack
May	Sudanese troops attack Aba in Congo
September	Commission of Enquiry on the south
October	Khalifa government formed; Southern Front formed; United National Front formed
November	President Abboud resigns; amnesty for overseas southerners; first SANU convention; Battle of the Streets (Khartoum)
December	Council of Sovereignty formed
1965	
February	More street battles in Khartoum
March	Round-table conference
July	Mahgoub government; Juba and Wau incidents
September	Bishops of Wau and Rumbek killed

October	Rebel attack on Takfika, houseboat burned (*Abu Anga*)
November	Communist Party suppressed
1966	
February	Anya-Nya changes tactics and becomes friendly to the people
April	Peace Villages established
May	Government offensive in south
July	Sadik Mahdi to be premier
September	Round-table report
December	Communist Party appeal fails; Osman coup
1967	
January	Socialist Party formed
April	Elections in the south
November	Khartoum riots
December	UDP formed (merger of Umma, NUP and UPD)
1968	
January	Amnesty offered to south – rejected
April	Elections in south
August	SSPG formed; Southern Freedom Front formed
1969	
March	SSPG becomes the Nile Provisional Government
May	Numeiry to power
June	June Declaration on southern autonomy
September	Anyidi Revolutionary Government formed (Tafeng); Sue River Revolutionary Government formed (Tawili); Sudan-Azania Government formed (Izbone Mendiri)
October	ANAF High Command Council formed
November	Numeiry's offensives in south begin
1970	
March	Aba incident
April	Death of Imam Mahdi
May	First Soviet aircraft arrive
1971	
May	SSU formed; secret negotiations begin
June	ANAF High Command Council meeting
July	Atta attempts coup
August	Lagu forms the SSLM
September	Steiner trial; elections begin
October	Numeiri becomes executive president
December	Major government offensive

1972
January	Last ANAF attacks
February	Autonomy agreement
March	Ceasefire
August	Autonomy ratified; People's Council for the South

1973
January	The Shenan conspiracy
March	BSO attack on Saudi embassy
May	Sudan becomes one-party state; southern autonomy confirmed
October	Fourth Arab–Israeli War
November	People's Assembly for the South
December	Abel Alier becomes president of the Southern Regional Assembly

1974
February	Lagu becomes inspector general

1975
March	The Akabo mutiny

1975
September	The Osman rebellion

1976
February	Army units desert at Wau
July	Libyan-backed revolution; Sudan–Egypt defence agreement

1977
February	Southern Air Force mutiny at Juba
April	Numeiry expels the Soviets

1978
April	National reconciliation agreement

1979
August	Student riots in Khartoum

1980
January	Numeiry's decentralisation plan

1981
October	National People's Assembly dissolved

1982
January	Death of el-Hindi
October	Charter of Integration (Sudan–Egypt)

1983
February	Appearance of the SPLM, SPLA and Anya-Nya-2
September	Introduction of Sharia law

1984
March	Air raid on Omdurman
October	Operation Moses begins

1985
March	Cease fire in the south – Peace Committee formed; general strike; army assumes power, Numeiry deposed; state of emergency declared
May	Decisive Justice Courts abolished
July	Sudan–Libya defence agreement
September	SPLA campaign against Bor and Nasir

1985
September	Mutiny and attempted coup
December	The name 'The Republic of Sudan' restored

1986
April	General election
May	The Sadik Mahdi government; the Koka Dam Declaration
June	The battle for Juba
September	SPLA shoot down a passenger aircraft
December	SPLA successes in battle

1987
January	Transitional Administrative Council
March	SPLA offensive
August	Transitional Charter
September	Anya-Nya-2 splits

1988
January	Emergency airlift of food to Juba
May	Government of National Unity
September	Drought replaced by floods; famine scare subsides

1989
May	SPLA declares ceasefire
June	Bloodless military coup brings General Bashir to power; Revolutionary Command Council established
July	Bashir forms a government
December	SPLA talks with the government

1990
April	Attempted military coup (the first of several)
August	Gulf crisis begins

1991
February	Sudan divided into nine states
August	SPLA splits into Torit and Nasir groups
November	Clashes between the Torit and Nasir groups

1992

January	National Transition Assembly formed
February	Economic Salvation programme
April	Successful government offensive in the south
May	The Abuja talks
September	Fighting between Torit and Nasir factions

1993

March	Government–SPLA ceasefire
April	SPLA-United formed
May	Ceasefire between SPLA-United and Torit faction
August	GHQ offensive against the Torit faction; Sudan placed on the list of states supporting international terrorism
October	Revolutionary Command Council dissolved; Bashir becomes president and head of state
November	Civil unrest due to fuel shortage

1994

January	IGADD talks begin
February	Sudan redivided into 26 states
August	Carlos the Jackal (terrorist) handed over to France

1995

January	Bashir calls for a jihad against the SPLA
March	SPLA cooperates with the NDA; SSIM congress in London; Uganda threatens Sudan
June	Opposition conference in Eritrea; attempt to assassinate Egyptian president
November	General mobilisation in Sudan

1996

January	UN resolution condemns Sudan for terrorism
March	General election (non-party)
April	A peace charter
June	Osama Bin Laden leaves Sudan
September	Bread riots in Khartoum

1997

January	Upsurge in fighting in the south
April	Fighting in the east; new chapter of cooperation
June	NDA terrorism
October	IGADD-sponsored negotiations
December	US secretary of state meets NDA and SPLA

1998

June	New constitution
August	US cruise missile attack on Khartoum

1999
  January   Multiparty system restored
  May   Ex-President Numeiry returns from exile

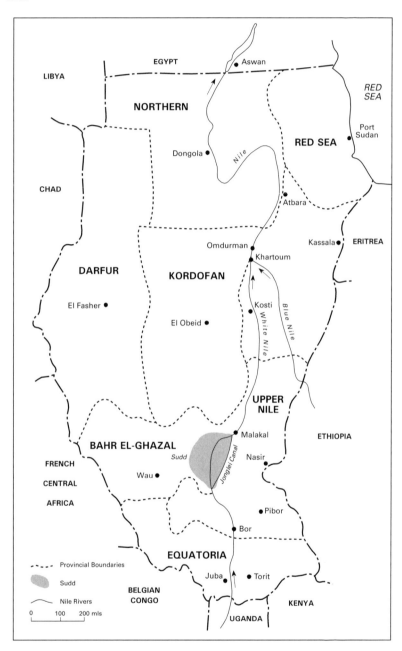

1 Sudan, 1956

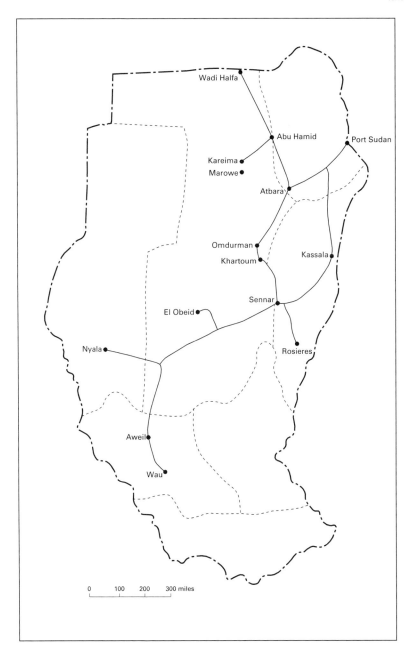

2 Sudan railways, 1956

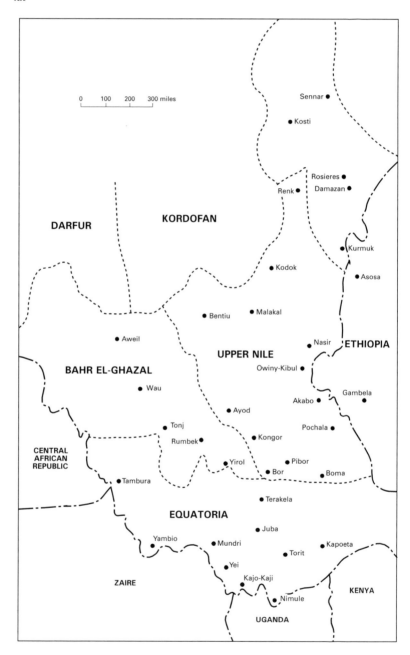

3 South-east Sudan, combat area, 1983–99

1
Independence

On 1 January 1956 the independent sovereign Republic of Sudan came into being upon the replacement of the colonial office of governor-general by a five-man Supreme Commission, consisting of four northern Sudanese and one southerner (Siricio Iro, who represented southern Sudan) and led by Ahmad Yasin, speaker of the Senate. Parades and other ceremonies were held to mark the occasion, and the new flag of Sudan was unfurled for the first time – a horizontal tricolour of blue to symbolise the two Nile rivers, yellow the deserts and green for agriculture. It was a joyous but dignified and low-key celebration compared with others I later witnessed in other parts of Africa. There was little rancour, except perhaps from Egypt, which had hoped to turn the Anglo-Egyptian Condominium (established in 1898) into an Egyptian dominion. However Egypt's wishes had been pushed aside by the USA and Britain, which already thought that Gamal Abdul Nasser, who had come to power in Egypt in November 1954, was getting too big for his boots. Sovereign recognition was immediately afforded by Britain, the USA and half a dozen other countries. Within days Sudan was granted membership of the United Nations and the Arab League.

There was only peripheral interest by the world at large in the fate of Sudan as it was remote to most countries and very remote to others, and had only been a bit player in recent international events. In Europe, where the Cold War was developing, Sudan tended to be seen as lacking strategical value, being undeveloped and seemingly poor in resources. However it was not completely overlooked as Western European countries and the Soviet Union sought to gain influence over the new state, and to prevent each other from doing so. The USSR looked on Sudan as its gateway to Africa proper, to where it was trying to export communism, while colonial powers such as Belgium, Britain and France hoped that Sudan would keep its gates firmly shut against the Soviets. The Arab League saw Sudan as the extensive eastern defensive bastion of the Arabic-speaking bloc, now involved in confrontation with Israel, the latter strongly supported by the USA. None wanted any of the others to gain paramount advantage over Sudan.

Sudan, now the largest independent state in Africa (over 2 506 000 square kilometers), had only a tiny population. The first ever census, taken in 1956, showed there to be 10 252 536 inhabitants, of whom 7 469 400 lived in the north and 2 783 136 in the south. Some 70 per cent of the people were 'Arabised northerners' and the other 30 per cent were primitive tribal southerners. There were 572 different tribes and 114 different languages, of which about 50 per cent were spoken in the south, an area of some 500 000 square kilometers.

The terrain varied from vast deserts in the north to savannah, scrub and hill tracts in the centre, to tropical forests and swamps in the deep south, while the Nile rivers made indelible lines on the map, flowing northwards into Egypt. Communications were extremely sparce. There were over 3000 miles of railway track, parts of which were remnants of Cecil Rhodes' dream of a Cape-to-Cairo trans-African railway. Roads ran between towns and development schemes, but not all were passable in bad weather and some were barely motorable at the best of times. Only parts of the Nile rivers were navigable, with cataracts blocking through traffic. There were only two towns of any size: Khartoum, the capital, set in a desert and with a population of about 87 000 people, and Omdurman, situated near the confluence of the White and Blue Niles and home to some 130 000 people. Sudan was barely developed economically, its principal exports being cotton and groundnuts. Sorghum (Indian millet, also known as dura) was grown widely as the people's staple food. Wherever the terrain allowed, tribal peoples, both settled and nomadic, maintained herds of livestock: cattle, sheep, goats, camels and horses.

Strategic position

Of the countries surrounding Sudan, some were independent and others were still under colonial tutelage. Most had predatory thoughts about parts of the newly independent republic as the national boundaries, which had been established in the nineteenth century by the European colonisers for their own convenience, often cut thoughtlessly and at times deliberately through tribal confederations or natural boundary features.

Sudan was bounded on the north by Egypt, which had shared the Condominium with Britain. Indeed in 1950 Farouk of Egypt had declared himself King of Sudan, a claim continued by Gamal Abdul Nasser when he had come to power in November 1954. Although deeply involved in the Arab–Israeli confrontation, Nasser had been scheming to make Sudan Egypt's own dominion when the British left. Nasser was not taking his failure too well, and was also involved in arguments with the Khartoum government over the division of the Nile waters.

To the east, Sudan was bounded by the Red Sea, with ports at Port Sudan and Suakin, providing maritime access to the world, and by Ethiopia, an ancient kingdom, briefly colonised for the first time by Italy just prior to the Second World War. Independence had been restored by the Allies after the war and Ethiopia was ruled despotically by Emperor Haile Selassie, who managed to retain his throne until 1974. In the south, Sudan was flanked by Kenya and Uganda, both under British colonial rule but with aspirations of independence, and the Belgian Congo, where thoughts of independence were not permitted. To the west lay a huge expanse of French colonial territory and the independent Kingdom of Libya, put together by the Allies after the Second World War and headed by King Idris. In short, Sudan was surrounded by instability.

Prior to independence British officials had established a colonial administration, based in Khartoum. Egyptians were supposed to be equally represented in the administration, but there was no doubt that the British had been in the driving seat. Sudan had been divided into six provinces: Northern Province, Darfur and Kordofan in the north, with the Blue Nile (formally Fashoda) and Kassala as sub-provinces; and Bahr el-Ghazal, Equatoria and Upper Nile in the south. Each of the provinces had been administered by a colonial governor with considerable local powers.

The Nile waters

The waters of the Nile rivers were of vital importance to life and agricultural development in Sudan and Egypt, and without them much of both countries would have been barren waste. Egypt's traditional fear was that the Nile waters might be diverted or reduced by the Sudanese. Small dams and irrigation devices began to appear in Sudan (and indeed in Egypt) as the country began to develop its agriculture potential and ever-increasing amounts of water were required. The purpose of the Nile Waters Agreement of 1929 was to allocate the Nile waters equitably between the two countries, according to their declared needs, but there were continual arguments, and accusations that one or the other was taking too much water. In August 1955 negotiations commenced in Cairo to settle the dispute. Sudan wanted Egypt's agreement to construct a small storage dam on the Blue Nile at Rosieres, near the Ethiopian border, which would increase Sudan's water supply by some 75 per cent; while Egypt wanted to construct a major dam above Aswan, adjacent to the Sudanese border and designed to increase Egypt's irrigated land area by about one third. This would also mean flooding large riverside areas in Sudan for about 100 miles upstream, which would render some 50 000 Sudanese homeless. Sudan would not agree, deadlock set in and international arbitration was sought. The problem remained unresolved for the moment, adding to Sudanese–Egyptian hostility.

Multiparty democracy

On 2 February 1956 an all-party government took office, led by Prime Minister Ismail al-Azhari, who also took on the interior portfolio. The British administration had encouraged the Sudanese to adopt a multiparty form of government in preparation for independence, and an interim government with limited powers had appeared in 1953, as had a wild tangle of political parties, the leaders of which were already bedevilling the country with their rivalry and quarrels. In the Muslim north, multiparty politics had really begun in the modern sense of that expressed in February 1938 with the formation of the Graduates' General Congress, a student political body. The congress had split in 1943, giving rise to two rival political – religious sects, the Ansar and Khatmia. Ismail al-Azhari had formed his Khatmia followers into the Ashikka (Islamic Brotherhood), whose motto was the Unity of the Nile Valley, and Abdullah Khalil had formed his Ansar supporters into the Umma Party (Community of the Faithful).

Political enlightenment had barely touched the neglected black south, but in view of the approaching self-determination of the country, a conference had been held in Juba in 1947 to promote fusion between northerners and southerners. This first ever attempt to sound out southern opinion had been a failure, mainly because southerners had been told that Arabic would become the sole national language. When an elected National Assembly had opened on 15 December 1948, consisting of 88 members, only 13 had been southerners.

In 1951 the Ashikka Party had split briefly over the issue of approaching self-determination, but the rift had soon been healed and the party had been renamed the National Unionist Party (NUP), still led by al-Azhari. In the same year the first southern political party had been formed by Buth Diu (a Nuer), Stanislaus Paysama (a Dinka) and Abdul Rahman (a Muslim), all southern politicians. The parties had eventually become known as the Southern Party. Other political parties had been formed, mostly in the Muslim north.

The interim government

In the elections for the new House of Representatives, which opened on 1 January 1954, the NUP gained 51 out of 97 seats and Ismail al-Azhari became interim prime minister. The Southern Party won only 12 out of the 26 seats allocated to the south, its leader, Stanislaus Paysama, blaming the poor showing of his party on the high rate of illiteracy and ignorance of democratic politics in the south, plus a deep suspicion of the Muslim north.

Ismail al-Azhari had been a regular officer in the Sudan Defence Force (SDF), reaching the rank of brigadier, and while his capability and efficiency could not be doubted, his manner was abrupt and he tended to remove personalities who disagreed with him, or even questioned his decisions. This was especially so within the NUP, but he also alienated members of his supporting Khatmia sect.

During the summer of 1955, relations between the Sudanese interim government and Egypt deteriorated, due to al-Azhari's increasing emphasis on independence and the Nile Waters dispute. The Egyptian press accused al-Azhari of waging a reign of terror in southern Sudan, where political opinion favoured federalism rather than a unitary state.

On 19 December 1955 al-Azhari's interim government approved four resolutions, which it was empowered to do under the interim agreement. The resolutions were (1) to declare Sudan as a sovereign independent republic; (2) to elect a Constituent Assembly; (3) to elect a five-man Supreme Council with head of state powers; and (4) to form a commission to consider the southern demand for a federal constitution. Al-Azhari only agreed to the latter resolution to gain southern voting support in the House of Representatives and as a sop to restless southerners – he had little intention of putting it into effect. He announced that the 'Sudanisation' of the administration and the armed forces had been completed, that all foreign (meaning British and Egyptian) armed forces had left the country, and that all was ready for independence to be declared on 1 January 1956.

The Kosti incident

The al-Azhari government had been in place in newly independent Sudan for just a fortnight when it was faced with the Kosti incident, which caused condemnatory headlines in the international press. In mid February demonstrations were launched by about 700 of the some 1000 tenant farmers participating in the Guda Agricultural Scheme in Kosti in the Blue Nile subprovince (about 200 miles south of Khartoum). The scheme was of several cotton-growing projects and the farmers were demanding an increase in their share of the profits, proper auditing of accounts and a say in management and sales policy. They refused to pick any more cotton until their demands were met. The strike and demonstrations continued, resulting in a major clash with the police on 18 February. Casualties were suffered by both sides. The police began to arrest the strikers, and on the 21st, 281 of them were locked in a cramped, unventilated room in a military cantonment. The next morning 192 of them were found to be dead, mostly from heatstroke and suffocation. Protest demonstrations were held in Khartoum, and the Sudanese press vociferously demanded the resignation of the al-Azhari government. An enquiry was held, but al-Azhari weathered the storm.

Defence

Under the Anglo-Egyptian Condominium the defence of Sudan had been entrusted to the Sudan Defence Force, a British-trained and originally British-officered colonial military force with a strength of about 5000, bolstered by British military detachments. By the early 1950s the SDF had been split into four separate regional military corps: the Eastern Arab Corps, the Central Arab Corps, the Western Arab Corps and the Equatoria Corps. All but the latter consisted entirely of Muslim soldiers, recruited from northern and central Sudan, while the Equatoria Corps was composed of non-Muslims from southern Sudan. Southerners had not been recruited into the SDF prior to 1910. As the Sudan Military College was producing over 60 graduate officers a year the Sudanisation of the army had been effected fairly quickly, but practically all senior and middle grade officers were Muslim, as indeed were the majority of the junior ones.

The Sudan Defence Force was in effect little more than a colonial gendarmerie. Its tiny complement had to keep order over a huge expanse of territory and patrol some 2500 miles of frontier, where cross-border tribal raids and cattle stealing had replaced slave raiding. Periodic tribal risings had to be dealt with, and intertribal quarrels sometimes had to be settled by force. The SDF was poorly equipped – apart from outdated British infantry weapons, its few guns and armoured vehicles were leftovers from the Second World War. Being extremely short of transport, it made much of its picturesque camel patrols. Soldiers were normally recruited on short-service engagements that could be extended. Military service was popular, so there was no recruitment problem.

The Torit mutiny

During the electioneering period prior to independence, several northern politicians made rash statements about what they would do when they gained power, including bringing the south more tightly into the proposed republic, which alarmed southerners. Also, the rapid pace of Sudanisation began to alarm the Equatoria Corps as more nothern officers were posted to it. A parallel process was taking place in the southern administration and the territorially based police service, which was adversely affecting morale. A great deal of publicity was give to a letter allegedly signed by Ismail al-Azhari urging his northern administrators to oppress and ill-treat southerners generally, prompting several protest demonstrations and strikes. A southern member of the House of Representatives was imprisoned after a dubious trial, which led to demonstrations in Nazra in Equatoria Province. In addition strikes broke out when northerners were taken on as employees at the Azande Development Scheme, displacing southerners. Discontent became manifest in the south.

The administrators in Khartoum decided to send detachments of northern troops to Juba in Equatoria Province, where two military clerks had been arrested and charged with conspiracy to mutiny. The subsequent arrival of some 500 troops at the only airstrip in the south caused considerable local apprehension. Somewhat unusually, it was decided in Khartoum that detachments from the Equatoria Corps should be sent to serve in northern Sudan, where there was also some unrest. On 18 August 1955 an Equatoria Corps company, based at Torit (the Corps HQ) was duly ordered to move to Khartoum, but the soldiers were reluctant to leave their families. A mutiny developed, allegedly led by Lieutenant Reynaldo Loyela. Armouries were broken into, soldiers went on the rampage and sympathetic mutinies broke out at Yei, Yambio and Maridi, all military posts in Equatoria.

Concurrently with the outbreak of the mutinies, thousands of tribesmen, in an apparently preplanned manoeuvre, attacked government buildings, northern military officers, officials, traders and their wives and children. At Torit all northerners were shot, apart from a few who took refuge in a Christian mission. For three days mutineers and rampaging tribesmen ran riot over a large part of Equatoria Province, one exception being Juba, which now had a part-northern garrison. In this frenzy of violence over 450 people, including women and children, were murdered and countless others injured, while thousands fled into the bush and forests as law and order collapsed. Some mutineers on their way to Torit, the centre of the mutiny, took a shortcut through Ugandan territory, where they were disarmed and interned by the Ugandan authorities

A state of emergency was declared, and British military transport aircraft were borrowed to airlift detachments of northern soldiers to deal with the mutines and restore order. This took some time as the majority of the 400 or so police officers in the province had joined the mutineers. Some mutineers fled into the forests, and even into adjacent Uganda, while others were persuaded to surrender by the British governor-general, Sir Knox Helm, who promised them a fair trial, clemency and safe conduct. But as he left Sudan on 13 December 1955, his post having been abolished, he was unable to keep his promises. On 3 November it was officially announced that 959 mutineers had either given themselves up or been apprehended (leaving about 360 still at large), and that over 3000 southerners had fled into Uganda.

The mutineers were tried by courts martial and civilian offenders by special courts (*Manchester Guardian*). Over 180 death sentences were passed and most were subsequently carried out. Included among those executed was Lieutenant Reynaldo Loyela, the alleged leader of the mutiny. Government figures became vague and contradictory. The mutiny and uprising had been confined to Equatoria Province (about 28 per cent of the southern region). The garrison at Wau (the capital of Bahr el-Ghazal Province), for example, had resisted calls to join in the mutiny, as had the garrisons in Upper Nile Province.

The special commission of enquiry appointed to determine the causes of the mutiny identified some of the reasons for its outbreak, and for the general discontent in the south. It confirmed that the mutiny had begun in Torit after southern troops had been ordered to move to the north – rumours were spreading that northerners were murdering southerners. Other suggested causes were the separatist policy of southern members of the interim House of Representatives, missionary allegations of Muslim hostility towards southerners, false hopes of military advancement by southern soldiers fanned by southern politicians who were hoping there might eventually be a separate southern army, and subversive propaganda by the Egyptian government.

Apparently, in July 1955 northern administrators in the south, had asked for additional northern troops to be rushed to Equatoria Province, indicating that the Equatoria Corps and the provincial police were ripe for mutiny, but there had been little positive reaction. Documents discovered several days before the mutiny had revealed the existence of a secret organisation, headed by a local tribal chief and a serving government official, but this had been ignored.

During the first days of September, SDF units reoccupied all the garrison posts in the south without resistance, but it was not until the end of the year that normal civil order was restored in the province. The Equatoria Corps was disbanded and a temporary ban was placed on the recruitment of southerners, but this was soon lifted as the new Sudanese Army began to expand. The newly recruited southerners had to serve in Arab Muslim units, which began to be posted to the south on a rotation basis. The only two secondary schools in the south, at Juba and Rumbek, were moved to the north.

The Sudanese Army

Upon independence the SDF was immediately renamed the Sudanese Army, and General Ibrahim Abboud, a long-serving regular officer, was appointed as its commander-in-chief, with Brigadier Ahmad Abdul Wahab as his deputy. Former corps areas became military districts, commanded by recently promoted northern officers. A start was made on increasing the strength of the army, obtaining modern arms and equipment and developing a tiny air force and a coastal naval element, but there were political difficulties, the main one being a shortage of military funding. It was true that the postwar cotton boom had brought large profits to Sudan, but much of the money received had been wisely spent on agricultural, irrigation and other development projects. The majority of these were in the north, the main one in the south being the Azande Development Scheme. Defence had a low priority.

The southern issue

Prime Minister al-Azhari's original independence government contained two southern ministers, Bullen Alier and Buth Diu, but both were soon dismissed for disagreeing with his southern policy. However southern members of the (now) National Assembly continued to support him in the hope that the constitutional committee, established in accordance with the December resolution, to examine the 'federal solution', would eventually reach a favourable conclusion. Meanwhile southern members continually complained that the south was being neglected and that funds for the Azande Development Scheme had been reduced. They continued to call for a plebiscite on the federal issue, but al-Azhari brushed this aside.

Change of government

On 26 June 1956 the People's Democratic Party (PDP) was formed in the National Assembly by Khatmia members who had broken away from the NUP after disagreements with al-Azhari, and also because a split had occurred in the party between those who favoured complete Sudanese independence and those who wanted closer links with Egypt. Twenty-one NUP National Assembly members switched allegiance to the new PDP, which was led by Murghani Hamza. On 4 July al-Azhari lost a vote of confidence in the National Assembly when the Umma Party and the new PDP voted against him, defeating his governing coalition. The following day Abdullah Khalil, leader of the Umma Party, became premier, forming a temporary coalition with the PDP. Khalil's Umma Party stood for 'positive neutrality', and he fended off attempts by the Soviet Union and the USA to gain influence in Sudan.

Premier Khalil refused a Soviet offer to take the unsold portion of the Sudanese cotton crop in exchange for Soviet arms, saying that he wanted agricultural machinery, not tanks. Nor would he allow the Soviets to stage an 'Atoms for Peace' exhibition in Khartoum. He also rejected proffered US aid under the Eisenhower doctrine, but later did accept some American technical assistance. Checks were made on every single US officer, government official and others who arrived in connection with this assistance to ascertain their political views and political connections, if any.

Southern National Assembly members had voted for Premier al-Azhari because they had been promised 'full consideration', which they had hoped would lead to federal status. They had demanded a referendum on this issue under UN auspices, but each time the question had been raised in the National Assembly they had been outvoted. They had continually complained that the south was being neglected, and that funding for the Azande Development Scheme had been being cut. When Premier Khalil came to power it turned out that he too had little time for federalism, and his administration continued to oppress the south.

In 1957 the Southern Federal Party, was formed by Izbone Mendiri, a southern member of the National Assembly. Mendiri declared that the new party would vote against the NUP, and that objectives were federalism for the south, an independent southern army, a separate southern economic development programme, and that English and Christianity be accorded equal recognition to Arabic and Islam. Eventually, in December, Khalil announced that the constitutional committee had given the southern claim for federal status very serious consideration, but had found that it would not work in Sudan and hence the issue would be dropped. This was a severe blow to all southerners, and turned the minds of some of their leaders to armed resistance.

Suspended government

The National Assembly was dissolved on 30 June 1957 to prepare for a general election, which was not held until February the following year. The ostensible reason for the dissolution was the dispute between the two main parties over how much cooperation there should be with Egypt, if any, but there were several other controversial issues at stake, and political leaders were now openly quarrelling with each other, with little semblance of dignity. The southern problem was hardly mentioned, although two southern members, Saturnino Lohure and Elia Lupe of the Southern Federal Party, openly campaigned for complete autonomy in the south. In the election the Umma Party gained 83 seats, the NUP 45, the PDP 27 and the southern bloc 37. Khalil remained premier, but adjourned the National Assembly until 17 November 1958. It had become not so much a case of bad government, but rather government by neglect, as ministers and members of the National Assembly became involved in corruption and other self-seeking pursuits. Personality clashes developed, with senior government officials often taking their lead from their masters in this respect.

The October crisis

Events reached crisis point in October after a politically tempestuous summer. Ismail al-Azhari, still leader of the NUP, wanted closer links with Egypt and criticised Khalil for accepting British military aid, holding back too much Nile water and aligning Sudan too closely with the West. The PDP was about to leave the coalition because one section of the Umma Party wanted to establish Sudan as an Islamic kingdom, with Abdul Rahman Mahdi as king. The cotton crop had been poor and there was difficulty selling it, and consequently there was a fall in the country's foreign exchange reserves. Khalil and al-Azhari were now deadly rivals, but both wanted to change the British legacy of multiparty democracy for a presidential form of government on the US model, each being ambitious to be the first executive president of Sudan. However they were beaten by events.

A military coup

On 17 November 1958 the Sudanese army, under the command of General Ibrahim Abboud, overthrew Khalil's government, dissolved the National Assembly and all political parties, and suspended the constitution. Very early in the morning armoured vehicles ringed Khartoum, troops occupied the airport (which had become increasingly important in reducing Sudan's remoteness), the radio station, the telephone exchange and government buildings, and soldiers were posted outside foreign embassies. Otherwise daily life in the capital seemed to continue as normal. The coup had been a complete surprise. Prime Minister Khalil and his ministers were woken early and given letters dismissing them from their posts. A dawn radio announcement told the people that the army had seized power in order to end political corruption and chaos. A state of emergency was declared, the Supreme Council, which had head of state powers, was dismissed and replaced by the Supreme Council of the Armed Forces, headed by General Abboud.

On 18 November at a press conference, General Abboud explained that the time was not yet ripe for Western-style democracy, that he did not want to hold power for long and that democracy would be restored within six to twelve months. There was to be no press censorship, but the media were told that they were expected not to criticise the new regime's policies. Only a few members of the Anti-Imperialist Front and the Trade Union Federation, both of which were regarded as communist motivated, were detained, but there were no other arrests and no subsequent political trials. Former ministers and National Assembly members were forbidden to enter government buildings, and the state of emergency conditions prevented demonstrations on the streets. In all respects it seemed to be a classic bloodless military coup.

Both Abdul Rahman Mahdi, leader of the Ansar sect, and Ali Murghani, leader of the Khatmia sect, expressed their approval. A government was formed on the 18th, headed by General Abboud and consisting of seven military officers and five civilians, all non-party men. The only southerner was Santino Deng, who had been a junior minister in the Khalil government. Abboud assumed the role of premier, with defence responsibilities, and his deputy commander-in-chief, Brigadier Ahmad Abdul Wahab, became minister of the interior and local government. Sudan had swung overnight from chaotic democracy to military dictatorship. The new regime was quickly recognised by foreign powers. On 30 November a huge barter deal was negotiated with communist bloc countries for Sudan's cotton crop, but the military government remained friendly with Western powers, obtaining aid, loans and credits from the USA, Britain and West Germany.

Ibrahim Abboud, aged 58, had been born in the Red Sea territory of the Hadendowa tribe, and had studied engineering at Gordon College, Khartoum, before entering the Sudan Military College to become a career officer in the Sudan Defence Force. During the Second World War he had served in Eritrea, Ethiopia and Libya with the Sudanese contingent of the British Army. He had been appointed deputy commander of the SDF in 1954 and commander-in-chief of the Sudanese Army in 1956. Brigadier Wahab, aged 43, had joined the SDF in 1938 and had also served in Eritrea. Neither had been involved in politics before the coup.

Ahmad Kheir, Abboud's minister of foreign affairs, outlined the country's foreign policy on 30 November. Among other things Sudan would support the right to self-determination of countries struggling for their liberty (meaning colonial territories still fighting for independence, mention being given to Algeria, Cyprus and the Cameroons); avoid military alliances that might endanger peace; combat all forms of racial discrimination (particularly relevant, owing to its own problems in the black south); support the use of atomic energy solely for peaceful purposes; oppose nuclear tests and the arms race; and seek close relations with both Arab and African countries, especially Egypt and Ethiopia. However it was suspected that much of this was purely for international consumption.

The generals' mutiny

On 2 March 1959, Brigadier Abdul Rahman Shenan of the Northern Command, supported by Brigadier Mohieddin Ahmad Abdullah of the Eastern Command, sent two companies of soldiers to the GHQ in Khartoum to present their demands to the Supreme Council of the Armed Forces. Shenan and Abdullah objected that the Supreme Council's policy was too pro-Western and demanded the dismissal of Brigadier Wahab, who was regarded as the 'strong man' of the Council. There had been some discontent amongst senior officers over the division of spoils after the coup, and the two brigadiers had been omitted from Abboud's military government. Abboud agreed to talk, and the soldiers were withdrawn from the capital.

As nothing seemed to be happening at GHQ, before dawn on 4 March Brigadier Shenan, with a battalion of his own troops and supported by a company of soldiers from Eastern Command, entered Khartoum, cordoned off the GHQ complex occupied certain key points and demanded to see Abboud. The latter assembled his senior officers immediately and the following day announced the appointment of a new Supreme Council. Some military members of the old Council had been excluded and new ones appointed in their place, including Shenan and Abdullah, both of whom also became ministers. General Abboud survived this military power struggle, stating that these top-level military changes were due to differences of opinion amongst senior officers over purely internal matters. General Wahab was included in the new Council, but was dismissed from it a few days later due to new pressures.

General Abboud then quietly set about gathering personal support, which culminated on 1 June with his announcement that certain officers, including Brigadiers Shenan and Abdullah, had been arrested and charged with inciting mutiny and conspiring with others to launch an armed attack on Khartoum with the aim of overthrowing the regime. A series of courts martial were held that were open to the public and broadcast in full on the public radio service. The verdicts and sentences, after their approval by General Abboud, were announced on 22 September. Six senior officers, including Shenan and Abdullah, were condemned to death, but their sentences were subsequently commuted to life imprisonment. The twenty other defendants were awarded terms of imprisonment or dismissed from the army, or both.

This caused a considerable upheaval in the armed forces, but it enabled General Abboud to promote his own men to senior positions. However the situation took some time to settle down and there continued to be occasional rumblings of discontent. One example occurred on 9 November, when an unsuccessful attempt was made to mount a coup at the School of Infantry in Omdurman, led by Lieutenant Ali Hamid. Hamid and four others were later found guilty and sentenced to death by hanging (instead of being shot, as was the military custom), it being said at the time that the military authorities could not be sure that members of the execution squads would obey the order to fire. Others found guilty were sentenced to terms of imprisonment and/or were dismissed from the army.

2
The Rejected South

Premier Khalil's rejection in December 1957 of the possibility of Sudan becoming a federal state had been a deep disappointment to southern politicians, and General Abboud's sweeping aside of all political parties and multiparty activities was an even deeper one. There was only one southern minister in the cabinet: Santino Deng, minister of animal resources. President Abboud (he soon assumed the style and dignity of that office) refused to believe there was a southern constitutional problem, and as a soldier was probably influenced by the Torit mutinies, having a traditional military prejudice against mutineers and referring to those still at large as 'outlaws'. He was convinced that they were being sheltered by southern tribes and his army carried out ruthless and brutal searches. For example in 1957, in the Yei district, soldiers blew up more than 700 village huts as a punishment for sheltering 'rebels'. At this stage the people of the south were as afraid of the rebels – who had probably forced the villagers at gunpoint to give them food and shelter – as they were of the harsh tactics of the army. They just wanted to get on with their normal lives and be left alone.

The missionary problem

President Abboud blamed Christian missionaries for trouble-making in the south. He suspected them of helping the rebels and actively opposing the government's integration policy. For their part the missionaries saw themselves as stemming the advancing tide of Islam, and protecting their flocks. In fact they had some cause to be wary as Sadik Mahdi (who had succeeded his father as leader of the Umma Party) had rejected the use of force in the south and suggested that the spread of Islam would solve the problem.

There were about a quarter of a million black Christians in the south. According to some there were about 200 000 Roman Catholics and 39 000 other Christian sects, although missionary organisations, who ran the elementary schools, liked to give the impression that there were double that number.

The Khartoum government moved against the missionaries and in 1947 all schools in the south were nationalised. Private schools which included those of the missionaries, were prohibited. In 1960 the Sunday Sabbath holiday was abolished in favour of the Muslim Friday. President Abboud was encouraged to pursue his campaign against Christian missionaries because many southern Sudanese refugees, especially those in Uganda to the south, were being supported by the Sudanese Christian Association, which was backed by several international Christian groups. From May 1962 foreign missionaries were required to obtain a resident's licence from the government and were forbidden to proselytise. In 1964 all Christian schools were finally closed down in the south.

A 'grass curtain' descends

President Abboud's abolition of all political parties came as another hard blow to southern politicians as it deprived them of a political platform and thus rendered them mute. Southern periodicals also disappeared, and little if anything of events in the south appeared in the national media. Although Abboud boasted that the press was not censored, this was only partly true. Southern political views, or indeed any reports of events in the south, such as military depredations and the harsh treatment of tribal peoples, did not appear in the Sudanese media. In this respect a blanket of silence or grass curtain descended on the south.

Southern politicians returned to the south empty-handed, but most remained in the open and on occasion a few individuals were arrested for alleged political activity. Meanwhile southern administrators and officials were squeezed out or withdrew from their jobs. In early December 1960 it was discovered that the government was planning to mount an operation on Christmas Day to arrest and detain them all, the intention being to 'behead' any developing southern political movements. Forewarned, many southern leaders went underground and then slipped away into exile, thus starting what became a large-scale exodus to adjacent states: the Central African Republic (which had become independent in August 1960), Ethiopia, Kenya and Uganda (the latter two still being under British colonial administration).

Some southern political leaders began to attract followers who were disillusioned and dissatisfied by the political suppression in the south. Furthermore a number of southern tribes wanted greater autonomy. This had found early expression at the Beja Conference in August 1956, when powerful confederations such as the Fur, the Funji and the Nuba tribes had insisted that Premier Khalil visit them for discussions. The idea had spread to other tribes who wanted to manage their own affairs, but the Khartoum government had taken little interest in the idea, which had been quickly forgotten when the Abboud government had come on the scene. The political seeds of independence had been sown, but it was not until 1960 that southern politicians began to turn to black African resistance groups across the border for sanctuary, sympathy and encouragement to strive for the right to manage their own southern affairs.

The formation of SANU

In February 1962 in Kinshasa (known until 1960 as Leopoldville, capital of the Congo) a group of southern leaders in exile formed a shadowy organisation called the Sudan-African Closed Districts National Union and revolutionary personalities began to appear on the scene to give political direction to the course of southern opposition. Joseph Oduhu became its first president, Marko Rume its vice president, William Deng its secretary general and Aggrey Jaden its assistant secretary general. It tended to be top heavy in titles and dominant personalities. Perhaps the real leader was Saturnino Lohure, who assumed the title of patron. The following year, after his release from detention, Dominic Muerwal replaced Marko Rume as vice president. The principle aim of this organisation was to obtain complete independence for the south, to be achieved by diplomatic and peaceful means. Oduhu publicly disclaimed the use of force or any connection with the 'armed rebels' lurking in the forests. This organisation provided information to the international media and sent petitions to the UN and the OAU, urging them to support its struggle against the Khartoum government, but neither organisation responded. The outside world did not want to know about the troubles in black Africa, which had entered its 'winds of change' phase.

In 1963 the organisation changed its name to the Sudan-African National Union (SANU), and after a number of moves it set up its HQ in Kampala, Uganda, which had already give sanctuary to other southern Sudanese refugees. However the SANU leadership was not united, there being divergent views and clashing ambitions and personalities. For instance, an element of SANU, influenced by William Deng, remained in Kinshasa for a while.

A guerrilla army

While the SANU leaders were quarrelling in exile, back in southern Sudan an embryonic guerrilla army was slowly taking shape under its own military leaders, without the aid or interference of southern politicians, who had been divorced from it since the late 1950s. Based on about 500 former members of the SDF, it included Equatoria Corps soldiers who taken part in the 1955 mutiny and others who had deserted because of fear or repression. The latter had stayed together in small groups, some developing on a tribal or regional basis, depending on where they had found themselves or had gravitated to for safety. Harassed by government troops, they were compelled to retain a semblance of military unity and discipline in order to survive, their success being due to the inclusion of a number of former southern officers and noncommissioned officers in their midst.

It can be said that the 'guerrilla survival' period was between 1955 and 1963. Their activities were scarcely removed from banditry as they had to forage aggressively for food. They were motivated more by a sense of injustice, injury and adversity, than by any sense of political awakening, and were still being hunted as outlaws. Initially they had only about 200 rifles and very little ammunition, having to rely largely upon bows and arrows, spears and machetes. This 'forest army' had a sudden boost in strength in 1961, when some 800 southerners who had been sentenced to imprisonment after the 1955 mutiny, and for military offences since, were released from prison. As most of them had no jobs or prospects they drifted towards the rebels. The guerrillas had one other disadvantage: their inferiority complex when pitched against northern Arab soldiers, as for centuries they had been the hunted, and Arabs the hunters.

They had no comprehension of real guerrilla warfare, which had become a military tactic for revolutionary political groups the world over in their struggle for independence. Rather their hatred of the northern regime manifested itself in the occasional ambush, sniping or minor raids for arms or food as opportunity offered. During 1961 and 1962 there were minor erruptions in southern Sudan, mainly the result of tribal dissidence and quarrels, which were settled by President Abboub's harsh reprisal policy. There followed a period of comparative calm, in which the rebels took stock of themselves and formed themselves into a fighting force.

Freedom fighters

The rebels in the south had come to realise that obtaining a satisfactory self-governing solution by peaceful means was doomed to failure, that SANU, with which they had hardly any contact, was just a diplomatic talking shop to which no one paid head, and that the northern dictatorship would continue to debar dialogue. Consequently independence would have to be fought for. Now with probably well over 1000 personnel, all with some military training and discipline, and being in forest-type terrain, the idea of guerrilla warfare was beginning to take hold. After all the northern army was very small for the huge area it had to cover and was poorly equipped, lacking combat and transport aircraft, vehicles and modern weaponry. Its blundering forays into the south had shown that it was neither powerful nor effective, and it suddenly dawned on the rebels that it could be a ripe target for guerrilla warfare.

There had been spasmodic, impromptu meetings between rebel leaders to discuss the idea of merging together, but some of the smaller groups remained fiercely autonomous. Eventually a number of leaders met together in a forest camp in early September 1963, and on the 19th they decided to form a combined organisation called the Land Freedom Army (LFA). The soldiers would be called freedom fighters. The LFA would be based on the British military model, with British-type military formations and ranks and English words of command – the only ones they knew. Emilio Tafeng, a former lieutenant in the SDF, commissioned from the ranks, was appointed commander-in-chief with the rank of major-general. Other appointments of existing territorial commanders were confirmed with appropriate formal ranks. Its lingua franca was to be English, a missionary heritage in the south. General Tafeng and half a dozen of his regional commanders met periodically and formed an impromptu GHQ.

The Anya-Nya

The NFA adopted the name of Anya-Nya for morale boosting purposes. In the Madi, Moru and Loyuko tribal dialects Anya-Nya means 'snake poison', and in certain other dialects it means 'poisonous insect'. It was hoped that the name would eventually serve to scare elements of the Sudanese regular army. Initially the Anya-Nya GHQ tended to hover around the Madi tribal terrain in southern Equatoria Province, between Nimule and Juba and adjacent to the Ugandan border. Later an Anya-Nya badge was devised, depicting a charging buffalo surrounded by two snakes, the whole being split by an arrow, signifying the strength of a buffalo, the deadliness of a snake and the accuracy of an arrow.

The Anya-Nya began to establish small bases and training camps in poorly accessible border terrain in countries adjacent to Sudan's southern frontiers. Attention was given to improving liaison between senior commanders, and to recruitment and training. For some time the Anya-Nya discussed which guerrilla warfare tactics to use against the 'occupying Muslim army' and its administration, including blowing up bridges, blocking roads, ambushing northern troops and punishing southerners who collaborated with the government or refused to help the Anya-Nya. It took some time for the campaign plan to materialise, but once it did it proved to be a hard, ruthless one that caused considerable hardship and suffering to ordinary people caught between two hard rocks. Government forces burnt down villages and huts and drove the inhabitants into the forests as punishment for harbouring or helping the Anya-Nya, while the latter razed villages and huts and drove villagers into the forests for collaborating with northerners. The result was an enormous increase in refugees, not only those with a political or military background, but also hordes of ordinary people. Trails of vandalised, burnt and deserted villages criss-crossed the forested terrain of the south.

The first serious NFA attacks were launched in September 1963, instigated by William Deng while the Anya-Nya proper was still meditating. The first took place on the 9th, when a small force assaulted and overran a border police post at Pachola near the Ethiopian border. The second was launched on the 19th against another police post this time at Kajo Kaji near the Ugandan border, which was also overrun. In both incidents several police officers were killed.

The united Anya-Nya assault was against a military barracks at Wau, on 11 January 1964. The attack was led by 'Captain Bernandino', a missionary-educated Dinka whose force consisted of just over 100 men, armed with British rifles, Sten guns and Molotov cocktails. The assault was beaten off by the garrison, which had been alerted by a premature bugle call, sounded before the freedom fighters were ready in their attacking positions. Bernandino and 60 of his complement were captured, and later he and two of his men were hanged. This failed opening to the planned guerrilla campaign badly affected morale and made the freedom fighters wary of attacking government positions, as their age-old inferiority complex overtook them again.

The attack on Wau caused the government to rush more troops to the south and to clamp more restrictions on movement in the southern 'closed district'. Many southern police, prison staff and minor officials were arrested on 12 February and later over a 100 of them were tried, convicted and imprisoned for subversion. The remaining southern government employees were ordered to move north. The sudden surge of nationalism that followed was such that practically all of them deserted their posts and many joined the Anya-Nya, which left an all-Muslim army and administration, giving the impression of being a foreign occupying force.

President Abboud also responded to the Wau attack by expelling more missionaries. Some 300 were deported soon after the attack, the reason given being that they were redundant as teachers and were being replaced by Sudanese. It was also announced that foreign traders would only be allowed to reside in provincial or district capitals in the south, where they could be kept under surveillance, and not in villages. This restriction was aimed at Syrian and Greek traders, who were suspected of helping the rebels.

Cross-border activities

On 8 May 1964 a small Sudanese military force crossed into the Republic of Congo to strike at an Anya-Nya camp near the town of Aba, from where it was thought the Wau attack had been mounted. Further reprisals were threatened. By this time the strength of the Sudanese Army had increased to about 20 000, still too small to cover the 25 000 miles or so of national frontier. The army was basically organised into four infantry brigades, one of which was stationed in Equatoria Province and reinforced as necessary. Additional units were sent to the other two southern provinces: Bahr el-Ghazal and Upper Nile. All told it was estimated there were over 8000 Sudanese soldiers in the south, certainly enough to make occasional punitive and deterrence raids into adjacent states, which individually lacked the military expeditionary potential to respond.

Uganda

The position of Uganda (which remained under British colonial administration until September 1967) was ambivalent as it gave refuge to southern Sudanese refugees but restricted their political activities, under British pressure. The *Daily Telegraph* reported in May 1964 that there were about 60 000 southern refugees in Uganda, 7000 of whom had arrived within the last few days, together with 16 000 cattle and 15 000 sheep. At this stage Uganda tolerated Anya-Nya activities within the refugee camps, but gave it no military aid as it hoped to attract UN cash for the upkeep of the camps. Belatedly, in May, the UN provided an initial grant. Joseph Oduhu, president of SANU, had been briefly detained in the Ugandan capital Kampala, for tying to recruit southerners from the refugee camps, while William Deng, secretary general of SANU, quickly left to avoid arrest, returning to Kinshasa (Congo), from where the Sudanese government tried unsuccessfully to extradite him. Deng then went to Geneva to mount a propaganda campaign against the Abboud regime, and during his absence Joseph Oduhu regained much of the authority Deng had been assuming. From Geneva, Deng alleged that Sudanese troops were frequently crossing into Uganda and Ethiopia, burning huts and committing atrocities. A few of the examples he cited had element of truth to them, but not all

Ethiopia

President Abboud concluded an extradition treaty with Emperor Haile Selassie of Ethiopia in May 1964, at a moment when relations between the two countries were better than was customary. However no one was extradited. Abboud had thought that the southern rebel leaders sheltering in Ethiopia would be handed over to him, but Haile Selassie wanted them to leave of their own accord, without political fuss, complications or reprisals. To this end he announced that all southern Sudanese refugees in his country would be deported to Sudan immediately, which caused large numbers of them to flee to Kenya or Uganda, thus conveniently lightening Ethiopia's refugee burden.

The fall of the Abboud regime

The northern Sudanese public was becoming restless about the mounting chaotic situation in the south and the failure of the Abboud regime to solve the problem, which seemed to have escalated from simple banditry and lawlessness to guerrilla warfare, with all its political implications. Guerrilla attacks and the consequent reprisals were becoming more commonplace, as were reports of atrocities and excesses by both sides, especially in the Torit area. Apart from the tussle between government troops and the freedom fighters, much of the south was unsafe for travel, especially by night, and neither people nor property were free from threat. As the Anya-Nya's planned campaign slowly took shape it did what it could to eliminate plain banditry and daylight robbery in its growing areas of influence, in an effort to bring about Mao Tse-tung's vision of guerrilla fish swimming safely in the sea of the people. So far it had only made tentative steps towards gaining the confidence of the people. On the other hand the army continued its heavy handed and ruthless operations, causing southern tribes and villagers to think that the freedom fighters might be the best of the bad lot.

On 7 September 1964 a commission of enquiry, set up to examine the unrest in the south, appealed to citizens to submit their views on the problem. This represented a chink in the heavy grass curtain of censorship that had screened all activities in the south since the Abboud regime had come to power, and prompted students at Khartoum University to organise themselves into discussion groups. The students criticised many aspects of the regime, despite express university orders not to do so. The commission, comprising 13 northerners and 13 southerners, was to make recommendations with the object of 'consolidating confidence and achieving stability', but it was not to infringe the principle of unitary government. The commission was authorised to visit the south and to interview anyone it chose – astounding freedom at that particular moment.

On 22 October the Anti-Imperialist Front, which had survived underground, held an unauthorised meeting of students at Khartoum University to protest against the government's brutal repression of the autonomist movement in the south. When the police attempted to break up the meeting they encountered violent resistance and opened fire, killing one student and wounding several others. Enraged students entered the city and sacked the offices of a government newspaper, whereupon a curfew was imposed.

Further student demonstrations erupted the following day and troops had to be called out to deal with them. The Umma Party issued a statement attacking the government's economic policy and the rising cost of living, and demanding a democratic constitution. It suddenly became clear that the banned political parties had not broken up in 1958, but had simply lain dormant and were now springing into action again, voicing their old cries. On the 24th demonstrations spread to other towns, including Omdurman, Juba and Port Sudan. The government closed Khartoum University and schools in affected towns.

The next day President Abboud appealed for order, promising an enquiry and punishment for those responsible. That evening three demonstrators were killed when the police again opened fire. Although students had originally taken the lead in these protests, other sections of the population quickly joined in, especially the banned political parties. The Communist Party (which had a strong influence on the Trade Union Federation), the United National Front (an alliance consisting of the

Umma Party, the NUP and the Islamic Parties) and some professional groups played a large part in the demonstrations. The leaders of the Ansar and Khatmia sects called for a return to democracy. It was an impromptu 'people's revolution'.

A widespread strike occurred the following day, in which some young military officers took part. Troops surrounded the presidential palace and the building in which the Supreme Council of the Armed Forces had been in session for several hours, forming a protective ring against rowdy demonstrators. On the 27th Abboud stated that a transitional government would be formed pending the adoption of a new constitution, but the situation remained uncertain owing to differences between senior officers. The following day the staff at Radio Omdurman went on strike, where upon the army took over the broadcasting station and announced that it would use force to disperse demonstrators. That day twelve people were shot dead on the streets. In the evening the United National Front came to an agreement with the newly appointed (expressly for the purpose) deputy commander-in-chief, General Abdul Rahman al-Makboul, that a civilian government would be formed, both agreeing that the essential issue was the integration of the south into the republic.

The Khalifa government

On 30 October 1964 a new caretaker government was formed by Khatim Khalifa, who became premier and minister of defence. The government contained representatives from each of the principal political parties, including the Communist Party, and certain other organisations. It included two southerners – Clement Mboro, deputy governor of Darfur Province, and Alfred Wol, but the latter was replaced almost immediately by Izbone Mendiri. The national emergency ceased on 7 November, when soldiers disappeared from the streets. Later it was stated that 36 people had been killed and over 100 injured during the crisis.

Almost immediately Khalifa clashed with President Abboud. On 8 November Abboud ordered the arrest of seven senior officers for submitting a note to the Army High Command calling for Sudan to cooperate more fully with the policies of Egypt. Khalifa protested that this was the first step towards dismissing all officers who had supported the 'people's revolution', but Abboud denied the accusation. Khalifa then ordered the arrest of seven former members of the Supreme Council and suspended the police commissioner. This led to another bout of street demonstrations, with people calling for army purges and the trial and execution of the army junta.

Another battle for the streets

On the evening of the 9 November 1964, troops belonging to an armoured unit barracked near Khartoum were preparing to take part in a night exercise, which immediately aroused suspicions that an army coup was about to take place. This coincided with a false announcement on Radio Omdurman (discovered later to have been planted by a member of the Communist Party but purporting to be from the United National Front) that armoured columns were moving out from their barracks and were about to take over the city, calling on all the people to rally to prevent this from happening. Mobs crowded the streets, put up impromptu road blocks and generally prevented vehicular movement. Despite appeals from members of the Khalifa government they refused to return to their homes.

Communists and their left wing allies also took to the streets and tried to assume control of the mobs, raising cries of 'arms for the people' and 'to the palace'. When the Ansar leaders realised that an attempted coup was in progress they reacted quickly, rushing huge numbers of their followers on to the streets to prevent it from happening. The 'battle of the streets' in Khartoum was won by the Ansar and lost by the communists. The importance of this impromptu intermob street fight – a very tiny blip in history – can be appreciated only if one realises that in November 1964, during the early stage of the Cold War, the threat of militant communism was very real and Moscow still regarded Sudan as its gateway to Africa. Khartoum had a narrow escape, as unearthed communist documents later illustrated.

Council of Sovereignty

The following day the United National Front called for the resignation of President Abboud, and on 14 November 1964 some 200 army officers petitioned the government to purge the army. On the 15th Abboud resigned, and was replaced by General Mohammed al-Khawad. On the 22nd Premier Khalifa released all military prisoners and detainees, including Brigadiers Shenan and Abdullah. A five-man Council of Sovereignty was formed on 3 December to replace the dissolved Supreme Council of the Armed Forces. The Council included just one southerner, Luigi Adwok.

This marked the end of a brief epoch in Sudan's modern history. Ibrahim Abboud had come onto the scene as a military dictator after his country had been subjected to almost three years of ineffective, bungling democratic rule following independence. His achievements included lifting his country out of economic chaos, introducing massive industrial capital, launching ambitious hydroelectric schemes and doubling the size of the Gezira project, but he had been unable to control his ambitious, quarrelling officers or unite the squabbling, self-seeking political leaders. His failure to recognise and resolve the southern problem had been the last straw in his downfall. By this time most of the older generation of army officers, educated and trained by the British, had left the service, almost the last being Abboud himself, who failed to realise that he had become a dinosaur. The generals' attempt to govern successfully and profitably having failed, they were being replaced by a new generation of middle grade officers who were more politically enlightened and had risen in rank and matured since 1955, during the 'grass curtain war' in the south.

3
Southern Politics

Premier Khatim Khalifa immediately turned his attention to the southern problem, and through Clement Mboro he tried to negotiate with southern leaders, appealing to both SANU and the Anya-Nya to suspend their antigovernment activities. Clement Mboro wrote to, among others, William Deng and nine southern politicians, three from each southern province, inviting them to Khartoum for discussions. On 11 November 1964, as a sign of good faith, Khalifa released a number of southern detainees and declared that Sundays and Christmas Day would again be recognised holidays. On the 12th Mboro managed to persuade the Anya-Nya to observe a month's ceasefire while he carried out a fact-finding mission.

A southern amnesty

Khalifa's new civilian government was of the mistaken opinion that the rebellion in the south had been directed solely against Abboud's military regime, and so its emphasis was one of reconciliation; for example soldiers in the south were forbidden to fire except in self-defence. During the ceasefire period Anya-Nya personnel were allowed to move about without restriction. Many visited towns and villages to recruit new members and intimidate those who were collaborating with the government. There were a few clashes with government troops and some minor reprisals, while the army stood by uncertain and demoralised, being denounced in Khartoum for its previous activities in the south.

Accompanied by Izbone Mendiri, Premier Khalifa went on a short tour of the south, and on his return on the 14th he announced an unconditional amnesty for all southerners who had fled the country since 1955, including those sentenced by the courts in their absence. He appealed to the exiles to return home to work for freedom and equality, and for them to put aside all racial, religious and political differences. He then made an offer to southern leaders that amounted to federal autonomy. However this was sharply rejected by SANU, which was now demanding complete independence. A SANU spokesman stated on 5 January 1965 that SANU would use all means to eject the 'Arabs' from the south.

More riots in Khartoum

On 6 December 1964 the aircraft bringing Mboro back from his tour of the south was delayed, and a rumour spread amongst the waiting crowd of welcoming southerners at Khartoum airport that he had been murdered by northerners. Up to a million southerners were employed in the north, mainly as labourers and in other menial work, a large proportion being in Khartoum. Eventually, when Mboro still did not appear, restless and suspicious southerners moved into the city and began to assault northerners, damaging vehicles and property. In retaliation crowds of angry northerners assembled and ran riot, attacking southerners. The rioting lasted until nightfall. Five people were killed and over 400 injured in this one-day riot, which demonstrated the depths of inherent hostility that existed between the people of the two regions and could explode at any moment. However for most of the time a live-and-let-live attitude existed in the cities and towns, with each group tending to keep within their own communities and to avoid open friction.

In Khartoum arguments arose over the date for the general election, with some accusing the communists of deliberately delaying their agreement in order to hang on to office as long as possible. The countercharge was that the Umma Party was planning to seize power by force. On 6 February 1965 rival mobs again clashed on the streets of Khartoum, with the communists calling on everyone to 'defend the revolution'. Their opponents were members of a paramilitary Ansar body, about 30 000 strong. The short political truce that was arranged for the duration of the British royal visit (8–11 February) broke down immediately after the queen departed, and hostile mobs again roamed the streets.

The British royal visit to Sudan had been arranged by President Abboud after his state visit to Britain, and despite the uncertain political situation in Khartoum it was decided that it should go ahead as scheduled. During the visit the Sudanese put on a spectacular 'desert durbar' at El Obeid, the capital of Kordofan Province. Over 40 000 camels and riders drew up in a vast square in the desert, and there was a march past of some 5000 camels, some ridden by descendants of tribesmen who had fought in the Mahdi's dervish army against the British in the late nine-teenth century. The Sudanese media depicted it as little more than a brief pantomime-like interlude in the political struggle, but hoped it would produce favourable aid and loans.

Khalifa resigned on the 18 February, but managed to form another government on the 23rd, being a coalition of right-wing parties and the Southern Front. Almost immediately Izbone Mendiri had to resign (for assaulting a government official) and was replaced by Gordon Muoriat, also of the Southern Front, which still had Luigi Adwok as its represen-tative on the Supreme Council. The Southern Front, which had been formed in Khartoum upon the collapse of the Abboud regime, consisted of southern students, government officials and employees. It was led by Gordon Abei and included Clement Mboro, Izbone Mendiri and Luigi Adwok among its membership. The Southern Front claimed to represent the whole of the south, and resented the government's invitation to SANU to meet and negotiate with it.

SANU divided

As the SANU leadership was divided and negotiations had been rejected, the next step could be armed resistance. At the first SANU convention, held at Kampala in November 1964, Aggrey Jaden was elected president general as the separate posts of president and secretary general had been abolished, and a 'shadow cabinet' was formed, in which both Joseph Oduhu and William Deng were given places. However neither of these men accepted the leadership changes. Oduhu returned to Kenya, while Deng, who had not been present at the convention, claimed that he was still secretary general and continued to speak for SANU in a forceful voice.

On 25 December 1964 Premier Khalifa announced that, after consulta-tions with SANU, meaning William Deng, general elections would be held in Sudan in March 1965. Deng then proposed a federal constitution for the south, which pleased the Khartoum government but was con-trary to SANU policy. He also demanded, in early January 1965, that Sudan should withdraw from the Arab League, retain its mem-bership of the OAU, introduce certain reforms and reinstate the dis-banded Equatoria Corps. This was followed by a letter from Deng on the 16th demanding a 'return to normal' in the south, the appointment of southerners to the government service and the police, and complete freedom for southern political leaders during the forthcoming electoral campaign.

There was a continual tug-of-war between right and left (there was no strong central party in Sudan). In January 1965, for example, the right (consisting of the Umma Party, the NUP and the Islamic Charter Front) succeeded – to the annoyance of the left – in terminating an arrangement for arms from Algeria and Egypt to be transported across Sudan for the use of rebels in Congo. In fact, I was told by the foreign minister that only five planeloads had been delivered. Another tussle occurred in the first week of February over the degree of autonomy to be offered to the south, with the left (the Communist Party, the Anti- Imperialist Front and pro-Egyptian members of the National Assembly) being prepared to give more leeway than the right.

To give southerners a chance to air their views, Premier Khalifa proposed that a roundtable conference be held in Juba on 15 February. At a SANU meeting in Kampala on 29 January it was agreed that negotiations should begin with the Khartoum government in Juba on that date, and that a three-man SANU committee, consisting of Elia Lupe, Michael Duay and William Deng, should speak for the south.

The first snag in the run-up to the conference was that the Southern Front insisted on being present. The Southern Front was still claiming to speak for the whole of the south and had just published a newspaper (the *Vigilant*), which upset SANU. Another snag was that some considered Juba to be an unsafe place for a conference, as elements of both the Anya-Nya and the army had not observed a ceasefire in that area. Southerners were reluctant to meet in Khartoum, fearing mob-ruled streets and the threat of danger from political opponents.

William Deng arrived in Khartoum on 27 February, insisting that he was the SANU leader and had come to make arrangements for the SANU delegation to attend the conference. There were suspicions that he lacked wholehearted SANU support because he had come alone. However he was tentatively accepted, especially when he said he was prepared to accept federation for the south rather than complete independence, which had been SANU's platform so far. Deng also agreed that the conference could be held in Khartoum, instead of in the south, as demanded by the Southern Front. Northern politicians smiled, sensing they had a southern 'moderate' to negotiate with. However when the SANU leadership in Kampala (Uganda) heard of this they refused to attend the conference, insisting that they alone should speak for the south, and not southern politicians who had no contacts there, and some of whom had only dubious southern roots. The Southern Front, however, urged the SANU element in Kampala to attend. Premier Khalifa would have welcomed a ban on all elements of SANU attending the conference as to his mind their presence would invite controversy.

More southern parties

This new era of political freedom in Sudan encouraged the formation of three more southern political parties during the first two months of 1965: the Southern Unity Party, formed by Santino Deng, who had been the sole southern minister in the Abboud government, a fact that did not endear him to many southerners; the Liberal Party, revived by Stanislaus Paysama and Buth Diu; and the Southern Peace Party. The first two were small and had little influence at this stage, while the third was simply a front for northerners. This proliferation of southern parties suited the government, which sought to divide and confuse the south.

The round-table conference

The conference eventually met in Khartoum on 16 March 1965 and was attended by delegations from the Southern Front, SANU and representatives of the northern parties. The official SANU delegation was led by Elia Lupe, and only after much discussion was William Deng accepted as a member, ranking only sixth out of nine. However Deng spoke up loudly and often, still insisting that he was the leader of SANU, so his exact position remained obscure. The government delegation went along with this as they saw him as a key moderate with whom they could do business. Aggrey Jaden, as president general, appeared only once: briefly on the first day, when he made a speech that was antagonistic towards the north. Also attending the conference were observers from Algeria, Egypt, Ghana, Nigeria, Tanzania and Uganda, who not only listened to the proceedings but also added their own criticisms, suggestions and comments.

Broadly, the southerners asked for federalism, with autonomy as an alternative, but the government proposed a form of regional government. The southerners wanted to involve the Organisation of African Unity, but the government insisted that this was a domestic matter. Nor would it agree to a referendum in the south, thus indirectly admitting that a referendum would inevitably result in an overwhelming vote for independence. Stalemate had set in by the 24th. At one point the conference was almost abandoned because news came through that a senior Dinka police officer in Upper Nile Province had murdered his Arab deputy.

When the conference ended on the 29th, no final decisions had been reached and only a few weak resolutions had been passed, including a 'return to normal'. Southerners were to be given governmental and administrative posts in the south and greater autonomy in education, religion and employment. At best it was merely an interim arrangement. A twelve-man committee of six northerners and six southerners was established to implement such resolutions as had been approved, and to report back in three months' time. Three of the southern seats were allocated to the Southern Front, and the other three to William Deng's section of SANU. No invitations had been issued to the SANU leadership in exile, and when one of its leaders, Peter Akol, arrived in Khartoum to demand a place he was turned away.

Elections

Southern politicians decided not to take part in the forthcoming elections, and after some hesitation the government announced that it would hold them in the north only. Those in the south would be delayed until the round-table committee came up with a solution. The elections in the north were held between 21 April and 21 May, during which time there was general rowdiness and some street violence in the cities. The Umma Party gained 75 seats, the NUP 54, the Communist Party 11, the Beja Tribal Association (a pro-Umma Party) 10, the Islamic Charter Front five, the PDP three and independents 15. Although there were no elections in the south, 21 southern candidates, including 14 Muslim merchants living in the south who had already registered for southern constituencies, claimed their seats by default, a decision that was upheld on legal appeal.

The Mahgoub government

The Khalifa government resigned on 2 June 1965 and a new Umma Party –NUP coalition was formed under Mohammed Ahmad Mahgoub of the NUP on the 14th. Sadik Mahdi, leader of the Umma Party, had allied himself with Mahgoub against the Communist Party because of slanderous remarks made about the Prophet Mohammed by a communist student. There was some policy dissension within the Umma Party as Sadik's chief rival for the leadership, his uncle, Imam el-Hadi al-Mahdi, wanted to turn Sudan into an Islamic state, and advocated a harder line against southern (Christian) rebels.

Premier Mahgoub proposed to allocate three ministerial seats to the south, the right to all three of which was claimed by both the Southern Front and Deng's SANU element, both claiming to speak for the south. The Southern Front then withdrew in pique, and so two of the seats were given to members of Deng's SANU: Andrew Wieu and Alfred Wol. Premier Mahgoub then appointed Buth Diu of the Liberal Party to the third ministerial post, but this caused Wieu and Wol to withdraw, alleging that Diu had no following in the south. Consequently Diu was the only southern minister in Mahgoub's cabinet for several months.

The only southerner on the Council of sovereignty was Luigi Adwok, who was now threatening to resign unless the government produced a satisfactory explanation for the burning of huts and several deaths in his home village in the south.

In June the Southern Front, which continued to claim wide support in the south, became a formally registered political party, with Clement Mboro as president, Gordon Muoriat as vice president and Hilary Logale as secretary general.

SANU splinters

Meanwhile in Uganda, the SANU-in-exile party was splintering, mainly due to personality clashes. In June Joseph Oduhu (released from detention), Saturnino Lohure, George Kwani, Pancrasio Ocheng, Marko Rume and others broke away to found the Azania Liberation Front (ALF), 'Azania' being the name of a sixteenth-century East African empire. The remnants of the party were left temporarily in the hands of Aggrey Jaden. Personalities continued to clash, and a little later Jaden was expelled from the SANU-in-exile rump, being unable to rally its members from his base in Uganda, many of whom were leaving to join the ALF. Jaden then formed his remaining followers into the Sudan African Liberation Front (SALF). Yet another offshoot was the Sudan African Freedom Fighters Union of Conservatives, but it soon disappeared.

Later in the year there was reconciliation when the remaining members of SANU-in-exile and the SALF were absorbed into the expanding ALF. Jaden became a vice president. Harmony did not reign for long, as in December Jaden was expelled from the ALF by President Oduhu for allegedly meeting William Deng in Nairobi to discuss the southern situation without Oduhu's permission. By this time the ALF was claiming political control over the revolt that had developed in the south, asserting that the Anya-Nya was its military arm.

The resurrected arms route

Meanwhile it was being alleged that when Khatim Khalifa was premier he had resurrected the illicit arms route across Sudan from Algeria and Egypt to Ethiopia and Congo, under pressure from the left, and that southern Sudan was becoming a supply route, base and haven for Eritrean and Congolese separatist rebels. (In 1962 Ethiopia had annexed Eritrea, with which it had been federated since 1952.) In May 1965, four former Sudanese officers were arrested, and Premier Khalifa confirmed that 18 tons of Czechoslovakian arms had been seized by the authorities at Khartoum airport. The arms had been flown in from Syria with the approval of the Sudanese government, and were destined for use by Eritreans fighting against the Ethiopian government, which in turn was giving sanctuary to southern Sudanese dissident political groups.

As soon as Premier Mahgoub gained power he stopped the transit of arms across Sudan. Later he personally stressed to me in an interview that no arms had ever been sent across Sudan to the Eritrean rebels, but was at loss to explain away the Khartoum airport consignment. On 26 July Mahgoub began a four-day visit to Ethiopia, the object being to seal the common frontier between the two countries and prevent illicit aid from filtering through to Sudan's southern rebels. This was followed on 10 August by the Sudanese foreign minister announcing that his government had undertaken to prevent Eritrean refugees in Sudan from engaging in subversive activities against the Ethiopian government, and as a sign of good faith an Eritrean 'rebel' was deported to Ethiopia. Mahgoub told me in another interview that he had personally discussed the issue with Haile Selassie, and it had been agreed that neither would allow refugee camps to be situated within fifty miles of the joint border, but the situation remained the same, as I saw for myself a few days later.

Illicit cross-border aid

In early July 1965 an ALF delegation visited Nairobi in Kenya to solicit aid from President Kenyatta. To counter this, in August Premier Mahgoub visited Kenya for talks. The Sudanese minister of information later issued a statement to the effect that Kenya and Tanzania had promised to crush any secessionist activity by southern Sudanese refugees in their territory, and that both countries wanted to see a united Sudan. Mahgoub also complained to the American ambassador in Khartoum that the government in Congo was passing on some of its US military aid to Anya-Nya groups sheltering in Congo, but this was flatly denied. ALF activities were restricted in Uganda, but they continued covertly, although Oduhu, now the leader of the ALF, was again detained by the authorities.

Communist Party dissolved again

Although the Communist Party only had about 5000 members it was becoming extremely active and influential, and Premier Mahgoub sensed danger. His opportunity to act came when a student publicly proclaimed himself proud to be a communist and an atheist, whereupon the Umma Party and the NUP demanded that the Communist Party be dissolved. On 15 November the National Assembly voted in favour of the motion, and on the 17th a student burned himself to death in protest. On the 22nd the Communist Party was again declared illegal.

Premier Mahgoub's strong coalition had quickly settled into office, and within weeks had several successes to its credit: winning a vote of confidence in the National Assembly; stopping the arms traffic across Sudan to the Congo; improving relations with Ethiopia, Kenya and Uganda over frontier and refugee problems; and driving the communists underground.

4
The Anya-Nya

The Sudanese army was largely designed for internal security, as a supplement to the police service and not – as in most countries – for defence against external enemies. Unconsciously perhaps, and almost as a matter of faith and tradition, Sudan still relied upon its remoteness, of being separated from potential predators by hundreds of miles of desert, scrub land and mountainous terrain. Roman legions and British armies had marched into its deserts, only to disappear.

During his administration Premier Khalifa declared on several occasions that the southern problem should be solved by diplomatic means, offering the south autonomy, almost to a federal standard. This was repeatedly rejected by southern leaders, who, since the appearance of the independent Republic of Congo on the African stage in July 1960, were scenting the possibility of complete independence. Under the cover of his placatory façade, Khalifa had gradually moved troops to the south, and eventually the towns in Bahr el-Ghazal and Upper Nile Provinces were fairly saturated with soldiery, which largely succeeded in preventing the outbreak of guerrilla warfare. Indeed even in Equatoria Province, the centre and mainspring of the revolt, the military presence restricted Anya-Nya activities. When the government was asked why it was building up military strength in the south, the answer was that it feared a Congolese invasion because the south was sheltering Congolese separatist leaders and refugees – a most unconvincing reply. In fact Khalifa had been preparing an offensive against the southern outlaws.

The Anya-Nya build-up

By the end of 1964 the strength of the Anya-Nya had probably risen to just over 5000, but only a small percentage had arms, their leaders having been unable to procure any for them, despite approaching several sources. As The Cold War progressed the Americans, British, French and Soviets were vying for influence over African countries, especially those that had just achieved independence, backing either the new government, or one or more of the armed opposition groups that had lost out in the struggle for independence. There seemed to be arms aplenty for those factions, but none for Sudan's black south, as the predator nations probably thought that country was on the verge of falling into their pockets. The battle for influence was still being fiercely fought in Congo, hence the Soviet-instigated arms trail across southern Sudan.

The Anya-Nya began quietly to hijack arms being transported across Sudan, but the number seized was small. However when the separatist rebels in Congo began to lose their battle with government forces and fled into southern Sudan, they either sold their arms to buy food or had them stolen by Anya-Nya freedom fighters. In this way several hundred automatic weapons and quantities of ammunition were obtained, enabling the the Anya-Nya to progress from the primitive spear, bow and arrow stage to a more modern guerrilla-like formation by mid 1965.

When Mahgoub became premier in June 1965 he appeared to relax the military saturation of the south and many northern soldiers were withdrawn. He also espoused a reconciliation policy, but his firm instruction was that law and order must first be restored. This was the year of the round-table conference, when Anya-Nya operations were at a minimum and both sides were interested in a political solution.

The Juba riots

This peace was shattered on 8 July 1965, when an incident occurred in Juba between a Muslim soldier and a southerner, in which the soldier was wounded. This caused the Muslin troops in Juba to run amok in the town. Soldiers cordoned off certain districts along the banks of the Nile, set fire to grass-roofed huts and shot the occupants as they emerged. Many people were drowned as they jumped into the river to escape. On the 10th there was an unsuccessful Anya-Nya attack on the army HQ at Juba. Southerners claimed that over 3000 huts had been burned, and according to official government figures, 1018 people were killed in two days (the population of Juba was then thought to be about 40 000). On the 12th the commanding officer of the Southern Command stated that his soldiers had opened fire on southern 'outlaws' attacking his HQ, and that 25 of them had been killed. Southerners alleged that this had been an attempt to eliminate them. All the customary claims, counterclaims and allegations.

The Juba incident gave credence to persistent southern claims that discipline was poor in the Muslim army in the south, that officers had little control over their men when they were away from their barracks and camps, and that soldiers were allowed to roam through forests and villages, killing and burning as much as they liked. Mahgoub insisted that this was not so, and that military discipline was good, both on and off duty. He discounted reports of army excesses as missionary propaganda. Some military officers, both senior and junior, told me that discipline was generally good and that they had full control over the soldiers at all times. They did admit that soldiers were occasionally given a free rein, but that they could be instantly brought to attention when required. They seemed to be like cobblers insisting that there was nothing like good leather. However a few days previously Premier Mahgoub had told me that he had found the army in poor shape. The evidence seemed to point to the probability of a policy of military reprisal that was separate from the political remit.

The Wau incident

The next major incident in the south occurred at Wau (the capital of Bahr el-Ghazal Province) on 11 July 1965, when Muslim soldiers surrounded the cathedral, where a marriage was taking place. Four Arab soldiers who were in the congregation were advised to leave by their fellow soldiers, who fired on the congregation as they were leaving the building. Seventy-five people were killed. Later the same day a strong detachment of the Anya-Nya attacked the army camp in a reprisal raid, but were beaten back at the alleged cost of about 70 freedom fighters. A government communique stated that the rebel losses amounted to about 250 dead. At both Juba and Wau a number of educated southerners had been killed, which gave rise to an allegation that the government was trying to eliminate them. A total curfew was imposed on the Provinces of Bahr el-Ghazal and Equatoria.

The *Vigilant*, the Southern Front's English-language newspaper, was suspended on 15 July after reporting the Juba and Wau incidents and printing a leading article holding the government responsible for the 'barbaric and brutal killing' at Juba, which was 'not an accident, but part and parcel of a plan to depopulate the South'. The article alleged there had been 1400 casualties, of whom 76 had been killed, and that the casualty list included 49 southern officials in government service. Oliver Albino, the SANU representative in Nairobi, alleged that government forces had also killed a further 700 or more civilians in the south, mainly at Mide in the Maridi district, and at Yandaru in the Yei district. On the 13th SANU appealed to the United Nations to intervene in the south, then to the Red Cross for help, and on the 20th to the OAU, but there was little response.

Mahgoub's brief attempts at reconciliation may or may not have been genuine, but after the Wau incident he took a tough line in the south, and July was a black month in that region. He stated that the outlaws must be subdued rather than negotiated with. The military mounted several operations, burning many villages and rendering numerous people homeless, many of whom fled into the forests. In particular, southerners alleged that Muslim soldiers had destroyed the few hospitals and medical centres in the south to prevent people from obtaining medical treatment. It was generally accepted that there were more deaths in this period from disease and medical neglect than from government weapons.

Mahgoub defined his method of coping with the situation in the south as first curbing external assistance, then discussing ways and means of bringing the people in the south under government control, and then reinforcing and re-equipping his army. He said that his initial policy was to contain the 'pockets of rebels' while he obtained more arms and equipment. He admitted, openly this time, that his troops were in poor shape, inadequately equipped and completely untrained for operations in the southern forests.

During July there were many clashes and incidents in the south. The claims and counterclaims are unverifiable, but it is sufficient to say that many lives were lost and much hardship was caused to the people, many of whom fled in fear. The number fleeing the area was sufficient to justify, in part at least, the allegation that the government's policy was to depopulate Equatoria Province. In general the Anya-Nya had freedom of movement in the countryside, their camps being either deep in the forests, where it was almost impossible for government troops to track them down and attack them, or in the mountainous terrain that bordered Kenya and Uganda, where freedom fighters were within easy reach of the frontier if danger arose.

On the 19th the minister of the interior called a brief amnesty and appealed to the rebels to desist from all acts of violence and surrender their arms within a fortnight, but when the time limit expired only five doubtful rebels had surrendered. Meanwhile the governor of Bahr el-Ghazal Province announced that some 500 persons were to be brought to trial for their part in the Wau incident.

Premier Mahgoub's antipathy towards the southern problem was now very obvious, and his army took note of his attitude and acted accordingly. Unable to strike at the elusive Anya-Nya, soldiers made the civilian population their targets – many villages were burned and their inhabitants scattered. For example it was alleged that on 20 July, troops fired on the small town of Rumek, killing several people; on 5 August troops marched into the village of Warwajok, a few miles from Malakal, and shot 187 inhabitants to prevent them from joining the rebels; and later in the month soldiers attacked a missionary station at Doleib Hill, at the junction of the White Nile and the River Sobat, as well as villages near Wau and Juba. Government news was relayed through Radio Omdurman, which stated that soldiers were attacking the rebels at various points, and giving official estimates of the casualties.

August was certainly another black month in the south, but it was not all one-sided. The Anya-Nya claimed to have opened fire on a military detachment at Katari near Wau, on 13 August, killing several soldiers, and then attacked a garrison at Bisellia, also near Wau. They also claimed to have burned down the police station, and to have besieged a military detachment at Tambura in the Wau area, whereupon paratroopers had to be flown from Khartoum to relieve it. The army was in the process of forming a paratroop brigade, with British assistance, and this was probably its first airborne operation.

Famine and disease

By the end of September 1965 Premier Mahgoub was openly admitting that a chaotic situation existed in the south, that the police, administration and education services were not functioning, and that provincial governors had little influence over events away from the garrison towns. Government oppression was particularly heavy in Equatoria Province, where most of the devastation and terrorism occurred. It was less heavy in Upper Nile Province due, I was told, to a more humane governor who kept stricter control over military activities in his domain.

It should be noted that by no means all the people in the south were involved in the rebellion against the Khartoum government. The three largest southern tribes, the Dinka, Nuer and Shilluk, living mainly in Upper Nile and Darfur Provinces and perhaps numbering well over one million, were standing aside and were not subject to military attack or harassment. The developing revolt was based entirely on the smaller tribes in Equatoria Province.

The breakdown of civil administration led to the spread of famine and disease. It was alleged there were at least 60 000 untreated cases of sleeping sickness and other diseases, as all the village medical centres and rural dispensaries had been abandoned. The wholesale destruction of villages entailed the destruction of crops and livestock, which naturally caused food shortages and many displaced refugees had to eke out subsistence existence in the forests. As the government seemed to have no plan to send emergency food supplies to the south, southern leaders were loudly claiming that the government was pursuing a policy of genocide.

A spat with the pope

As Christian missions, churches and schools seemed to be suffering badly at the hands of the government military repressors, the Pope was prompted on 9 August 1965 to appeal directly to Mahgoub to find a peaceful solution. Mahgoub replied sharply that he had already asked the rebels to lay down their arms, suggesting that if they continued to attack the southern population it was the Pope who should appeal to the rebel leaders. The Pope persisted, and in response to a further appeal to the Sudanese government, on 3 September he received a reply from Sadik Mahdi, leader of the Umma Party, pointing out that a 'group of irresponsible people, professional and lay-persons' were doing all they could to turn the southern problem into a crusade, and that the government was opposed to such an attitude as African states were 'multi-religious'. He suggested that the Pope should consider the Africanisation of his clergy in Sudan.

During September the Bishops of Wau and Rumbek were killed in the disturbances, which brought protests from several international Christian missionary organisations. The secretary of the Church Missionary Society in London estimated that half the churches in the south had been destroyed, that the majority of those serving or working in the various religious orders had decamped to the forest, and that whole communities had been forced to flee to escape murder, torture and wholesale destruction. The Sudanese chargé d'affaires in London replied that several priests had been found in possession of arms, and that missionaries had encouraged and sheltered the rebels. According to Mahgoub's estimates, 90 per cent of southerners were animists, 5 per cent were Muslims and 5 per cent were Christians.

Rainy season, 1965

In October 1965 the Anya-Nya claimed that during an attack on Taafika it had defeated a company of government troops and burned a river steamer (the *Abu Anga*). In retaliation the soldiers were said to have entered Warwajok (previously attacked in August) and killed all the male villagers. With the advent of the rainy season, military activities on both sides slackened off. One exception was a government attack on an Anya-Nya camp near Wau on 24 November, after which the LFA's activities in the two provinces amounted to little more than pinpricks for several months. Some 15 000 troops remained, smothering potential rebel activity, while the major Shilluk tribal federation remained firmly on the government's side.

In November Mahgoub announced that the rebellion had been completely suppressed in both Bahr el-Ghazal and Upper Nile Provinces, and that he had decided to send southern members of the National Assembly on a fact-finding mission to these provinces. In early December Mahgoub modified his statement, saying merely that the situation in the south had improved, and that the rebellion would be crushed by the end of the year. He also reiterated his commitment to a peaceful solution within the framework of a unified Sudan. An offer by President Nkrumah of Ghana to mediate was rejected on the ground that the southern problem was an internal affair.

Meanwhile Mahgoub had forged a good relationship with Milton Obote, president of adjacent Uganda. Obote had visited Sudan in 1963, and in successive years had taken part in several reconciliation attempts. A few joint Sudanese–Ugandan military exercises had been undertaken, but these had tended to be 'sweeps' and had had no lasting effect. Nor had they plugged the gaps in the joint frontier, as had been hoped.

Lifting the grass curtain

The Sudanese government's strenuous efforts to suppress all news of the rebellion in the south, about which little was known by the outside world, continued to be successful until adventurous journalists began covertly to enter the south from adjacent countries, making clandestine journeys to meet the Anya-Nya and report back on what was actually happening. Two such individuals, Anthony Carthew and Keith Kyle, did much to open up southern Sudan to the world's gaze. The government estimated that the Anya-Nya consisted of about 8000 armed and trained men, but Carthew of the *Daily Mail* put it at fewer than 5000 men with about 100 rifles and one bazooka. The Anya-Nya had limited freedom of movement in Equatoria Province, and there was only scant liaison between isolated groups. There was also little sign of the tribes being turned into Mao Tse-tung's 'sea' in which the guerrilla 'fish' could safely swim, as at this stage the Anya-Nya were burning as many village huts and killing as many villagers as were the government military forces. 'The smell of burning was always in my nostrils' (Carthew, *Daily Mail*).

Military aircraft

The Sudanese government was having difficulty developing an air force, which was essential to transport troops across the huge distances between towns, for reconnaissance purposes and for aerial activity against Anya-Nya camps. During the latter part of 1965, several bombing raids were made against Anya-Nya camps, but little damage was done. A rumour that British pilots were being recruited by the Sudanese was unfounded, but some Arab mercenary pilots were briefly employed, and the British did train Sudanese pilots. Military airstrips were constructed near garrison towns by northern soldiers. In January 1966 the Sudanese government again appealed to the Anya-Nya to surrender themselves and their arms, by which time some parts of the south had reverted to tribal administration and yet others had become 'free-fire zones' in which government troops shot at anyone they saw.

The southern military HQ was situated in Maridi. The town was filled with civilians, resettled under military protection, but they were not allowed outside the military perimeter to cultivate their vegetable plots. Schools remained closed and all essential supplies came in by air, a military transport aircraft flying daily between Maridi and Juba, about 200 miles by road. Occasionally a military convoy was organised for bulk supplies, but it required a large military escort, and as bridges along the road had been destroyed, heavy bridging equipment had to be carried along to place over rivers to enable the vehicles to cross. In Equatoria Province the army was consolidating the towns, and the Anya-Nya the countryside.

The Anya-Nya changes tactics

By February 1966, as its leaders prepared for the long struggle ahead, the Anya-Nya had begun to develop its own military framework and administration. Furthermore its policy towards the inhabitants of the south had changed. Suddenly they were wanted as friends, and were to be treated as such. According to Keith Kyle, who spent four weeks in the south in early 1966 and was the first Western journalist to enter Equatoria Province officially, the Anya-Nya HQ was at the border town of Akobo, about seven miles from the Ethiopian frontier in an area inhabited on both sides of the border by the Nuer tribe, the sector on the Ethiopian side being only 'lightly administered'. The Anya-Nya had three camps on the Ethiopian side, each containing 400–500 men, who conducted raids into Sudan for cattle, grain, arms and recruits. These camps had been poorly coordinated, but a couple of months previously a delegation of the Azania Liberation Front (ALF) had established an overall command under Colonel Nyingeri Ajulo. The ALF was beginning to flaunt its rank structure.

The political and military GHQ of the revolt was situated deep in the forest, somewhere between Maridi and Yei, away from roads that were monitored from the air by government aircraft and approachable only by secret trails. From there orders were sent out to the military commanders of regions and sectors, and instructions issued to administrators appointed to run rural areas under Anya-Nya control. One of the senior ALF military commanders at the GHQ was Colonel Joseph Lagu, who frequently left the camp to organise arms supplies in Uganda. There seemed to be hardly any border crossing problems. Senior ALF officers hovered around the Ugandan towns of Arua, near the Congo border, Gulu, the chief northern administrative centre, and Kitgum, which controlled the arms trail from the Kenyan port of Mombasa through sparsely inhabited parts of Kenya and Uganda into Equatoria Province.

Peace villages

In April 1966 Premier Mahgoub toured the south for a first-hand assessment of situation. During his travels he met the chiefs of the major tribes, who asked for arms to protect themselves against the Anya-Nya. A small number of rifles were issued to certain of them. They also asked for army protection, which caused Mahgoub to launch a programme whereby 'peace villages' would be set up away from the fringes of the forests, where people could live in peace under the protection of army guns. This programme was slow to get under way, and was never really a success.

On his return to Khartoum, Mahgoub announced a 'Month of the South Campaign' and appealed for national unity. He said that some 'normal services', such as policing, had been resumed in the south, but admitted on 15 May that the rebels were imposing taxes and had set up their own tribunals. However he emphasised that the security forces were there to enforce the law. Northerners suddenly appreciated the fact that it was necessary to appeal to and win over the southerners. Mahgoub urged government-backed and government-subsidised chiefs to do all they could to restore their tribal authority

The Anya-Nya command structure

During 1966 a few political leaders in exile returned to southern Sudan, but they met with a mixed reception as the Anya-Nya military commanders did not welcome their authority being encroached upon. Two of these were Joseph Oduhu and Aggrey Jaden, uneasy partners who both claimed to lead the ALF. In the spring, Jaden had attempted to form the first provisional government of the south, but had been unsuccessful as general support was lacking and the idea was viewed doubtfully by the Anya-Nya. At that time Oduhu had been under arrest in Eastern Equatoria after a difference of opinion with Saturnino Lohure. Lohure subsequently sought the leadership, and although he remained a prominent political figure this prize eluded him. He had been early to throw in his lot with the Anya-Nya, but was eventually killed by them on 25 July 1966. Mahgoub scoffed at the attempt to form a southern government, describing it as 'children at play' and denying that it had any effect on his policies.

Premier Sadik Mahdi

On 25 July 1966 Mahgoub was replaced as premier by the leader of the Umma Party, Sadik Mahdi, a well-educated, 30-year-old, pro-Western politician who became allied to President Azhari's NUP. His appointment caused a split in the Umma Party and right-wing members broke away under the leadership of Mahdi's uncle, Imam el-Hadi al-Mahdi, whose aim was to institute an Islamic state. As some members of the Umma Party refused to serve under Mahdi he was not able to form a government until December. Although he was regarded, especially by the West, as an enlightened leader, his attitude towards the south was much the same as that of his predecessor.

Pacification with persuasion

Sadik Mahdi continued Mahgoub's policy of containing the rebels and retained the peace village programme, but placed restraints on the army in the south. Soldiers would no longer be allowed to shoot people at random in the 'free-fire zones', destroy crops or confiscate cattle. His declared policy was to crush the rebellion and bring about a dialogue with all elements favouring a political solution. He was able to carry William Deng of SANU along with him.

Mahdi dismissed the unpopular southern minister Buth Diu from the government, worked for elections in the south and coined the phrase 'pacification with persuasion'. He told his North African Muslim partners in the UN Economic Commission for Africa that his government wanted to join the East African Group, which was seen as heresy by the Muslim northerners in Sudan and further antagonised his uncle and the right wing of the Umma Party. However the statement was not taken too seriously, being considered merely a political gesture towards the southerners.

Some elements of the army in the south were not too happy about the way the war was being fought, the way it was depicted in communiqués and the fact that impromptu, covert military groups were appearing. One of these was the Soldiers and Officers Front, and it is interesting to note that soldiers took precedence over officers in this secret organisation. In 1966 this group produced a pamphlet entitled *The Battle for the South is against Imperialism*, which attributed the killings at Juba and Wau to the army's lack of positive motives for fighting and a spirit of despondency amongst them The government, which frequently ignored advice from serving officers with experience in the south, did not heed this warning and continued to issue misleading communiqués.

Government offensive

A major sweeping operation was conducted by the army in the south between 6 and 20 May 1966 against a major (unnamed) Anya-Nya centre in Equatoria Province. There were a dozen or so centres by this time, several in remote, abandoned mission stations. Afterwards a government communiqué claimed that a prominent Anya-Nya leader (unnamed) had been killed and 528 rebels had been taken prisoner, obviously designed to rebut allegations that northern soldiers did not take prisoners. There had been several similar operations, but few had netted many prisoners. One reason why few prisoners were taken by government forces was that the Anya-Nya intelligence network was good, and it invariably obtained prior notice of government operations. Therefore the Anya-Nya were able to vacate their camps in plenty of time, either to return later when the military operation ended or to move to a fresh site. Remote, abandoned mission stations were favoured by the Anya-Nya as they usually consisted of several buildings and were ideal to house a HQ staff and base. Government troops were often at a disadvantage owing to lack of intelligence about activities in the southern forests. They did not know the local dialects, whereas the Anya-Nya invariably had members of local tribes in its ranks, who were able to obtain instant information about Muslim forces in the area.

Round-table conference report

In September 1966 the round-table conference report suggested that a centralised form of government no longer suited Sudan. The report was not made public, although copies were circulated to the political parties. This was not the answer that Premier Sadik Mahdi wanted, so he established a constitutional draft committee to consider the southern problem.

In December a constitutional crisis arose, pitching the High Court against the Constituent Assembly over the latter's banning of the Communist Party and the unseating of communist deputies in November 1965. The communists had appealed against this decision to the High Court, which on 22 December 1966 upheld their appeal. At an emergency meeting the following day the Constituent Assembly refused to reinstate the communists or declare the Communist Party legal. Police had to be called in to eject hostile demonstrators and the protest spilled into the streets. The government launched an appeal against the High Court's decision, and in turn the High Court sought protection from the constitution. There the matter rested for a while.

It should be mentioned that the Communist Party was the only political organisation to be really in touch with the people, to know what they thought, felt and wanted. The other political parties were aloof and remote, being in touch only with the small middle class and even smaller upper class, and lacking contact with ordinary people in the street.

An attempted coup

On 28 December 1966 Lieutenant Hussein Osman and a contingent of other young communist army officers tried unsuccessfully to seize the presidential palace and the central post office. Osman had persuaded about 300 officer cadets to take part in this venture in an attempt 'to end the state of constitutional anarchy'. About 400 people were arrested, including Osman, Colonel Gaafar Mohammed al-Numeiry (in charge of Eastern Command), Abdul Khalik Mahgoub (leader of the banned Communist Party) and former Premier Mohammed Ahmad Mahgoub, who denied that the Umma Party was in any way involved in the attempted coup. The left-wing newspaper *Akhbar al-Usbu* was banned. On 1 January 1967 all the civilians who had been arrested were released, and later some of the military officers were also freed.

President al-Azhari called the attempted coup 'a childish deed by a young officer', and Premier Mahdi still refused to permit the re-establishment of the Communist Party. However to placate sections of the rowdy crowds still on the streets, on the 21st a Socialist Party was allowed to appear, which unofficially absorbed a number of former Communist Party members.

Lieutenant Osman and certain other officers involved in the attempted coup were sentenced to long terms of imprisonment. Numeiry was released on 9 January and sent to command the Infantry School at Omdurman. He was told there would be no further promotion for him, which I was later informed by his friends had turned him into a determined revolutionary.

Eritrea, Ethiopia and Chad

Relations between Sudan and Ethiopia continued to improve on the surface at least, and a joint boundary commission demarcated the full extent of the frontier between the two countries. The next bonding move was a state visit by Emperor Haile Selassie to Sudan on 23–6 February 1967, during which communists and Eritrean refugees staged hostile demonstrations. The NUP and the Islamic Charter Front refused to take part in the reception ceremonies. According to Sudanese estimates about 7000 Eritrean nationalists had fled to Sudan as the result of Ethiopian military operations against them. At the end of the visit it was announced that Ethiopia and Sudan would sign a treaty on the refugees, with the option of repatriation or removal from the border regions, However in April the Sudanese minister of the interior stated that the Ethiopian government had decided to evacuate all villages along the Sudanese border, and to move the Eritreans living in them to areas within reasonable reach of army and police posts. He reaffirmed that Sudan would not interfere in the internal affairs of neighbouring countries. In practice very little changed.

Relations between the government of Sudan and adjacent Chad, a large country (1.2 million square kilometers) that had gained independence from France in 1960, were mercurial and each harboured the other's dissidents. In mid 1966 the president of Chad had accused the Khartoum government of harbouring the Chadian Islamic government-in-exile. Periodic border friction had occurred between the two countries, but relations had improved by September. The Sudanese government was accepting dissident refugees from several countries and allowing them to live in special camps run by the army, being fully involved in African international power play and seeming to enjoy this form of intrigue.

Elections in the south

Elections in the south began on 8 March 1967 and ran for about three weeks so that all voters would have enough time to get to the polling stations, some of which were set up in remote forest and bush areas. To help the illiterate (the great majority) the various parties used symbols to identify themselves, such as familiar animals, but there was still much confusion. Despite the Anya-Nya's boasts that it would prevent voting from taking place, this only happened in three out of 36 constituencies. The constituencies in question were adjacent to the Ugandan border and government troops were unable to enforce control over them for the purpose of the elections, even temporarily. The elections were boycotted by the Southern Front, but as it was ensconced in Khartoum and had little contact with the people in the south it was a meaningless gesture. The results were 15 seats for the Umma Party, 10 for William Deng's SANU (all in Bahr el-Ghazal Province) and one for the Liberal Party, represented by Buth Diu. Twenty-one National Assembly members had already been seated by default in 1965.

Mahgoub returns as premier

Premier Sadik Mahdi was defeated in a vote of confidence in the National Assembly on 15 May 1967 by a coalition formed by President Ismail al-Azhari and Imam el-Hadi al-Mahdi, Mahdi's rival. Mahdi had some southern and tribal support, so as a counter the imam put forward the idea of a presidential form of government, on US lines. However on the 16th Mohammed Ahmad Mahgoub formed a government, thus resuming his former role as premier. His government contained Buth Diu of the Liberal Party, Hilary Logale of the Southern Front and Alfred Wol of SANU. The Umma Party was still of the mistaken belief that William Deng's SANU had a considerable intellectual following in the south, and decided to favour it. SANU dithered between supporting federation or secession. Later, in December, the Umma Party, the NUP and the UPD merged to form the Unionist Democratic Party (UDP).

Black central movements

Previously, in April 1964, Philip Ghabosh Abbas, a member of the Nuba tribe and former clergyman, had become the leader of the General Union of Nubas (GUN), and he had subsequently succeeded in bringing together five separate black African organisations under his leadership. Abbas claimed that together these organisations represented some four-million non-Arabised Africans in the north. These he welded into the United Sudanese African Liberation Front. Abbas claimed that he had organised a coup against Premier Mahgoub, due to be sprung on 29 May 1969, but that he had been forestalled by Numeiry. Abbas then fled Sudan, his dream of a black-power federated bloc in Central Sudan – which he hoped would eventually dominate the whole country – having been shattered. However it has to be said that the feasibility of black Africans taking over an Arab capital and Arab-inhabited terrain was extremely doubtful anyway.

Meanwhile the reappearance of Mahgoub as premier brought no comfort to the southerners, who remembered the repressive measures he had introduced during his previous terms of office. Indeed, as they feared, he reintroduced his former harsh laws and regulations, which gave virtual licence to his soldiers in the south to keep order as they thought fit. He also introduced some new measures to cope with unrest. From the government's point of view the security situation in the south had worsened during 1967.

In the foreign field, the six-day Arab–Israeli War in June 1967 was also a watershed for Sudan, as it severed its diplomatic relations with the USA and certain other Western countries, coming out openly against Israel. A Sudanese infantry battalion was sent to the Suez Canal area, and even though it arrived after the hostilities had ceased it was instructed to remain in place at Port Fuad in Egypt. Americans and Westerners in general were eased out from their positions in Sudan.

5
Numeiry to Power

On 10 January 1968 President Ismail al-Azhari announced that all who had taken part in antigovernment uprisings in previous years, including the some '45 000 Sudanese' (a large underestimate) who had fled from the south, would be granted amnesty if they returned and gave themselves up. Not one took advantage of the offer.

During the first quarter of 1968 the now regular pattern of small guerrilla-like operations interspersed with government reprisals continued. On 28 April it was reported in government communiqués that 500 rebels from Ethiopia had crossed into Upper Nile Province and attacked government security forces, who had killed 80 of the attackers and wounded 74. After this the tempo of activity in the south slackened off considerably.

Revolutionary momentum

So far the revolutionary momentum in the south had been slow to develop, largely due to the lack of strong, clear-sighted leadership. However the Anya-Nya had become a recognisable guerrilla force and was about to enter a protracted stage of guerrilla warfare. It was operating independently of the politicians who claimed to have authority over all or parts of it, and Anya-Nya commanders in the field remained autonomous. For example Colonel Joseph Lagu, the regional commander in Eastern Equatoria, had established his own independent command structure and would not cooperate with either the nominal commander-in-chief, the other regional commanders or any of the southern politicians.

The various southern political parties and factions had differing aims and did not collaborate with each other. The section of SANU led by William Deng and the Sudan Unity Party, led by Philemon Majok, now advocated a united Sudan, while the Anya-Nya in the field were fighting for complete independence. A compromise solution was put forward by the Southern Front, led by Clement Mboro, to discuss federation, provided the south was granted the right to self-determination, while most southern politicians in exile supported either federation or independence.

Southern Sudan provisional government

In an attempt to prevent further splintering and to achieve unity, in August 1968 a number of southern leaders met in the town of Angudri in Eastern Equatoria to form a southern freedom government. The governmental structure that Aggrey Jaden had attempted to put in place had never really taken shape, and was certainly never effective. However this meeting resulted in the appearance on 18 August of the Southern Sudan Provisional Government (SSPG), headed by Jaden, who assumed the title of president, his deputy being Gordon Mayen. The object of the SSPG was to govern and to establish an administration in areas under Anya-Nya control or influence, but as it lacked support from Eastern Equatoria, the Zande region and the Moru region, its task was a difficult one from the start. Ignoring dissenting and fractious southern leaders living in the north, the south or in exile, it hoped it would gain prestige and strength from the fact that it was actually operating in the south as a guerrilla government in the forests, but almost immediately local hostility forced the SSPG to move westwards from Eastern Equatoria to Bungu, near Yei.

The SSPG assumed, without any real foundation, authority over the Anya-Nya and decreed that its commander-in-chief, General Tafeng, would be directly responsible to President Jaden. The name of the Land Freedom Army was changed to the Anya-Nya Armed Forces (ANAF), but in practice the SSPG had only nominal authority over the ANAF in Central and Western Equatoria. The Eastern region still would not cooperate, while the regional commanders in Bahr el-Ghazal and Upper Nile Provinces remained remote and aloof.

By the end of 1968 the strength of the ANAF had probably risen to about 10 000, less than one fifth of whom possessed firearms of any sort. With this increase in size came the problems of desertion, indiscipline, individualism and banditry. Camps were established to provide basic military training, but many of the recruits, after completing their initial training, did not report to the detachments to which they had been posted and instead returned home with their weapons to fight in tribal wars. There were reports of ANAF platoons refusing to carry out operations, of suddenly turning on a rival tribe, or of merely disintegrating as they fought amongst themselves over a tribal issue. There were many cases of theft of cattle, goods and produce, of abduction of women, of deliberate arson and destruction of huts or villages when thwarted, and sometimes of the murder of people they were supposed to live amongst and protect.

Generally ANAF fighters were neither politically motivated nor disciplined and it seemed that no steps had yet been taken to provide them with political indoctrination, which is so essential in a guerrilla-type army. Central authority was weak and often ineffective, and all depended on the personality, calibre and skill of the local commander, be he in charge of a region or a platoon. There still remained a few extrovert, flamboyant, sabre-rattling Anya-Nya commanders who had little regard for the feelings of the people, or for the cause for which they were supposed to be fighting.

When establishing its administration the SSPG took up the idea put forward by Izbone Mendiri in 1965 of dividing the south into nine regions, each under a regional commissioner and subdivided into separate districts with district commissioners or chairmen, who would be responsible to the regional commissioners. In turn the latter would be responsible to a combined military and political HQ, which the SSPG was trying to become. Districts were organised into village councils, and an attempt was made to train home guards as protection against the excesses of government troops. Mendiri had already established markets in the Bari and Moru areas, both of which were under ANAF influence.

Internal differences

The SSPG was not a happy organisation, being continually rent with quarrels and jealousy as smaller tribes such as the Bari and the Laturo resented Dinka domination. Differences arose between Aggrey Jaden, a Bari, and Gordon Mayen, a Dinka, and friction increased as the months passed, which tended further to divide the SSPG into two hostile camps. In September 1968 Jaden openly complained that he was not being supported and respected as president of the SSPG, alleging that Vice President Camillo Dhol, a Dinka, was working to depose him. Without Jaden's knowledge, some of his supporters solicited ANAF support, and managed to win over General Tafeng and some of his officers to their side to help oppose the Dinka majority in the rampant tribalistic struggle within the SSPG. The friction became so severe that in early 1969 Jaden, fearing his own safety, decamped to Nairobi. Jaden had always followed a cautious line and had been accused of indecisiveness by his own supporters, who were disappointed that he had not made a firmer stand against Dinka dominance within the SSPG.

The Nile Provisional Government

The SSPG continued unsteadily under the leadership of Mayen until a convention was held in March 1969 near Yei, which many of Jaden's supporters refused to attend. At the convention southern Sudan was named the Nile State, and the name of the SSPG was changed to the Nile Provisional Government. Mayen was elected its first president. The policy of the Nile Provisional Government, still dominated by Dinkas, was to prosecute a 'war of liberation', to fight for complete independence and to work for southern unity

The Anyidi Revolutionary Government

Having failed to oust Mayen from the presidency of the Nile Provisional Government, General Tafeng, together with a small group of ANAF officers and several prominent southern politicians, formed the Anyidi Revolutionary Government on 15 September, Anyidi being an old trading post in the south. Assuming the title of president, Tafeng was joined by Jaden, who returned apprehensively from exile to become Tafeng's foreign minister. Another prominent southern politician, Aliaba Loboka Surer, became its minister of finance and information. The Anyidi Revolutionary Government was tribally motivated and had really been jolted into existence by the overwhelming Dinka majority in the Nile Provisional Government.

The Sudan-Azania Government

Around the same time in Western Equatoria, near the Congo border in the Zande region, a Zande separatist movement led by Michael Tawili appeared. It was called the Sue River Revolutionary Government and the area it claimed to govern became known as the Suer Republic. The River Sue flowed northwards from the vicinity of Yambio, near the Congo frontier, passing through Wau before flowing into the Sudd (a section of the Nile river side that was almost impenetrable as it was choked with undergrowth and reeds).

At about the same time in East Africa, Izbone Mendiri formed the Sudan-Azania Government. So it can be seen that by the end of 1969 there were three southern governments in the south itself, all claiming to represent the south; one southern party in exile (the Sudan-Azania Government); and three southern parties in the north – the Southern Front, SANU and the Sudan Unity Party. In all seven parties were claiming to represent the south.

Elections – April 1968

Meanwhile a general election had been held in Sudan from 18–25 April 1968, the results being declared on 6 May. The UDP had gained 101 seats, the pro-Sadik Mahdi branch of the Umma Party 38, the pro-imam branch of the Umma Party 30, SANU 15, the Southern Front 10 and others 11. During the election the imam had openly challenged his nephew, Sadik Mahdi, and so split the Umma Party. The PDP had boycotted the election. Santino Deng, Buth Diu and William Deng had failed to be re-elected. Allegations of electoral irregularities, bribery, coercion and corruption were rife, as was deliberate confusion of the already bewildered illiterates, who had had to rely on pictorial symbols to guide them. It was also alleged that many southerners had been detained in the peace villages, and told how to vote before being released.

Mohammed Ahmad Mahgoub formed another coalition government, consisting of the UDP, the Umma Party (pro-imam) and the Southern Front. The two southern ministers were Clement Mboro and Hilary Logale, and Jervase Vak, a southerner, succeeded Philemon Majok on the Supreme Council.

On the 5th, the day before the election results had been made public, William Deng, leader of a SANU element, and some of his supporters had been ambushed and killed on the road from Rumbek to Wau after refusing a proffered military escort. Southerners alleged that he had been deliberately murdered by northern soldiers. This was denied by the government, which a week later, when Deng's death was announced on Radio Omdurman, blamed 'outlaws' for his death. Premier Mahgoub was convinced that Alfred Wol, a Dinka, was responsible for the murder, having lost his seat to one of Deng's candidates in the election. Wol denied the accusation.

An executive presidency

The constitution had been foisted on Sudan upon independence by the British and reflected their own, with a purely ceremonial head of state (the president) and political power being vested in the premier of the day, who could be removed if he lost a vote of confidence in the National Assembly or was swept away by the polls. The ambitious Mahdi family, looking ahead, wanted something more substantial. It wanted to change the constitution and introduce an executive president.

On 12 April 1969 the Umma Party, which had resolved its differences and reunited, issued a series of demands: that the imam should become executive president, that Sadik Mahdi should be premier, that the Umma Party should have a greater proportion of ministerial posts, and that the present UDP–Umma Party coalition government should continue in office. The UDP would not agree. On the 23rd Premier Mahgoub resigned, but said he would remain as caretaker until the two main parties came to some agreement, but no progress was made.

The period between 1964 and May 1969 is often regarded by Western commentators as one of ideal democracy in Sudan, but in fact it was one of continual political squabbling over the yet to be established post of executive president. There were several contenders for this dazzling prize, the main ones being Ismail al-Azhari, the current president, Sadik Mahdi (who as a constitutional president had little political power), and his uncle the imam. Later Mohammed Ahmad Mahgoub told me that the Mahdis seemed to think that the rule of the state was a booty to be inherited and divided between them.

A bloodless coup

On 25 May 1969 a military junta headed by Gaafar Mohammed Numeiry overthrew the Mahgoub caretaker government in a bloodless coup. A Free Officers' (sometimes referred to as a Young Officers') Movement had been in existence within the armed forces since 1957. A pale copy of the Egyptian model, for years it had been ineffective, but now at last it had suddenly sprung to life. Most of the top senior officers in the armed forces were out of the country, on either official or private business, so the chosen time was opportune. The coup took place at 0200 hours, and at 0600 hours Radio Omdurman announced the takeover and the list of new ministers. The coup had been well prepared. Mahgoub later insisted to me that President Nasser had been behind the plot.

Born in 1930, Numeiry had entered the Sudan Military College, becoming a second lieutenant in the Sudan Defence Force in 1952. He had attended the Sudanese Staff College and later the US Command and General Staff College. A leaked CIA observation on him during this period was that 'if there is to be revolution in Sudan, this officer will probably lead it'. After his punitive period of command in the Infantry School, Numeiry had served with distinction in Equatoria Province.

Numeiry formed a Revolutionary Council under his chairmanship, and proclaimed the establishment of the Democratic Republic of Sudan. He stated he had taken power because the contemporary history of Sudan had been nothing but a series of catastrophes, and because too many political parties with selfish motives had been in power for too long. Numeiry had been in command of the Khartoum garrison and had therefore been well placed to carry out the coup. Although he had probably been involved in at least three previous plots or attempted coups, so far he had not been regarded as having any political thirst for power, despite having been arrested in December 1966 after the failed attempt to topple the government of Sadik Mahdi.

The only civilian on the Revolutionary Council was Babiker Awadalla, a lawyer and reputed to be anti-American, who was appointed premier. Awadalla had taken part in the overthrow of President Abboud and had subsequently refused the post of premier, becoming chief justice instead. In May 1967 he resigned when his decision regarding the illegality of the Communist Party was overruled. The Awadalla government contained only one southerner, Joseph Garang, a well-known member of the Communist Party who had little contact with or sympathy for the south, being more of a communist at heart than a southerner. Also in the Awadalla government were several members of the new Sudan Socialist Party, formed in January 1967 after the Communist Party had been banned.

On the 26th Numeiry suspended the constitution, abolished the Supreme Council, National Assembly and Civil Service Commission, and ordered the dissolution of all political parties. He took over the defence portfolio and promoted himself to the rank of major general, retired over twenty serving officers (mostly senior to himself), dismissed over 30, and promoted selected officers and appointed them to key posts. The new Revolutionary Council issued stern warnings to prospective counter-revolutionaries, and gave notice that saboteurs and strikers would face the death penalty.

The new government's declared policy was to work for a 'modern Sudan' and follow a neutral policy in foreign affairs, but on the 27th premier Awadalla stated that his government would support 'liberation movements', naming the Palestine Liberation Organisation. Southerners were disappointed as his declaration leaned positively towards the Arab bloc and away from the African one. On the 31st Numeiry announced there would be no return to multiparty democracy, but nor would there be a communist-type regime. This disappointed those who thought that Numeiry had left-wing leanings. Numeiry also stated that 13 officers had been dismissed, and that 64 former political leaders and civilians remained in detention. The following day some detainees were released, including Clement Mboro and Hilary Logale, but censorship was imposed. Several thousand people in Khartoum demonstrated in favour of the new regime.

The Soviets arrive

When Numeiry first came to power his main opponents were the Ansar seat and the Umma Party, so he wooed the communists and gave in to many of their demands. During July and August 1969 several plots to overthrow him were exposed, and there were other rumblings of discontent below the surface. So far no Soviet military advisers had been active in Sudan, but Numeiry now opened the door to them, adding to the discontent. In an interview on 1 August in *Le Monde*, Numeiry said that his regime had numerous and powerful enemies, naming them as the Islamic Charter Front and the Ansar and Khatmia sects, in other words the traditional, the conventional and the religious. In terms of numbers, the Ansar sect, for example, claimed a following of three million. Press censorship, which had been eased to some extent was tightened again in October.

In the weeks following the coup there was some sweeping nationalisation of both Sudanese and foreign firms, which was interpreted as a sop to the communists, with whom Numeiry, from initial weakness, was forced to work. A further weakening of contacts with the West followed, but Numeiry admitted that the absence of diplomatic relations with the USA was having a dampening effect on the economy.

On 26 October Numeiry reshuffled his government. He assumed the premiership and retained his chairmanship of both the Revolutionary Council and the Defence Ministry. Awadalla, who was pro-Marxist but not a member of the Communist Party, became deputy chairman of the Revolutionary Council. This new government contained two southerners: Joseph Garang, an ardent communist, and Abel Alier, a Dinka Protestant lawyer from Bor in Upper Nile Province.

Several senior officers were arrested in December for anti-revolutionary activities. Numeiry announced on 12 December that another plot against his government had been foiled, claiming that an American aircraft had landed in eastern Sudan, allegedly to prepare for the arrival of foreign accomplices of the Muslim Brotherhood, a pan-Middle East

Islamic political organisation. He admitted that elements of the former political parties were active underground in Khartoum and in adjacent countries. On 13 January 1970 the new defence minister, General Khalid Hassan Abbas, claimed that the army had foiled yet another attempt to overthrow the government, this time by an anti-revolutionary organisation with the collaboration of Brigadier Abdullah Mohammed Aden, one of the officers who had been retired after the 1969 coup. In March another plot was foiled, said to be the tenth in as many months.

The Aba Island incident

Tension continued to rise between Numeiry and the Ansar, led by Imam al-Mahdi, and on 27 March 1970, when Numeiry was on his way to Aba Island in Blue Nile Province, the traditional seat of the Ansar sect, an attempt was made to assassinate him, causing him to abandon his planned visit. According to Numeiry, as he was leaving an airfield near Kosti the Ansar had launched a machine-gun attack. On three previous occasions he had been prevented from passing through Kosti, which was near Aba Island. A government delegation was sent to Aba Island to see the imam, who told them that Numeiry must resign, which caused Numeiry to declare publicly that the Ansar, led by the imam, was about to plunge the country into civil war.

On the 30th Numeiry, with about 40 000 troops and some armoured support moved against the 30 000 or so Ansar assembled on Aba Island, which was about 30 miles in length, extremely narrow and normally had a population of about 9000. Numeiry's order to surrender was rejected by the imam, so Sudanese troops, supported by aircraft, attacked the island. The following day the defence minister stated that Aba Island had been recaptured after 36 hours of bitter fighting in both Aba Island and Omdurman, that the rebels had surrendered or been captured, that large quantities of arms and ammunition had been seized, and that pockets of counter-revolutionary rebels were still being mopped up and houses searched. The government admitted to the loss of 40 of soldiers, but did not know the extent of the Ansar casualties.

Numeiry was not without foreign support. On the day of the battle the governments of Iraq and Egypt had expressed their willingness to help, while Libya had gone further and sent a token military force and some aircraft to Sudan. (In 1960 King Idris of Libya had been deposed by Colonel Moamar Gaddafi, a revolutionary officer who was friendly with President Numeiry.) It was also suspected that Egypt had sent some of the combat aircraft and pilots that had taken part in the attack.

(Mahgoub told me that Sudan then had neither aircraft nor the pilots to fly them.)

Death of Imam Mahdi

On 1 April 1970 President Nasser sent his vice president, Anwar Sadat, to Khartoum to steady the rather shaken young revolutionary officers and assure them of Egypt's support. Ansar members who had fled to Europe later claimed that Aba Island had been attacked by 25 MiG aircraft, some flown by Egyptian pilots and others by Soviet pilots, and that surface-to-surface missiles had been fired at them from Kosti. The Ansar made exaggerated claims about the number of losses on both sides, but independent sources estimated that there had been about 1000 deaths all told.

The imam, who had asked for a period of grace to prepare himself for surrender, slipped away with several companions in two vehicles, but on the 31st they were all killed by frontier guards when attempting to cross into Ethiopia at the Kurmuk checkpoint. The Sudanese foreign minister alleged that plans for the imam's insurrection had been drawn up in February 1970 at a conference in Jedda (Saudia Arabia), where the Umma Party, the Ansars' political arm, had been given the task of implementing them. Numeiry said that the struggle against the Ansar would revert to being a political one, and that there would not be an all-out military offensive, but did admit that Mohammed Salih Omar, leader of the Muslim Brotherhood, was being sought by the police.

Radio Omdurman announced that over 300 persons, including a number of foreigners, had been arrested for implication in the insurrection, including Brigadier Hamid. Hamid and a number of others were charged with training members of the Ansar in the use of firearms. Sadik Mahdi, former leader of the now dissolved Umma Party, who had been under arrest since June 1969, was sent into exile in Egypt to prevent him from being elected imam in place of his deceased uncle. Numeiry also expelled Abdul Khalik Mahgoub, leader of the Communist Party. On 7 April amnesty was given to the inhabitants of Aba Island, but not to the rebels who had been arrested or escaped.

Purge of the Communist Party

Having dealt with the Ansar–Umma Party threat, Numeiry was still faced with hostility from the Communist Party, which was the largest in any Arab country at the time – the government put its strength at about 10 000, while the party itself claimed to have influence over one million people. In November 1970 Numeiry dismissed three of the original members of his Revolutionary Council: Colonel Babiker al-Nur, Major Osman Hamadalla and Major Hashem Atta, all of whom were suspected of leaking details of confidential government discussions to the Communist Party. Numeiry then began to purge all communists from his administration, and on 12 February 1971 declared that he would destroy the Communist Party.

The Soviet Union sent a delegation to Khartoum to intercede on behalf of the Communist Party, but Numeiry was not moved. On 17 May he banned the Students' Union, the Women's Organisation and the Youth Organisation (all communist groups) and five leading communists were banished to Kodak in Upper Nile Province. On the 25th he announced that the Sudanese Socialist Union (SSU) was to be the country's sole permitted political party, and that its 20-member central committee, under his chairmanship, would prepare for its first congress, to be held before the end of the year.

Unwittingly, Numeiry had forestalled a Soviet-organised plot to seize power in Khartoum, and in fact the KGB had been working to gain control over the Sudanese Communist Party and the Sudanese trade unions. Nonetheless, on the annual Independence Day parade (28 May), Soviet SAM-2 anti-aircraft missiles and other Soviet weaponry were displayed for the first time, and Sudan continued to accept economic and military aid from the USSR, and to trade with that country.

Communist take over

Suddenly, on 19 July 1971, the Numeiry government was overthrown by a group of left-wing officers led by Major Hashem Atta. An armoured detachment, supported by presidential guards, surprised Numeiry and members of the Revolutionary Council and placed them under arrest: it was all over in twenty minutes. A Beirut report stated that the real leaders of the coup were Brigadier Abdul Rahman, commander of the Presidential Guard, and Colonel Abdul Moneim Riad, commander of the Third (and only) Armoured Brigade, who were soon in full control of Khartoum. Be that as it may, on the 20th it was Atta who announced the formation of seven-man Revolutionary Council, which was to be the sovereign body of the Democratic and Independent Republic of Sudan.

Atta promised democracy for all popular organisations and home rule for the south. He banned all the political groups set up by Numeiry, revoked all his edicts and released about 50 political prisoners. The ban on the four communist organisations – the Trade Union Federation, the Students' Federation, the Women's Organisation and the Youth Organisation – was lifted, control of the police was taken over by Khalid Ibrahim (who had been retired on 30 March 1970), several ministers were arrested and newspapers were banned, with the exception of the English-language *Nile Mirror*, then edited by Joseph Garang, a southern communist.

There were others who claimed to be coup leaders, two being Colonel Tigany Babiker and Major Osman Hamadalla. Colonel Nur, who had been the Sudanese Defence Attaché in Kampala until Milton Obote had asked that he be recalled because of his political activities, later said the coup had been in preparation since February 1971, and that it had a left-wing character but was not communist. Nur and Hamadalla had been in Britain and were returning home by airliner, but when the plane entered Libyan air space it was ordered to land. Both Nur and Hamadalla had just been interviewed on the BBC African Service, and had mentioned how and when they would be travelling The pilot refused to land in Libya and asked for permission to land in Malta. This request was refused when the Maltese realised that the aircraft was still in Libyan air space, so the pilot had to land at Benina airport in Libya, where the two Sudanese officers were detained.

Meanwhile there was resistance to the Atta government on the streets of Khartoum, with large demonstrations for the return of Numeiry. Consultations between the governments of Libya and Egypt ended on the 21st with the decision to back Numeiry rather than Atta. Indeed that day a prominent Egyptian editor, Ahmad Hamroush, flew from Cairo to Khartoum, to plead for Numeiry's life. However the Soviet ambassador had hastened to congratulate Atta on his coup. Iraq was possibly the only Middle Eastern country glad to see Numeiry ousted – then at odds with most of the other countries, Iraq instantly recognised the Atta government and dispatched a delegation to congratulate him. The plane carrying the Iraqi delegation was denied permission to land at airports between Baghdad and Khartoum, but as the plane was running short of fuel, it was eventually given permission to put down at Jedda in Saudi Arabia. When coming in to land the aircraft hit some high ground about ten miles from the town and crashed, killing ten people on board and injuring others. There was no suspicion of sabotage.

According to Egyptian sources the Atta coup had been organised by the Communist Abdul Khalik Mahgoub from his refuge in the Bulgarian embassy in Khartoum, where he had sought asylum after his escape from prison at the end of June, but this was formally denied by the Bulgarian ambassador. The Egyptian newspaper *Al Ahram* also alleged that Mahgoub had taken advantage of the absence of the defence minister, who was visiting Moscow, and the head of the air force, who was visiting Yugoslavia. It further alleged that the Atta plotters had sought to make contact with 'opportunist elements' in the armed forces, but had only succeeded in subverting the armoured brigade and the presidential guards who had arrested Numeiry. Other garrisons in the country stood by and waited to see what happened – none joined Atta, despite his appeals to them.

Numeiry returns to power

On 22 July 1971 the Sudanese troops serving in the Suez Canal zone, now up to brigade strength, were flown back to Khartoum in Libyan Anatov transport aircraft. Although they were not involved in any action, their presence was favourable to Numeiry and detrimental to Atta. Later that day Radio Omdurman announced Numeiry's return to power, stating that forces loyal to him, led by Lieutenant Mohammed Ali Kerbassi and other officers who had refused to join Atta, had seized the bridges over the Nile between Khartoum and Omdurman and arrested the leaders of the Atta coup. The bridges over the Nile were key strategic points, and hence revolutionary targets. They were also a barometer for trouble – the presence of soldiers to guard them signalled danger in the air. Numeiry himself then broadcast to the people, blaming the communists for the coup against his regime.

There were conflicting reports about how Numeiry's return to power had happened, and confusion reigned for a while. The fact was that the successful countercoup was conducted by just three T-55 tanks, commanded by a warrant officer with non-commissioned officers as crew, which made a frontal attack on the presidential palace. Within minutes of the assault over 30 officers loyal to Numeiry, who had been detained by Atta in a guest house, were killed. Thus it was not Sudanese officers who had rallied to the rescue of Numeiry in this vital hour, but the soldiers of the armoured brigade. Their motive had been religious, as they were concerned about the grip that communism was getting on the country, to the detriment of Islam. Major Atta immediately called for 'popular resistance to foreign interference', but was arrested in the early hours of the 23rd.

On the 25th on Radio Omdurman, Numeiry described in detail his experiences during his two days of detention in the presidential palace, and how during the final loyal attack he and Farouk Abu Eissa, his foreign minister, had narrowly escaped death. Later Numeiry stated that a total of 38 persons had been killed and 119 wounded in the countercoup.

Numeiry's vengeance was swift and deadly. He passed a death sentence on Major Atta, Colonel Ahmad and Colonel Hussein, whom he considered to be the coup leaders, and immediately had them shot. He then ordered the arrest of all those suspected of having taken part in the coup, together with all known communists, who were tried by special military courts. On the 26th Colonel Nur and Major Hamadalla, who had been handed over by Colonel Gaddafi of Libya, were executed. Also hanged that day was Shafei Ahmad el-Sheikh, secretary general of the Trade Union Federation and deputy leader of the (Communist) World Federation of Trade Unions. Sheikh, a founder member of the Sudanese Communist Party and a member of its Central Committee, had taken part in the 1964 revolution and had been detained under the Abboud regime. Joseph Garang, a communist and minister for the south, was dismissed on the 24th and hanged on the 26th.

Abdul Khalik Mahgoub, secretary general of the Communist Party, was hanged on the 28th. Numeiry claimed that Mahgoub had confessed that the coup had been planned by him and the Central Committee of the party during May 1971. Mahgoub had also been arrested after the unsuccessful coup of December 1966, but released on 2 January 1967. On coming to power in 1969, Numeiry had formed a a 'tactical alliance' with the communists for expediency's sake against the Ansar, but in April 1970 he had expelled Mahgoub from Sudan. Mahgoub had returned from exile in Egypt in June, whereupon he had been placed under house arrest. In November he had been sent to prison, from where he had escaped on 30 June 1971, taking refuge in the Bulgarian embassy. It was reported that on 27 May twelve people had been executed, and that more officers had been imprisoned or dismissed.

Numeiry publicly thanked the governments of Libya and Egypt for providing practical aid to help him crush the rebellion. He was so grateful that he said his government was prepared to join the proposed Arab Federation (of Egypt, Libya and Syria) when a single-party state had been established in Sudan, which he thought might be in 1972. The Organisation for Communist Action, a Marxist–Leninist group, based in Lebanon and reputedly a KGB front organisation but claiming to be independent of both Moscow and Peking, asserted that Major Atta's regime would not have collapsed without the open intervention of the governments of Egypt, Libya and Syria, a view unofficially confirmed by the three countries themselves.

On the 27th the Soviet ambassador protested to Numeiry about the treatment of Soviet citizens in Sudan, while Numeiry accused the Iraqi government of being implicated in the Atta coup, but this was formally denied. The following day all diplomatic bags leaving the Sudan were seized and searched by the government, and as a result 83 officers were held for trial and over 1000 civilians were arrested. When the Kremlin put through a frantic top-level telephone call to Numeiry asking him to spare the lives of the arrested communist leaders, Numeiry's reputed reply was 'They were hanged this morning'.

Still obsessed with Atta's coup and the conduct of the Sudanese communists, Numeiry continued to arrest alleged communists and to purge the armed forces and judiciary of all those who might have been involved. In addition to the some 1400 arrests already announced, another batch of about 700 communists were detained in Upper Nile Province on 7 August. A mutineer soldier who had shot and killed a loyal officer was executed, bringing the official total of those executed to almost 20. Over 50 military officers had been retired or dismissed from service, as had ten judges. All those convicted were automatically deprived of their political rights, and three men accused of helping Abdul Khalik Mahgoub to escape from detention were given long prison sentences.

On 29 July Numeiry stated that there was no evidence of Soviet implication in the Atta coup, and that he did not wish for any deterioration in relations with the Soviet Union. When asked about the 1800 Soviet personnel in Sudan, he replied that the Soviet experts had come to Sudan to train the army in the use of modern equipment but were on the verge of leaving because their mission was completed, and that some had left before the coup. He said that the majority were military technicians, rather than military tacticians. However on 5 August Numeiry again declared that 'There is no place in Sudan for communism' and that 'We will not accept the Soviets as colonisers'. The failure of the Atta coup was generally regarded as a considerable setback for Soviet influence in the Middle East.

President Sadat of Egypt wrote a personal letter to Numeiry, pointing out the need to safeguard Arab–Soviet relations and strengthen Arab friendship with the Soviet camp. However on 10 September, in a speech not publicised in the Arab states, Numeiry attacked the USSR and alleged that all East European countries, with the exception of Yugoslavia, had, on the instructions of Moscow, cooperated in the attempt to overthrow him, and it was only after the failure of Moscow's 'conspiracy' in Egypt, led by the former vice president, Ali Sabry, that the conspirators in that country had tried their luck with the Atta group in Sudan. Following his estrangement with the USSR, Numeiry sought to improve relations with communist China, whose government had congratulated him on his return to power. Previously (August 1970) Numeiry had visited China and obtained a promise of loans amounting to some $35 million to build a textile factory and improve roads.

Further repressive action followed, and in early August press censorship was again imposed and certain unions were dissolved by decree. East German nationals were expelled and Soviets had to remain in their quarters. Periodic executions continued, but by September Numeiry had begun to release detainees in batches. More than 1500 were still being held. One of those released was Clement Mboro, who had been sentenced to four years' imprisonment for customs offences in 1971.

Presidential constitution

Once he had settled the Atta coup, Numeiry set work to reorganise his own house. He reshuffled his government and dismissed ministers who had been associated with communism or were suspected of having left-wing sympathies. Abel Alier succeeded the executed Joseph Garang, and two newly installed southern ministers were Luigi Adwok and Tobi Madot. On 2 August 1971 Numeiry announced that a referendum would be held in the south.

On 13 August the Revolutionary Command Council promulgated a new provisional constitution, under the terms of which the president would also be commander-in-chief and would hold office for a six-year term, with executive powers similar in many respects to those held by the president of the USA. The Revolutionary Command Council and the cabinet were dissolved. There was only one presidential candidate, Numeiry, and voting began on 15 September. The results were announced on 10 October, when it was declared that 98.6 per cent of the votes cast were for Numeiry, who was formally sworn in as the president of Sudan on the 12th. Thus the dream of the Mahdi family had been snatched by an upstart army officer.

On the 14th Numeiry appointed a 26-member government, from which some former members had been dropped. Those who remained had their portfolios reshuffled. The new members were mostly university professors. There was one woman, Mme Nafissa el-Amin, who became minister of culture. The south was not forgotten, and one of the three vice presidents, Abel Alier, was male minister for the south. Southerners were also appointed to the governorships of the three southern provinces: Luigi Adwok for Upper Nile Province, Tobi Madot for Bahr el-Ghazal Province and Hilary Logale for Equatoria Province.

Numeiry's next step was to resurrect the Sudanese Socialist Party (SSP) and make Sudan a one-party state. This was done in October 1971, and Major Maamoun Abu Zeid became the party's secretary general. No other political party was allowed to operate in Sudan. Thus Numeiry had not only survived a series of revolts and insurrections, but had also managed to change the constitution of his country to ensure his political survival. Multiparty politics in Sudan had so far only brought quarrelsome in-fighting.

6
Lagu Unites the South

Shortly after he first seized power in 1969, Numeiry said that the south was capable of self-rule within the framework of a unified state and true socialism, which was the simplest requirement of regional rule. This was followed by the June 1969 Declaration, in which he stated that he would grant the south local autonomy and implement a social, economic and cultural programme that would be similar to the proposals discussed between President Ismail al-Azhari and southern leaders earlier in the year. However Numeiry stressed that there must always be a unified Democratic Republic of Sudan.

There were varying reactions to Numeiry's declaration. The Nile Provisional Government rejected it flatly, stating that it would continue to fight for independence, but on the 24th Fahan Utur and Ahmad Mogan, the Ugandan-based leaders of the ALF, expressed their willingness to travel to Khartoum to discuss the proposed autonomy. On 22 July Gordon Mayen, leader of the Nile Provisional Government, changed tack and said that he would be prepared to negotiate with the Numeiry government, but that he would like the OAU to use its good offices to resolve the conflict. At the end of the month the newly formed Anyidi Revolutionary Government, headed by General Tafeng, stated that any agreement reached in Khartoum by the Nile Provisional Government would be valueless as his government stood for complete independence. Aliaba Loboka Surer, his minister of information, added that his government refused to recognise Gordon Mayen.

Anya-Nya activity

Apart from spasmodic guerrilla incidents there had been little real Anya-Nya activity for several months, the reason being that the southern leadership in the field was undergoing a traumatic phase of splintering and quarrelling, there being no main centralised source of direction. It is almost true to say that the only incidents that occurred were ones of tribal differences and banditry. The largest incident acknowledged by the Khartoum government took place in April in Bahr el-Ghazal Province, but this had nothing to do with the Anya-Nya, being a clash over tribal grazing rights. Over 100 people were killed and many were injured before government security forces brought the situation under control. The most notable insurgent incident announced by the authorities was that 12 rebels had been killed when attempting to sabotage a railway line, but neither place nor date were mentioned.

In late May 1969 the commanding officer in charge of the south stated that there had been no major action for some time, claiming that the Anya-Nya had been broken and dispersed into small groups. He added that the Anya-Nya had been smuggling in weapons from refugee camps in Uganda. Numeiry stated on 1 August that there could be no military solution to the rebellion in the south, explaining that his own experience in the south (he had commanded the Equatoria Military District from November 1966 to December 1967) had brought him to this conclusion, which was why he was proclaiming the right of the south to autonomy. He said that all members of his Revolutionary Command Council agreed with him in this respect, but he once again stressed that the unity of Sudan must not be jeopardised.

While presenting a stern face to the Anya-Nya, Numeiry made some attempt to mollify and help the population, enforcing a strict code of better military behaviour towards the people. Attention was given to improving the security of the peace villages, and in the interest of community relations, efforts were made to reopen medical centres and hospitals, repair bridges and introduce agricultural projects to provide work for southerners and tempt them to leave the forests and return to their former villages. However these measures were slow to start and southerners were generally suspicious and automatically hostile to whatever the Khartoum government proposed.

Numeiry rearms

Although he publicly professed that there could be no military solution to the southern problem, Numeiry did not actually dismiss the military option and set about obtaining modern arms and increasing the size of his armed forces, which had been badly shaken by their violent forays into politics and much weakened by the subsequent purges of officers.

The structure of the army, inherited from the Anglo-Egyptian Condominium, had remained on the British pattern, and the majority of its weapons were out-dated British ones.

Numeiry's initial tactical liaison with the left caused his government to be smiled upon by communist powers; for example the Soviet Union was eager to provide small amounts of arms and aircraft, to be accompanied by large numbers of advisers, instructors and technicians. Moscow still regarded Sudan as its gateway to Africa. Although the amount of military equipment eventually received from the Soviets was extremely small in comparison with the huge amounts sent to adjacent Egypt, it did give Numeiry the extra capability he needed to combat the Anya-Nya. It also gave him a problem in that there were now two types of arms and equipment to cope with, British and Soviet, which disrupted the simple standardisation the Sudanese armed forces had enjoyed until Numeiry came to power. With two types of ammunition and spares, instruction was made more difficult.

Soon the Soviet Union began to limit its military aid and increase its conditions. There had been no Soviet advisers in Sudan before Numeiry came to power, but by the end of his first year in office there were well over 1000. Earlier, when the need for military aircraft and helicopters to cope with the southern insurrection had become apparent, the previous Sudanese government had approached the Americans, who had been hesitant and unhelpful, so when diplomatic relations with the USA had been severed in 1967 a Sudanese delegation had been sent to Moscow with a military shopping list. In August 1968 the Sudanese government, then led by Premier Mahgoub, had concluded a large arms deal, reputedly valued at $150 million, a huge sum in those days for a country with such a comparatively small economy. The Sudanese were to have received military aircraft, tanks and other armoured vehicles, but none had been received by May 1969 when Numeiry seized power. The few Soviet light weapons possessed by the Sudanese had been obtained through the influence of the illegal Communist Party.

Owing to further negotiations and delays it was not until February 1970 that the Sudanese armed forces began to be equipped with Soviet military material, and even then the process was slow. Eventually the Soviets took Sudan's cotton crop in exchange for the armaments and sold it on the world market at a great profit, an unexpectedly capitalistic act by a communist power and one which upset the Sudanese.

In the meantime Sudan accepted some Soviet equipment, plus instructors, from Egypt, mainly for the air force, which was concentrated at three main Sudanese air bases: at Wadi Saidna, about 20 miles north of

Khartoum; Juna, about 30 miles south of Khartoum; and Jebel Aulia, also south of the capital. It was frequently alleged that Egyptian and later Soviet pilots flew operational sorties from these three bases to the south.

Sudanese army expansion

During 1969 the strength of the Sudanese army hovered around the 26 000 mark, consisting basically of four infantry brigades, each with four infantry battalions, together with three artillery, one armoured and one paratroop regiment, with supporting subunits and back-up administration. Manpower in this voluntary army had increased only slowly, and the accumulation of modern weaponry had been patchy and slow. Some light aircraft, light armoured vehicles and 12 modern field radio sets, the latter of a type on trial in Britain but not on general issue, had been obtained on the occasion of the royal visit in 1965, when unauthorised promises had been made that the British Foreign Office, despite Ministry of Defence resistance, had insisted be honoured. At this moment the basic communication system of the Sudanese armed forces consisted of the field telegraph, which had originally been installed in the country in the nineteenth century. I was told that apparently only two of the 12 sets worked, but the Sudanese radio operators, thinking they were at fault, were too proud to admit their failures. This type of radio set had not been adopted for use in the British army.

During the next 18 months there was an unquantified influx of Soviet weaponry, including transport and fighter aircraft, modern tanks and artillery, and anti-aircraft weaponry. The strength of the army increased to over 36 000. Two more infantry brigades were formed, one of which served in rotation in the Suez Canal Zone, and three anti-aircraft regiments were set up. The latest versions of MiG combat aircraft were flying overhead, as were Soviet Mi-8 helicopters, and modern Soviet tanks were openly displayed for prestige purposes.

Soviet military doctrine

Generally the Soviet attempt to teach and impose their military doctrine of massive might on the battlefield was pretty much a failure with the tiny Sudanese armed forces, and damaged their efficiency. The Soviets persistently intermixed politics with training, which grated on the ears of the religious-minded Muslim Sudanese. Pilot training for MiG fighter aircraft took place in the USSR and was a two-year course. As the trainees had first of all to acquire a working knowledge of Russian, the time lag for producing qualified pilots was long. Included in the course was a thick wad of political training and indoctrination, which the Sudanese students considered both time-wasting and irrelevant, but the Soviets remained inflexible on this point.

Numeiry's offensive

In September 1969 a government communiqué announced that, in an action against the Anya-Nya at Pibor in Upper Nile Province, government forces had killed 97 outlaws and seized large quantities of illicit arms. This was a lead in to Numeiry's major offensive, which did not really get under way until November. During December a government attack was made on an Anya-Nya base near Torit, where according to the *New York Times* up to 50 soldiers were killed 'in a battle of unusual size, which had been in progress for several days'. About the same time the Anya-Nya attacked and overran the nearby border post at Kaya.

However the *Christian Monitor* claimed that during the last three months of the year the army had massacred all or part of the population of entire villages. For example in Marial Aguog in Bahr el-Ghazal Province 'all 700 inhabitants were machine- gunned', and at the police post at Ulang, south of Nasir in Upper Nile Province, where government troops were active, some '2000 people were killed and their cattle driven northwards'. These incidents may have happened, but the casualty estimates seemed to be overexaggerated. A government spokesman said the allegations were 'missionary hallucinations'.

Aerial activity

On 29 December 1969 a bombing raid by three MiG aircraft was made on the town of Nyerol in Upper Nile Province. A cattle enclosure was struck and it was said that several thousand cattle were killed. After this the Sudanese Air Force, using Soviet aircraft, came increasingly into action, bombing, machine-gunning and firing rockets at Anya-Nya camps and bases. In addition Soviet helicopters were used to provide close support to attack troops, and were frequently used to lift them forward to surround villages, assault Anya-Nya bases and camps or block escape routes.

A rumour soon spread that many of the Soviet aircraft were being flown by Egyptian or Soviet pilots. This was repeatedly denied by all concerned, but there was probably some truth in the allegation as the first Soviet aircraft had reached Sudan in May 1969 but the first Soviet-trained Sudanese pilots were not due to return to Sudan until April 1970, so the pilot shortage had to be filled somehow. A rumour that mercenary pilots of other nationalities were employed does not seem to have been substantiated. Both Egyptian and Soviet personnel were employed in training and technical roles, and also as advisers to the Sudanese air force.

The government insisted that it was not carrying out random bombing raids, and that aerial action was only taken against outlaw camps. It also stated that some of the villages in the south had to be protected against outlaws, and that many of the inhabitants were hiding in the forests, too scared to return to their homes. Returned southern refugees were often placed in peace villages under military supervision, and it was alleged that the bodies of some of them, with gunshot wounds in the back of the head, had been found floating down the Nile.

In May 1970 the government claimed to have captured 502 rebels (it was still trying to counter the allegation that its troops did not take prisoners) and quantities of arms and ammunition of British, West German and Israeli origin. In July the Anya-Nya again attacked the rebuilt police post at Kaya, and it was alleged that at Banja, on the Sudan–Congo border, a church had been set on fire and almost 30 people had been burned to death inside it, while others outside had been killed. Complaints and allegations about the behaviour and activities of the army in the south poured out, but they were usually ridiculed by the Khartoum government, which blamed inflated missionary propaganda and pointed out that the locations and dates were omitted from the southern reports. Examples included eleven villages being destroyed in one day near Juba, the killing of 34 people and the torture of others at a funeral at a missionary station, and the killing of 95 people at a mission station during August.

ANAF commanders had begun to send action reports to the local periodicals and news sheets that occasionally appeared in the south in order to advertise both themselves and their command. Several were written in a vague conversational style, rather than the precision required for a military report, and were often boastfully naive and imaginative. The example below is quoted from a report by the Upper Nile ANAF Command HQ, signed by Stephen Lam, minister of information in the Nile Provisional Government, covering the period August to December 1970, which presumably would have been approved by Colonel Joseph Akwon.

In August, the ANAF attacked the Arab District HQ at Akabo, killing 16 northerners, and losing one man themselves – that month the

ANAF also attacked the District HQ at Nasir, and occupied the town for 24 hours, killing 24 Arab soldiers, and losing one Captain themselves – in October the ANAF overran the government station at Burmah, manned by two platoons of government troops, killing 102 Arabs, of whom 40 were killed when the truck in which they were riding overran a mine, for the loss of seven ANAF killed and 17 wounded – and in November, the ANAF attacked and overran two platoons at a government post near Keir, when four Arabs were captured with their arms.

This was probably founded on fact, but was overembroidered and imprecise.

In May 1970 the Sudanese Association of Southern Exiles was formed in London and began to produce a quarterly journal in English, called the *Grass Curtain*. The journal was jointly edited by Mading de Garang and Lawrence Wol-Wol, and for the first time brought the Sudanese southern problem to international attention.

Israeli involvement

Rumours had abounded since the Arab–Israeli War of 1967 of Israeli intervention in the south and Israeli aid to the Anya-Nya, reinforced by government allegations that Israel was supplying arms to the ANAF, flown in by night in unmarked aircraft from either Ethiopia or Uganda. The arms were said to be Soviet-made weapons captured from the Egyptians, and the alleged destination was a camp at Owiny Ki-Bul in Eastern Equatoria, about ten miles from the Ugandan border. Certainly, during 1969 and 1970 a small number of Soviet arms reached the Anya-Nya, but there was no substantiation of the rumour that Israel was running training camps for the ANAF.

There had also been contact between Israel and Uganda since the 1967 war, as Israel was making a determined effort to gain influence with certain African states, both diplomatically and by providing expertise and technical aid, with the object of removing the need for similar help from northern Arab countries. Israel managed to establish military training missions in Ethiopia, Congo and Uganda, and as Israelis were also training the Ethiopian police, this provided them with the opportunity to help southern Sudanese insurgents. Israel had been hoping to use Uganda as a base to transport military equipment to the ANAF, but had only limited success as during 1970 President Milton Obote became more friendly with President Numeiry.

In January 1971 General Idi Amin, the Ugandan inspector general, seized power from President Obote, who sought refuge in Tanzania. Amin ejected the Soviet military training missions that were operating in the country and brought in an additional Israeli one to train his air force, and so another opportunity presented itself to Israel to help the ANAF. Prior to the coup Amin had been in contact with the Anya-Nya, and is said to have secretly visited Colonel Lagu at his HQ in Owiny Ki-Bul, accompanied by Israeli officers on several occasions, and to have assisted the ANAF by allowing supplies to cross the Ugandan border into southern Sudan. Later, when Obote was warming towards Numeiry and cooling towards the Anya-Nya, Amin was said to have personally and covertly ordered Ugandan officers to facilitate this illicit traffic.

Several months before the coup Amin had recruited about 500 southern Sudanese mercenaries to help him overthrow Obote, and once in power he increased this mercenary detachment to about 1300 armed men, to counterbalance the threat posed by the dubious loyalty of the small Ugandan army, consisting of only about 3000 servicemen.

Owiny Ki-Bul

On 25 January 1971 a large government force occupied Owiny Ki-Bul in Eastern Equatoria which had long been Colonel Lagu's GHQ. The ANAF evacuated in a great hurry and established a new camp in the Immatong Mountains area. Lagu's excuse for withdrawing without a fight was that Owiny Ki-Bul was set in open country, and successful defence would not have been possible against government aircraft and superior weaponry, and that the retreat had been in accordance with conventional guerrilla tactics. Lagu's new GHQ also given the name Owiny Ki-Bul – was the war cry of the large Acholi tribe, which spread across the southern frontier into Uganda – which tended to cause some confusion both to the Anya-Nya and to the Sudanese army's intelligence branch. The old site came to be referred to as the 'real Owiny Ki-Bul'.

The real Owiny Ki-Bul remained garrisoned by government troops, and for a while also housed a detachment of Ugandan troops loyal to Obote and hostile to Amin. In August 1971 a Ugandan military reconnaissance plane flew low over the real Owiny Ki-Bul, and when fired upon it took evasive action. It is believed that President Amin was a passenger. Later, in December, the Khartoum government warned Obote that he must moved his armed force, now down to about 200 men, from the real Owiny Ki-Bul, and they disappeared early the following the year.

Apart from probable Israeli help, the insurgents in the south had fought alone until the appearance on the southern scene of Rolf Steiner, a German mercenary, fresh from his involvement in the civil wars in Congo and Biafra. Steiner's trial in Khartoum between 5 August and 12 September 1971 attracted international publicity, and put the southern insurrection on the world map almost for the first time. Steiner stated that the Israelis had bases in Ethiopia and Uganda, some only eight miles from the Sudanese border, that they had established a training camp inside southern Sudan, and had been involved in laying mines in rivers. He also stated that Numeiry had personally helped the deposed Obote by allowing him to recruit and train his band of armed Ugandan exiles at the real Owiny Ki-Bul.

Born in Germany in 1931, Rolf Steiner had belonged to the Hitler Youth and the Nazi storm troopers. After the Second World War he had joined the French Foreign Legion, seeing action in Indo-China and Algeria, and then become a white mercenary in Africa. At his trial in Khartoum he stated that he had first visited the south in July 1969 to discuss the situation and to help build a radio station and an airport, but his services had been rejected by the ANAF so he had attached himself to General Tafeng in November. He had been given the rank of colonel (later major general) and the task of raising, and commanding, an army of between 20 000 and 24 000 men for Tafeng's newly formed Anyidi Revolutionary Government. He had applied for citizenship of the Republic of Anyidi.

When the Anyidi Revolutionary Government ceased to exist in April 1970 he had again been rebuffed by the now uniting Anya-Nya. Steiner denied that he had ever collaborated with the Anya-Nya, which was probably true, but admitted his involvement with the Anyidi Revolutionary Government. After a period wandering restlessly about the south, unsuccessfully offering his services, in early November he had crossed over into Uganda, presumably with the intention of travelling to Europe, but had been immediately arrested in Kampala, where he had been kept in detention for three months while President Obote decided whether or not to hand him over to the Sudanese government. Obote later said that he had rejected a West German extradition application for Steiner, but had eventually complied with an OAU ruling and Steiner had been handed over to the Sudanese on 10 January 1971. A fortnight later Obote had been overthrown by General Amin.

On the 18th Steiner was presented at a press conference, at which the secretary general of the OAU expressed the hope that this was the beginning of the end of white mercenaries in Africa. Steiner was the first to be arrested and brought to trial. He had kept a full and frank diary and extracts were read in court. He also gave a long rambling discourse of implausible accusations. One witness, Brigadier Khalifa Karrar, claimed to have led a raid on an Anya-Nya camp, where Steiner was alleged to be at the time, but Steiner denied this. Ex-President Obote declined to give evidence, asserting that his life would be in danger if he did. Although charged with numerous counts, Steiner was only found guilty of initiating war against the Sudanese government, inciting war and distributing medical drugs. His death sentence was commuted by President Numeiry to 20 years' imprisonment.

Steiner had made hardly any impression on the south, which in general seemed embarrassed by his former presence there, but in view of his experience, some of his comments on this semi-secret war are of interest. He argued that the whole southern revolutionary movement was plagued by disunity, personal conflicts and a lack of both military and political coordination. Of the southern guerrillas, he said they fought very well against each other, but against Arabs they were psychologically inferior. After a few months' training at Anya-Nya camps many deserted with their arms, preferring to fight in their own tribal areas, under their own self-appointed colonels. They were never happy or confident away from their own localities, and several of his own carefully planned attacks had ended in confusion with one or more of the 'resistance platoons' fighting its own private war, or simply not fighting at all.

Numeiry's community programme

Concurrently with his military offensive, President Numeiry continued with his community programme to help people in the south in order to win them over to his side. Efforts were made to improve communications by repairing roads, bridges and buildings, but there was a shortage of money for the purpose. However Numeiry's state visit to China in August 1971 resulted in the Chinese government giving him loans that enabled this programme to commence, but it made slow progress.

Despite the dearth of medical facilities in the south, Joseph Garang (minister for the south and later executed) claimed some improvement in this sphere, citing the completion of a 60-bed hospital in Gogeal in Bahr el-Ghazal Province, new health and dental centres in Wau and eye-clinics in Nasir and Doro, the ongoing construction of a hospital in Kodok and a new school for medical assistants in Juba. In general the government had some success in population centres that were protected by troops, but absolutely none in the countryside. A start was made to reclaim deserted agricultural land, and about 40 resettlement areas were opened in Equatoria Province. Garang also claimed that progress had been made with other projects, including a large rice-growing scheme in Aweil in Bahr el-Ghazal Province, a jute scheme in Tonj, a tomato farm in Wau and the revival of coffee plantations in Maridi, Oba, Mitika and Kargulla.

Lagu unites the south

Out of the morass of quarrelling southern personalities, one arose to tower above the others. He was Joseph Lagu, who had become commander-in-chief of the Eastern Equatoria region and whose name became synonymous with the military struggle in the south. Born in 1931 of the Madi tribe in Moli, a village in Equatoria Province about 40 miles from Nimule, Lagu was the son of a lay preacher at an Anglican mission. He had been educated at mission schools, and when the Rumbek secondary school had moved to Khartoum, Lagu had gone with it. Afterwords he had briefly attend Khartoum University to read law. He later told me that he had had the choice of either law or the army for a career, having been accepted by both, but had chosen to enter the Sudan Military College because its term commenced earlier. He had been commissioned in May 1960, eventually to be posted to Shendi, north of Khartoum. On 4 June 1963, while on leave in the south, he had defected to the Anya-Nya, thus exchanging his rank of second lieutenant for that of colonel. He explained to me that he had been gazetted as a lieutenant while on leave, from which he had not returned and thus had never officially worn his second pip.

When I asked him why he had defected, he explained that the situation had become such that southerners regarded the army as an enemy force bent on suppressing their political aspirations. Units in the south were never looked upon as part of the national force, but as an army of occupation. Consequently he had felt unable to remain in a force that was used to suppress his own people. He would not be drawn on the precise reason for his abrupt defection, or what act or slight had provoked him to change sides, but the carrot of rank, coupled with political acumen and ambition, cannot be overlooked.

His initial post with the Anya-Nya was that of special functions, which he himself likened to that of a minister of defence, working with General Tafeng and politicians who still had some authority in the resistance movement. He held this position for over a year, adding the responsibility for the whole organisation to his brief, but in October 1964 it began to splinter. He then took over the Eastern Equatoria region and built up an efficient, self-contained, independent regional command.

Lagu had a pleasant personality and was intelligent and energetic, but he lacked the breadth that comes with continued formal military education. A natural leader who attracted followers, he was anticommunist and favoured Western-type democracy. From December 1968 he began to work independently, taking no orders or instructions from political leaders, and eventually the Anya-Nya grouped around him as he made his bid for power. Politicians realised they were not attracting enough followers to their individual banners, so either dissolved their parties or went in to exile, thus allowing him a free hand to lead the continuing struggle in the field. Some politicians gave him moral support, while others simply kept quiet.

ANAF High Command Council

In October 1969, when Lagu considered that Anya-Nya unity was almost complete, he formed the Anya-Nya Armed Forces High Command Council. Its objectives were to control and direct military operations, to obtain and distribute arms and military materials, and to administer the civilian population under Anya-Nya control or influence. As the struggle continued, Lagu constantly complained that the armed forces of the several southern governments, such as they were, spent more time and energy struggling against each other for recognition and supremacy than they did fighting against the northern government. The council was scheduled to meet once a year, but was not able to convene for some time.

Lagu's main opponents were the southern politicians, all of whom were anxious to gain control over the ANAF, but Lagu knew they would bring confusion rather than cohesion, so he ignored them from his autonomous, aloof position in the Eastern Equatoria region. He did at one stage, after initial differences, liaise in Kampala with Joseph Oduhu, who somewhat over-enthusiastically claimed that the Anya-Nya was under his leadership. For some months Lagu was engaged in a struggle for authority with his nominal superior, General Tafeng, but operating from his secure guerrilla base at the real Owiny Ki-Bul, Lagu outsmarted him.

The Anyidi Revolutionary Government collapses

Having consolidated his own position in Eastern Equatoria, Lagu turned his attention to uniting the Anya-Nya in his region. He began with the failing Anyidi Revolutionary Government, whose tiny army, briefly commanded by Rolf Steiner, was cooped up in a small area that was squeezed on one side by a small group of guerrilla fighters from the Nile Provisional Government, and on the other by Lagu's warriors. In April 1970 Lagu persuaded General Tafeng and Tafeng's deputy' Colonel Frederick Magot, to join him and place whatever armed forces they could bring with them under his command. This caused the collapse of the Anyidi Revolutionary Government and was a key victory for Lagu. Magot became Lagu's chief of staff and had a seat on the ANAF High Command Council, which Lagu was shaping to suit his own plans and ambitions. It was also the first stage of Tafeng being pushed into obscurity.

The Nile Provisional Government

In June 1970 Lagu engineered a coup against the Nile Provisional Government, headed by Gordon Mayen and based near Yei. First he won over Samuel Abujohn, its chief-of-staff, whom he formally appointed as commander of the Western Equatoria region. Abujohn placed his Anya-Nya element under Lagu's command, On 23 May Stephen Lam, Mayen's minister of information, announced that as Mayen had failed to attract southern politicians to his banner, Mayen had disbanded his own government and intended to work to establish a National Liberation Front, to be controlled by the ANAF High Command Council. This was another key victory for Lagu, who had now gathered all the effective military and political resistance elements in Equatoria Province into his own hands, a somewhat unusual situation in that the political organisation was subordinate to the military command.

From his GHQ (still called Owiny Ki-Bul, but now somewhere in the Immatong Mountains), Lagu obtained a firm hold on the ANAF in Equatoria Province, and as his grip tightened, weaknesses and shortcomings were rectified. He gained control over the illegal arms supply that filtered across the borders, which enabled him to dole out weapons and ammunition selectively to the ANAF detachments, being quick to withhold them for insubordination, tendencies towards regionalism and plain banditry. However he seems to have had some difficulty arranging meetings of the ANAF High Command Council. The first scheduled one – not held until June 1971 – was not a success due to poor staff work. For example Colonel Emmanuel Abur, commander of the ANAF in Upper Nile Province, was unable to reach the meeting place before the departure of Colonel Akwon, the ANAF commander in Bahr el-Ghazal Province. Both men had given their allegiance to Lagu.

Although efforts had been made to organise a civil administration in the territory under Lagu's control or influence, and to establish courts, schools and medical centres, little real progress had been made. Lagu turned his attention to this and appointed Elisapana Mulla, a former southern government official, as the commissioner for Equatoria Province. Mulla started a civil administration training college in Langayu, about 40 miles from the Ugandan border.

7
Autonomy and Consolidation

In the latter part of 1970 and the first part of the following year, Colonel Lagu consolidated his successes and was able to call another meeting of political and military leaders in August 1971 at Owiny Ki-Bul in the Immatong Mountains. At this meeting he formed a political party, the Southern Sudan Liberation Movement (SSLM), which was to be subservient to the ANAF and of which he became chairman. Lagu also promoted himself to the rank of major-general and took the post of commander-in-chief of the ANAF, thus holding the top military and political appointments in the Anya-Nya. Colonel Samuel Abujohn became deputy commander of the ANAF. During the course of the meeting Lagu rejected a suggestion that a government-in-exile be formed, saying that the time was not yet right. He had not yet brought all the excited southern politicians under his influence, and feared they might gang up against him if such a sovereign body developed, which would simply provide an arena for top political infighting. Also present at the meeting were Mading de Garang, the Anya-Nya representative in London, and Lawrence Wol-Wol, the Anya-Nya representative in Paris, who were both in favour of forming a government-in-exile.

Lagu once explained to me that his masterplan had been first to gain control of the entire Anya-Nya movement in the south, then to produce a single political party to take care of wayward politicians, and finally to concentrate on developing armed resistance. Lagu continued to resist pressure from southern politicians in the south, the north, and in exile to form a government-in-exile. I suspect even then that his thoughts went further than southern independence, as such a platform would be too small for his ambitions.

Lagu appointed Elia Lupe, formerly of SANU, as chief commissioner of the south, and Elisapana Mulla as commissioner for the Upper Nile

Province, the post of commissioner for Bahr el-Ghazal being left vacant for the moment. Dishan Ojwe became police commissioner. A few prominent southern politicians, some from former 'governments', agreed to work in Lagu's administration and were given ministerial-type jobs. One was Aliaba Loboka Surer, former minister of finance in the now defunct Anyidi Revolutionary Government, who became commissioner for education. Surer set about organising small forest schools, each to cater for about 200 pupils, and a teacher training centre was established, but the general shortage of books, writing paper and teaching aids was a hindrance. Felix Ibui, an experienced medical assistant, was appointed commissioner for health and began to establish small medical posts and forest dispensaries, as well as training staff to man them. His problem was an almost complete absence of drugs, medicines and equipment. Lagu now virtually had a small government functioning under his control.

Lagu next made contact with prominent southern politicians in exile, some of whom had been representing the south in their own way, either acting on their own or for one or other of the southern 'governments'. His aim was to win them over and absorb them into the SSLM, and in some cases to formalise their existing appointments. For example Mading de Garang remained in London, Lawrence Wol-Wol in Paris, Dominic Mohammed in Washington, Angelo Voga in Kampala and Job Adlier in Addis Ababa to act as Lagu's overseas representatives.

Air attacks

Beginning in 1971, the Sudanese armed forces brought their improved weaponry into action against the ANAF, and in January it was claimed that MiG aircraft and helicopters machine-gunned and rocketed villages near Magawe, in the Palwar area in Eastern Equatoria. The ANAF admitted that a forest hospital had been destroyed. The following month there was an air raid on the real Owiny Ki-Bul, occupied by the Anya-Nya, which lost 12 men. A later government air raid on a school at Akabo caused several civilian casualties, which provoked the ANAF into a punitive attack on a police post. In reprisal the army shot a number of southern prisoners they were holding there. Southerners were now claiming that Soviet troops were accompanying the Sudanese army and air force on their missions, which was probably true, but only to a small extent. When Lagu's GHQ was at the real Owiny Ki-Bul it was targeted on several occasions by the Sudanese air force. Lagu claimed that in one instance a government combat aircraft had been shot down by the

ANAF, the Soviet bodies in the wreckage being identified as such by dental evidence.

Southerners also alleged that government troops had changed their tactics from open killing to kidnapping individuals from their homes, killing them and throwing their bodies into rivers in the hope that 'outlaws' would be blamed for these crimes. On the other hand, while the ANAF soldiers were a little better trained and disciplined than previously, they still committed atrocities and the government insisted that the Anya-Nya was still not taking prisoners but simply shooting all captives.

Numeiry also had military problems, being very short of junior officers, espeically after Atta's attempted coup, when over 200 of them were dismissed from the service. He filled this gap by selecting long-service warrant and non-commissioned officers, invariably a little weak on education but skilled in tactics, military routine and man-management, and sending them on special 'crammer' courses at the Sudan Military College. In this way he created a solid corps of junior officers who were loyal to himself because they owed their status and promotion to him and no political affiliations.

In general, Sudanese regular officers tended to lack breadth of experience, especially after the expulsion of the Soviet advisers and technicians. Lack of funds meant that Sudanese officer cadets were no longer sent to Sandhurst, the British officer-producing establishment, so their horizon was initially limited. When the Soviets were expelled the British returned briefly to staff the Sudan Military College, which accepted a few officer-cadets from adjacent countries, including Uganda. In answer to a query about the low ratio of southern officers in the Sudan armed forces, the chief-of-staff, General Mohammed Abdul Gudir, replied that there were over 3000 southerner soldiers in the Southern Command, and that since the 1969 revolution several had reached the rank of colonel, adding that the army in the south had a black majority, which consisted not only of men from the Nuba Mountain area but also southerners.

High Command Council Conference

After much delay the Second ANAF High Command Council Conference was held in October 1971 at Owiny Ki-Bul in the Immatong Mountains. Several decisions were made, the main one being to dismiss Samuel Abujohn (deputy commander-in-chief of the ANAF and commander of the Western Equatoria Region), reportedly because he had developed an uncooperative attitude towards the High Command, lacked seriousness about his work and was given to insubordination. According to some sources, he had plotted to overthrow Lagu and take his place. Abujohn was replaced by Colonel Joseph Akwon, commander of the Upper Nile region, who was promoted to brigadier and became Lagu's deputy commander-in-chief while retaining his regional command. Colonel Habakuk Soro, deputy commander of the Western Equatoria region, was promoted to regional commander. The ANAF High Command Council now consisted of Colonel Lagu, Brigadier Akwon, Colonel Frederick Magot (the latter as chief-of-staff and secretary) and Colonels Soro and Abur.

The next step was to formally divide the ANAF into three territorial brigades: the 1st Brigade, commanded by Colonel Magot in Equatoria Province; the 2nd Brigade, under Brigadier Akwon in Upper Nile Province; and the 3rd Brigade, led by Colonel Abur in Bahr el-Ghazal Province. Equatoria Province was to remain in three military parts, the eastern one – Lagu's power base – under Lagu, the central one under Colonel Magot and the western one under Soro.

Major northern offensive

Numeiry engaged in secret diplomacy with adjacent states to persuade them to stop sending supplies to the ANAF and harbouring southern resistance refugees, but he had less than moderate success as he himself gave sanctuary to diverse groups of exiled dissidents.

For some months the north had maintained three brigades in the south, totalling over 14 000 soldiers and about 6000 armed police. The strength of the brigades was reinforced at the beginning of December 1971 in preparation for a major offensive. The object was to prevent ANAF activities spreading over into Bahr el-Ghazal Province, where so far there had been few incidents compared with Equatoria Province. Two main government thrusts were made, one in the vicinity of Yei and the other towards Rumbek. The Anya-Nya, in true guerrilla fashion, avoided a set-piece battle and gave way before the advances. Northern troops followed closely, chasing Anya-Nya units across the border into Uganda.

On the 15th an official spokesman in Kampala stated that fierce fighting was taking place inside Uganda, but the following day President Amin said that the Sudanese troops were now withdrawing. Amin invited the Sudanese government to discuss with him the matter of the joint frontier, which had been closed since 1969. He also said that he was willing to reestablish diplomatic relations with the Khartoum government, which had been severed when Obote was deposed. On the 27th Peter Gatworth, a southerner and Numeiry's minister for southern affairs, made contact with Kampala.

On 5 January 1972 the real Owiny Ki-Bul camp, now occupied by government troops but still housing remnants of Obote's Ugandan armed exiles, was attacked with mortar and gunfire by units of the ANAF, but the latter were beaten off. They attacked again about a fortnight later, but with no better fortune.

Secret peace negotiations

Despite the fighting, northern and southern delegations had been conducting secret negotiations since May 1971 through the good offices of the World Council of Churches, helped by the UNHCR and others. These negotiations were brought to a head in February 1972 when the two delegations met in Addis Ababa.

On the 12th General Khalid Hassan Abbas, the Sudanese defence minister, resigned, as did a few senior Sudanese military officers, including the chief-of-staff and Major Maameum Zeid, secretary general of the Sudanese Socialist Party. All were protesting strongly against the peace talks, which were scheduled to begin the next day. Numeiry threatened that if there were any more resignations he would dissolve the executive committee of the SSP.

In Addis Ababa the government negotiators were led by Abel Alier, a vice president and Numeiry's minister for the south, while the southern team was led by Izbone Mendiri, a former minister in the Khalifa government (1964). Mendiri, who had been in exile since 1965 and had headed the short-lived Sudan-Azania Government, was a member of neither the SSLM nor the ANAF. Within the southern delegation, Mading de Garang represented the SSLM and Colonel Frederick Magot the ANAF.

The negotiations foundered almost as soon as they began as the southerners demanded a separate army, claiming that this was essential if they were to defend themselves against reprisals. Haile Selassie stepped in and invited the delegates to his palace, where he personally, and in the name of the OAU, guaranteed the well-being of the southerners. The southern delegation was persuaded to abandon its demand, and in return the government agreed to grant a greater degree of autonomy than it had originally intended.

Agreement on autonomy

On 26 February 1972 an agreement was reached for southern Sudan to have full autonomy within the Republic of Sudan. The agreement was initialled on the 28th. There was to be an interim 18-month regional government, after which elections would be held for a regional assembly. Gordon Mayen, leader of the Liberation Front and living in exile in Zaire (Congo had been renamed Zaire in October 1971), denounced the agreement, describing it as an 'Arab fraud' that had been agreed to by certain southern delegates representing only themselves. The government of Zaire promptly expelled him and he moved to Belgium. Later he was invited by Numeiry to return to Sudan, but he declined.

Lagu, as commander-in-chief of the ANAF and leader of the SSLM, after listening to reports from the southern delegates, welcomed the autonomy agreement on 1 March, saying that in general terms he was quite satisfied with it, and adding that the majority of the Anya-Nya leaders welcomed it. On the 3rd President Numeiry formally issued the decree granting autonomy to the south 'within the framework of the Republic of Sudan', declaring a general amnesty for all southerners who had taken part in the rebellion, and stating that he had ordered the armed forces to cease fire.

However, despite Lagu's remarks not all southerners were content with autonomy. Many wanted complete independence, and the Anya-Nya themselves were under the impression that that was what they had been fighting for all these years. It was not until 6 March that Lagu felt able to order the ANAF to cease fire, which they did, but in many cases very reluctantly, the fighting continuing right up until the deadline. Credit is due to Lagu for being able to persuade reluctant personalities and elements of the SSLM and the ANAF to accept this agreement. To give southerners confidence in the government's promises, Numeiry, accompanied by Abel Alier, his minister for the south, began a ten-day tour of the south to explain the terms of the agreement and meet the people.

On 19 March Numeiry formally promulgated his amnesty, and the following day he lifted the state of emergency in the south (in force since 12 August 1955). An international commission – composed of observers from Ethiopia, Uganda, Zaire, the Red Cross, the World Council of Churches, the UNHCR and others – would oversee the ceasefire and the arrangements for the repatriation of refugees.

Ratification

The original date for ratification of the agreement had been 12 March 1972, but Lagu asked for more time as he had to allay the doubts and suspicions of some of his supporters. It was eventually ratified on the 27th in Addis Ababa in the presence of Haile Selassie, who had done much to bring the agreement about. Lagu said that the southerners would cooperate with the government once they were recognised as full citizens of Sudan. He also issued a warning against eventual Sudanese accession to the much discussed Arab Federation, and indeed the settlement had been a setback for Sudanese pan-Arabists.

President Numeiry made changes to his government, removing pro-Egyptian and pro-Arab ministers and replacing them with men who took a softer line with southerners. He brought in two southern ministers, Lawrence Wol-Wol, who had latterly been the SSLM representative in Paris, and Samuel Norbay. That month the government stated that there were still 1521 people in detention, but that there had been no subversive activity for six months.

The Provisional Council

On 6 April 1972 Numeiry appointed Abel Alier as chairman of the Provisional Council, which was to administer the south until a regional assembly could be elected. The 12-man council was a wide mix that included the governors of the three southern provinces (Luigi Adwok, Tobi Madot and Hilary Logale), Joseph Oduhu (now prominent in the SSLM), Michael Tawili (former leader of the now defunct Sue River Revolutionary Government), Izbone Mendiri (who had headed the Sudan-Azania Government), Elia Lupe (the SSLM's chief commissioner) and Mading de Garang. Aggrey Jaden became executive director of national resources of the south, and Clement Mboro became chairman of the Repatriation of Refugees Committee.

Fusing the armed forces

According to the autonomy agreement, about 6000 ANAF personnel would be absorbed into the Sudanese armed forces in their current rank, and the remaining 4000 would be taken into either the police force or the prison service, or returned to their former occupations. It was assumed that in February 1972 the ANAF was about 10 000 strong. The strength of the Sudanese army in the south was given as 15 000. For a transitional period the southern army would be placed under the command of a commission, to be composed of equal numbers of northern and southern officers and responsible to the central government. It was planned that the southern army would be reduced to about 12 000 men, half southerners and half northerners. There was also to be an armed police force, plus a paramilitary force of frontier guards, to total about 3000 men, all southerners.

On 12 June it was suddenly claimed that the ANAF was actually 25–30 000 strong, the majority of whom wanted to be absorbed into the Sudanese regular armed forces at their current rank. The bulk of the ANAF had retained their weapons (mainly British rifles, Soviet grenades and Czech automatic rifles) and remained in the forests in their military formations, but they were now becoming impatient. Eventually a figure of 12 000 was agreed upon and a six-year integration plan was worked out. During the first two years there would be separate subunits, containing all southerners in the ranks. During the next two years the southern subunits would be incorporated into northern units and vice versa, and during the last two years final integration would be completed.

General Lagu produced a list of his officers, and after the list was authenticated the officers were sent on refresher courses to bring them up to regular army standards. Those who failed were given another chance, and eventually the majority of the officers were accepted. A similar programme was adopted for those claiming to have been warrant and non-commissioned officers. A somewhat similar integration programme was introduced for the prison service, the police and the civil administration.

The south remained a closed area, and no foreign journalists were allowed to enter to report on the chaotic conditions. A start was made on clearing mines from roads and bridges, and the roads were gradually improved. General Fatlalla Hamid, the Sudanese commander of the south, worked with Lagu and they made frequent tours of the south together, visiting the towns and speaking to the people, explaining their new autonomous status and persuading them to accept it and cooperate.

Refugees

The government undertook to facilitate the return of refugees, of whom according to UNHCR figures, there were about 20 0000, some 70 000 in Uganda. The Khartoum government announced that the repatriation of 180 000 refugees would be completed by the end of June the following year, when it was stated that 143 000 southern refugees had already arrived back in Sudan from Ethiopia, the Central African Republic, Uganda and Zaire. Voluntary repatriation was virtually completed, except for the Sudanese refugees living in three camps in Uganda under UN auspices.

Foreign relations

Meanwhile, after the conclusion of the agreement with the south and when the suppression of the Communist Party had run its course, the rift with Egypt and Arab-bloc countries increased as the Khartoum government tried to mend some fences with its African neighbours.

Official state visits had been exchanged with Ethiopia, with which relations had been poor as each accused the other of sheltering and aiding its dissidents. Sudan was in fact harbouring the leaders of the Eritrean Liberation Front, now locked in a vicious armed struggle with the Addis Ababa government. Numeiry had visited Ethiopia in November 1971, and Haile Selassie visited Sudan in January 1972. Minor border arrangements were made between the two countries, on much the same lines as previous ones, which had been blithely disregarded. This time the joint border was tightened up selectively. The Sudanese government agreed not to harbour or help the Eritrean activists, and during 1972 Eritrean leaders were deported from Khartoum and the frontier town of Kassala, where they had become ensconced. The two heads of state began to smile at each other again.

Meanwhile Khartoum was talking to Kampala for the first time since the joint border had been closed in 1969. The border was reopened and President Amin sent a delegation to Khartoum, resulting in a Sudanese–Ugandan defence pact in June 1972. The displaced ex-president, Milton Obote, was still hovering in the region, so Amin needed firm allies. Despite this, Amin's obvious leaning towards Arab Muslim states caused some apprehension in Sudan, especially as Amin was receiving considerable economic and some military aid from Gaddafi, who sent aircraft and troops to help him repel an invasion from Tanzania by Milton Obote's supporters in mid September.

Relations with Britain, severed since 1970, improved when that country promised to pay compensation for nationalising British Commercial interests, and were formally resumed in March 1973, when British aid was granted and agreements were concluded for technical aid and cultural exchanges, which included Sudanese students studying in Britain. President Numeiry then paid an official state visit to Britain.

Conspiracies against Numeiry

On 19 July 1972 it was discovered that members of the dissolved Umma Party and the Islamic Charter Front were conspiring against Numeiry. The conspiracy also involved army officers, and indicated a deep current of dissatisfaction with his decision to grant autonomy to the south. Afterwards Numeiry criticised his ministers, saying that he was searching for the best way towards 'true democracy'.

The People's Council

Numeiry announced on 12 August 1972 that a 207-member Sudanese People's Council would be created for the purpose of drafting a new constitution. Elections would be held for 175 of the seats and the remainder would be filled by nominated members. The council, which included 18 women, was duly formed on 4 October. Numeiry then ordered his cabinet to resign, which it did in its entirety, as did the governor of the Central Bank and the secretary general of the presidential palace. On the 9th Numeiry announced the formation of a new cabinet, in which he took the positions of premier and defence minister. The same day he nominated Professor Nazir Dafalla, a former vice chancellor of the University of Khartoum, as chairman of the People's Council. Opening its first session on the 12th, Numeiry declared that it would have full freedom to debate, criticise and issue directives to the executive.

Worsening relations with Egypt

During September and October 1972, Sudan's relations with Egypt deteriorated. Cairo criticised Numeiry for dropping pro-Egyptian ministers from his new cabinet, and also for refusing to allow the transit of Libyan troops by air across Sudanese territory to Uganda. The Sudanese government had also given an order that the number of Egyptian students at the Khartoum Branch of Cairo University must be reduced from about 2000 to 500, and that the Egyptian director of this branch be expelled. In response the Egyptian government announced on 29 September that all the Egyptian staff, numbering about 300, would be withdrawn from Sudan. Despite an interim settlement of the dispute and the brief return of the Egyptian director, the latter was again expelled on 22 October. The previous month the Sudanese government had ordered the closure of two Egyptian state import–export undertakings in Khartoum.

In retaliation Egypt asked the Sudanese government to withdraw its some 2500 troops from the Suez Canal area, where they had been stationed since the 1967 Arab–Israeli War. Furthermore President Sadat ordered the return of the Egyptian instructors at the Egyptian Military College, established near Khartoum in 1967, together with all Egyptian servicemen stationed in Sudan, mainly naval staff at Sudanese naval bases on the Red Sea, and at certain air bases. It was a tit-for-tat spat between two presidents. In a speech on 24 October Numeiry stated that he would welcome an Egyptian initiative to restore confidence between their two countries, but the Egyptian president ought not to think that Sudan would take orders from Egypt.

Another conspiracy

On 26 January 1973 it was announced in Khartoum that retired Brigadier Abdul Rahman Shenan and several soldiers had been arrested for conspiring to kill Numeiry and others. In March 1959 Shenan had led his unit against Abboud, forcing Abboud to accept him on the Supreme Council of the Armed Forces. Later Shenan had been imprisoned until November 1964. He had subsequently been elected to the National Assembly, but had lost his seat in 1968 and retired from the army. This time he was sentenced to three years' imprisonment.

A new constitution

After being ratified by the People's Council and approved by President Numeiry, the new constitution for the Republic of Sudan came into force, after a referendum and elections, on 8 May 1973. It authorised a presidential form of government and the only permitted political organisation was to be the Sudanese Socialist Union (SSP). The autonomy of the three southern provinces was confirmed. Islam was to be the state religion, but it allowed for Christianity as that was the 'religion of a large number of citizens'. The government's latest assessment was that in the south there were 1 per cent Muslims and 12 per cent Christians. Detention without trial was made illegal, and Numeiry released the last 47 detainees, including Communist Party leaders and Sadik Mahdi, the former premier.

Numeiry had proposed in May 1971 that the SSU should be formed and become the country's sole political party, and it was established in October that year, with Major Awad Maameun Zeid as secretary general. Its original charter had been drafted by a mixed committee of nationalists and communists, and to embrace the principle of national unity, under which neither class struggle nor liberal democracy would be permitted it included the elimination of all forms of exploitation, improved welfare conditions and equal rights for women. Of the south it said that the 'rebellion' and 'imperialist intrigues should be foiled', and that a peaceful solution should be sought, based on regional autonomy. The amended charter of the SSU was approved on 3 January 1973 by the party's Constituent Assembly, attended by some 900 delegates.

On the 10 May 1973 a 14-member cabinet was formed, with Numeiry once again becoming premier and minister of defence. On the 23rd in response to a 'mass request', he withdrew his offer to resign as president of the Republic and the SSU. He also cancelled the price increases on petrol, sugar and certain other items that his government had imposed a few days earlier. The People's Committee dissolved itself, and the National Assembly reverted to having only legislative and advisory functions.

Disturbances in Khartoum

During the last week in August 1973, while Numeiry was away from his country on a state visit to Algeria, there was a spate of disturbances in Khartoum, Port Sudan and Atbara, mainly by students, who were demanding that the army return to barracks and leave politics to the politicians, but the root cause was Muslim discontent at the granting of autonomy to the south. A state of emergency was declared in these cities on 9 September, and Numeiry hurried back to his capital.

Southern Regional Assembly

The 60-member Regional Assembly for the South was to include 30 members elected on a territorial basis (for which elections took place in November), 27 representatives of provinces, regions and professional bodies, and three nominated members. A 13-man executive, to be known as the People's Assembly of the South, replaced the Supreme Council of the South, more commonly known as the Regional Assembly. At its first meeting on 15 December 1973, Abel Alier was elected as president.

During his 19-month tenure as head of the Supreme Council of the South, Abel Alier had made some considerable achievements. He had resettled some 859 000 displaced persons, including about 220 000 returning refugees. It was estimated that about 1 190 320 people had emerged from their refuges in the forests or returned from exile, and that only about 31 000 remained abroad principally in Uganda, where many had struck new roots. Farmers and agriculturists had been given tools and seeds to help them restart cultivation, and work had progressed on improving roads and bridges, financial help being obtained from the Khartoum government and international sources.

The main factor in this was the growing atmosphere of confidence and the eradication of fear chiefly due to good liasion and cooperation between Abel Alier and General Lagu. The comparatively smooth process of integrating the ANAF into the Sudanese regular armed forces was also due largely to these two southern leaders. Huge, colourful posters were posted all over the south, depicting a Muslim northerner and a black southerner walking together and bearing an inscription in both Arabic and English: 'The north and south go hand-in-hand'. However these posters were not much in evidence in the north.

Lagu appointed inspector general

On 3 February 1974 Lagu was appointed inspector general of the Sudanese armed forces. This was mainly an advisory post and did not involve direct command of troops. This was a shrewd move by President Numeiry, as by making Lagu nominally responsible for the whole of the Sudanese armed forces he removed him from his narrow southern military power base, where he could have made trouble if the promise of autonomy was not met. However Lagu had hoped for something better, and he later told me of his disappointment. He had hoped to become Sudan's defence minister, a rather forlorn hope for a Christian in a predominantly Muslim country. The suspicion that Lagu regarded the south as a small platform for his personal ambitions was confirmed.

8
Terrorism and Treachery

At about 1900 hours on 1 March 1973, eight Palestinian terrorists from the Black September Organisation (BSO) burst into the Saudi Arabian embassy in Khartoum, where a high-level diplomatic function was being held to bid farewell to the departing US ambassador, George Moore. When they realised what was happening the Soviet, French and British ambassadors managed to escape over the compound wall in the initial confusion, but five other senior diplomats were not so fortunate and were held hostage. They were Sheikh Abdullah al-Malhouk, the Saudi Arabian ambassador and doyen of the Khartoum diplomatic corps; George Moore and his successor, Cleo Noel; Guy Eid, the Belgian chargé d'affaires; and Adly al-Nasser, the Jordanian chargé d'affaires. A number of wives and children were also held.

In return for the safe release of the hostages the BSO terrorists demanded the release of Abu Daoud (a Palestinian terrorist leader) and 16 of his accomplices, who were being held in a Jordanian prison, plus some Palestinian Fedayeen (freedom fighters) who had been in Jordanian detention since 1970, Sirhan Bishara Sirhan (who had killed US Senator Robert Kennedy and was being held in an American prison), all the Baader-Meinhof members being held in West German jails, and all female guerrilla fighters being held in Israeli prisons.

Palestinian terrorism

Despite being a member of the Arab League and a majority Muslim country that refused to recognise the State of Israel, Sudan remained on the periphery of the Arab–Israeli struggle, a reluctance that irritated Egypt. In spirit and sympathy, Sudan was on the Arab side in this struggle, allowing the Palestine Liberation Organisation (PLO) and other resistance groups to have offices and collect funds in Sudan. It also maintained a token detachment of troops in the Suez Canal area, but did not want to be tied too tightly into the anti-Israeli Arab bloc, having a southern window looking into black Africa.

The Israeli victories in 1956 and 1967 made it obvious that Arab states were no match on the battlefield against Israel, which was armed with modern weaponry and supported by the USA. The Palestinian reaction was to resort to 'armed struggle', a euphemism for terrorism, which burst on to the international stage in 1968. There were several active groups, carrying out spectacular aircraft hijackings, seizing hostages and attacking Israeli embassies. The 1970s were the heyday of international terrorism, especially in Europe and the Middle East, where such notorious groups as the Baader-Meinhof gang in West Germany, the Red Brigades in Italy and a number of Palestinian ones operated dramatically and effectively.

The Black September Organisation was named after the month in 1970 when Yasir Arafat's Palestinian guerrillas had been driven out of Jordan by Jordanian armed forces. It had been a black month for the Palestinian fedayeen, in which fellow Arabs had deliberately fought against them. In November 1971, BSO commandos assassinated the Jordanian foreign minister in Cairo, and the following month attempted to assassinate the Jordanian ambassador in London. The next major operation occurred in May 1972, when a BSO team of two men and two women hijacked a Belgian airliner and forced the pilot to fly to Lod airport in Israel. All the passengers and crew were held hostage, and the highjackers threatened that if their demand for the release of a hundred Arabs in Israeli prisons was not met within 24 hours, the aircraft and all on board would be blown up. A period of negotiation followed, ending after a few hours when an Israeli special force team made a successful surprise attack. Despite their failure to achieve their ends the BSO, having charged into the lions' den, regarded this as a spectacular, morale-boosting exploit. Red Cross personnel, who had been involved in the negotiations, were blamed for betraying them.

The next BSO operation was even more spectacular. On 5 September 1972 a group of eight BSO commandos seized nine members of the Israeli team at the Olympic Games in Munich (Germany) and demanded the release of 200 Arabs in Israeli detention, Kozo Okamoto (a Japanese terrorist operating with a Palestinian terrorist group who had opened fire at Lod airport on 25 May 1972 killing 20 people and wounding another hundred, and was now in Israeli hands) and two German urban terrorists, Andreas Baader and Ulrike Meinhof, who were in West German detention. They also demanded an aircraft to fly them and their hostages to an Arab capital. Eventually helicopters were provided to take the terrorists and their hostages to the 'waiting passenger aircraft', but were fired upon by security forces. In the mêlée one helicopter went up in flames. The death toll for this exploit was 17. Three BSO commandos survived and were taken into West German custody. That was the track record of violence and death of the terrorists who entered the Saudi Arabian embassy in Khartoum.

The embassy seige

Inside the embassy the BSO terrorists waited for their demands to be met, threatening to blow up the embassy and all inside, including themselves, if any rescue attempt was made. George Moore, Cleo Noel and Guy Eid were tied up, even though Eid had been wounded in the initial attack, but the rest of the hostages were not restrained in this way. The governments that were the subject of the terrorists' demands refused to comply, and so a period of suspense set in. On the second day the terrorists dropped their demands on the governments of the USA, West Germany and Israel, but insisted on the release of Abu Daoud, a high-level BSO operator and planner, and those in Jordanian detention.

On the evening of the second day the attitude of the terrorists suddenly hardened on receipt of a radio message (monitored by the Sudanese security service): 'Why are you waiting? The blood of the Palestinians is waiting for vengeance.' The two Americans and the Belgian were untied, given pens and paper and told to write their last letter to their families. They were then taken to a cellar and shot. The Saudi ambassador was allowed to phone the Sudanese minister of the interior to tell him that Moore, Noel and Eid had been executed.

On the third day the terrorists tried to bargain with the Sudanese government, but President Numeiry insisted on unconditional surrender. That day a man and his wife, friends of the Saudi ambassador, walked into the besieged embassy and demanded the release of the ambassador's wife and her four children. The children were freed, and although the terrorists said that Mrs Malhouk could leave as well, she chose to stay with her husband.

Eventually, at 0600 hours on 4 March, after a 60-hour seige, the terrorists received a message from the BSO HQ (then in Beirut) ordering them to surrender, which they did and all surviving hostages were released unharmed. Arab and Israeli hints of retaliatory executions probably caused this change of plan. President Numeiry said that the terrorists must stand trial, something that no Arab government had been bold enough to do so far. The bodies of the two Americans were flown to the USA, and that of Eid, a naturalised Belgian born in Egypt, was flown to Cairo for burial. On the 4th King Hussein of Jordan, confirmed the death sentence on Abu Daoud.

President Numeiry openly accused Fatah (led by Yasir Arafat and said to be the largest Palestinian resistance movement) of instigating the incident, it being previously thought that the BSO was a completely separate organisation. He blamed the planning of the operation on Kawaz Yassin, the Fatah representative in Khartoum, who had diplomatic status and had left Sudan in a Libyan aircraft for Tripoli a few hours before the terrorist attack on the embassy began. Numeiry also alleged that Yassin's assistant had driven the BSO terrorists to the embassy in his own vehicle and had actually led the assault himself.

Arafat immediately refuted all these allegations, issuing a statement denying that either the PLO or Fatah had been in any way involved in the operation and accusing Numeiry of 'launching an American-inspired campaign' against the Palestinian guerrillas. He added that he had asked Abu Yusef, one of his senior leaders (who was later killed by the Israelis in their Beirut raid in April 1973), to conduct a Fatah enquiry into the embassy killings, but this was only for public consumption as no such enquiry was held. The Khartoum incident was not mentioned by any of the media in Libya, Syria and Iraq and in Egypt only brief mention was made, with the even briefer criticism that it had been 'the latest in a series of mistakes made by the Palestinian organisation'. This illustrated the fluctuating isolation that Sudan periodically suffered in the Arab world.

Operation Tariq

On 7 March 1973 the Sudanese security authorities made public an eight-page BSO battle plan, entitled Operation Tariq, complete with a map showing the layout of the Saudi embassy, which they had seized together with many other incriminating documents when they raided the PLO offices in Khartoum. The plan had been written by Kawaz Yassin (also known as Abu Marwan), and gave details of the precise tasks allocated to each of the terrorists. For example one man was to command the initial assault squad, another to read a statement to the diplomats, another to control the telephone communications to and from the embassy, another to select the diplomats to be killed, another to act as executioner, and so on. Omar Haj Musa, the Sudanese information minister, said that six Sudanese named in incriminating documents would also stand trial, adding that 'We will give him [Arafat] the facts. It was his men and an al-Fatah car. And the plans were found in the Fatah leader's drawer after he fled the country before the attack. We want them to give us the men who fled.' He also indicated that the weapons had been provided by Libya.

Haile Selassie

On the 9th the Sudanese security authorities stated that the main target of the BSO operation had been Emperor Haile Selassie, who was visiting Sudan at the time. Pretending to be Saudi officials, the terrorists had telephoned Haile Selassie's secretary several times, both before and during the diplomatic party on 1 March, to try to persuade him to attend, or even put in a brief appearance. Haile Selassie, who had played such an important part in finding a solution to the southern problem, had been invited to Sudan as a guest of honour at the First Sudanese National Unity Day celebrations, held on the same day as the embassy party. The invitation to the Saudi reception had been politely declined by the emperor.

President Numeiry alleged that Fatah activities in Sudan were directed against his regime and were particularly aimed at disrupting his good relations with the Ethiopian government, saying 'We have documents to prove that Fatah men in Khartoum work more to foment troubles in Ethiopia, than for the cause of Palestine.' This was true, and the BSO's real aims had been to create a rift in the improving Sudanese–American relationship, isolate Sudan from black Africa, and seize and kill Haile Selassie.

Numeiry banned all Palestinian organisations and their activities within Sudan, and put the 'BSO Eight', as they became known, on public trial, despite being urged by his fellow Arab states not to do so – Numeiry was stubborn. After a number of postponements, in July 1974 the BSO Eight, who all pleaded guilty, were convicted and sentenced to life imprisonment, which Numeiry commuted to seven years' imprisonment. He then ordered that they be handed over to the PLO to serve their sentences, and they were spirited away from Sudan. The USA immediately recalled its ambassador from Khartoum.

The Ramadan War

The fourth Arab–Israeli War, which began on 5 October 1973 and lasted for 23 days, was known to the Arabs as the the Ramadan War and to the Israelis as the October War. The Arab forces caught the Israelis by surprise when they crossed the Suez Canal and broke through the Israeli Bar Lev Line. For four days it was touch and go for the Israelis, who were saved when a sudden, last minute, massive infusion of sophisticated American weaponry and other essential military items was airlifted in, after which the Arab troops, using Soviet weaponry, were gradually pressed backwards until a ceasefire was negotiated. Both sides claimed victory over this watershed in the ongoing Arab–Israeli struggle.

The USA and the USSR, power brokers and arms suppliers to one side or the other, were given pause for thought, both realising that if they did not stop fuelling the conflict they might ignite a Third World War. Sudanese armed forces played only a minor, peripheral role in the war, and its effect on Sudan was minimal.

The Shenan conspiracy

Meanwhile President Numeiry continued to rule a politically divided country, studded with frequent rumours and reports of plots against him, some, but not all, motivated by his rival for power, exiled Sadik Mahdi, former leader of the outlawed Ansar sect. On 26 January 1973 it was announced the Kheir Shenan (a retired brigadier) and several military personnel had been arrested, allegedly for conspiring to assassinate Numeiry and other leading personalities. At a large rally organised by the SSU, Numeiry blamed the communists, the Muslim Brotherhood and Arab nationalists. The whiff of conspiracy lingered for the remainder of the year, and suspected plotters were arbitrarily arrested. Shortly afterwards Numeiry confirmed that Sudan and the USSR would exchange ambassadors so that relations, strained since July 1971, could return to normal. In January 1975 Numeiry dismissed almost a dozen ministers for 'errors, laxity or negligence', or refusing to implement his decisions. The following month he reshuffled his cabinet, retaining the foreign affairs partfolio for himself and stating that he intended to reorganise the governmental structure.

The Akabo mutiny

On 1 March 1975 Numeiry, accompanied by Colonel Gaddafi of Libya and other northern and southern notables, visited Wau in the south to attend the celebrations marking the third anniversary of the Addis Ababa Accord. There a group of former members of the Anya-Nya symbolically laid down the old Soviet-made weapons they had used in the civil war days, and in exchange were given modern national army ones. The reaction came the following day at Akabo near the Ethiopian border, where southern troops mutinied, killing Colonel Chow (a southerner) and several other officers. Fighting broke out between loyal soldiers and mutineers, military reinforcements were rushed to Akabo, and the fighting rumbled on for some time.

The Sudanese government initially played down this incident, describing it as a minor mutiny and saying little about it. However in July it announced that eight mutineers had been executed and another 48 sentenced to terms of imprisonment. In fact it had been an attempted military rising of some magnitude, designed to spread throughout the south and initiated by Numeiry's exiled enemies to destablise the region. According to Ethiopian officials in Gambela, western Ethiopia, more than 10 000 Sudanese, both military and civilian, had fled into the Ethiopian province of Ilubabur between March and July, being hunted by the Sudanese army. According to refugee sources, more than 200 people had been killed in the fighting and about 150 rebel troops, former Anya-Nya members, had been disarmed, some of whom were later executed. A rebel leader speaking from Ethiopia accused the Sudanese government of continually violating the 1972 agreement, and declared that the rebels would continue to fight against the Arabs until southern Sudan was free. This was one of the first signs of major southern unrest, so far largely concealed by censorship

Economic stimulus

Sudan's national economy remained in a poor state, but an economic stimulus was provided by the reversal of the nationalisation measures taken in 1970 in most branches of production (except banks). The Arab Fund for Social and Economic Development was supporting Sudan in a ten-year plan to increase agricultural productivity, especially groundnuts, cotton and sugar for export, and there was talk of more land being irrigated and more wheat being grown. Sudan could not feed itself, and food had to be imported. Both Numeiry and Sadik Mahdi, were influenced by the dream that one day Sudan would become the granary of the Middle East. Oil exploration projects on land were being pursued, but not too enthusiastically as agriculture dominated future plans, but the Sudanese agreement with Saudi Arabia to exploit resources in the Red Sea was welcomed, and a joint commission was formed.

The Osman rebellion

Early in the morning of 5 September 1975 a rebellion against President Numeiry began, led by Colonel Hassan Hussein Osman, commander of a paratroop regiment. Osman's followers seized the Omdurman radio station, announcing themselves to be members of the National Front, which comprised both communist and right-wing religious opposition groups. They demanded that the cabinet and the Sudanese Socialist Union be instantly disbanded.

In a statement read for him over the radio, Osman denounced the revolution that had brought Numeiry to power in May 1969, declaring that instead of bringing freedom and independence it had brought chaos and disorder, that corruption was everywhere and that high prices and poverty had replaced prosperity. He accused Numeiry of suppressing all freedom of thought and education, and condemned him for nationalising the press, closing the Islamic University and suppressing freedom at the University of Khartoum. At the same time it was announced that an armoured brigade was moving against the presidential palace in Khartoum.

Numeiry, who was about to leave Khartoum to visit flooded areas of Kassala Province, learned of the rebellion at 0300 hours and immediately called on the rebels to surrender. Major Abu Kassem Ibrahim, minister of agriculture, and deputy secretary general of the SSU, led a tank offensive against the occupied Omdurman radio station, and regained it from rebel control after a two-hour battle, during which a number of rebels were killed or wounded.

The second rebel group, waiting to attack the presidential palace, was routed by loyal troops, and skirmishes took place in parts of Khartoum throughout the day. Colonel Osman, wounded in the fighting, was arrested and taken to hospital. In these two skirmishes, the government stated that five loyalist soldiers and three rebels were killed.

General Bashir Mohammed Ali, army commander-in-chief and defence minister, broadcast that day that loyal troops were crushing every rebel position that stood against them or was connected with the plot, adding that 'we shall uproot communist and sectarian corruption'. Abu Kassem Ibrahim accused the outlawed communists and Muslim Brotherhood members of having planned the abortive revolution. Numeiry announced later the same day that the rebels would be given a just trial. He also had several ministers arrested, saying that they had planned to execute him but that his early start for his visit to Kassala had enabled him to avoid capture. Alleging that Sadik Mahdi was behind the attempted revolution, he called upon the people to seek out the enemies of the revolution and 'the real motivators backstage and underground'. Police reported that a cache of arms and ammunition had been found in the students' residential quarters of Khartoum University, and further searches revealed huge sums of money in US dollars. The university was closed until further notice. Special courts were to be established to try the rebels, and the People's Assembly voted in favour of special powers to detain suspects. Numeiry addressed a specially arranged rally outside the presidential palace, asserting that the attempted revolution had been directed by a group of Sudanese political exiles, some living in Libya. He shouted 'Brother Gaddafi where did the cash found at the University come from?'

Later, in November, Major Hamid Fathalla was arrested when trying to flee the country. A huge sum of money was found in his possession. The special state security courts tried over 140 persons accused of being involved in the rebellion and in January 1976 Colonel Osman and others involve in the plot were executed by firing squad, as were several soldiers, while others received prison sentences. Numeiry had survived another attempt to remove him by force.

The Libyan-backed revolution

The next attempt to remove President Numeiry by armed force occurred in July 1976 with Libyan assistance. It was quickly suppressed by loyal troops, although there was considerable loss of life and damage to property in Khartoum. It began at 0500 hours on the 2nd, a few minutes after Numeiry had arrived back at Khartoum airport after visiting the USA and France. With him was Amadou Mahtar M'Bow, director general of UNESCO. Grenades suddenly exploded in several parts of the city and a group of armed civilians firing shots advanced towards the airport. Alerted to the danger, the president, his VIP guest and the other members of his party managed to escape to a village some miles away, from where he organised resistance.

Meanwhile loyal troops battled on the streets of Khartoum against the armed invaders, reinforcements being quickly sent in from Gezira and other garrisons by Kassem Ibrahim. The street battles lasted almost two days and were won by loyal troops. The cost to the invaders was heavy. Throughout, messages of loyal support had been sent to Numeiry by army commanders, and also by Vice President Abel Alier, head of the southern regional administration.

On the 3rd Numeiry announced that an attempt to take over the government by a foreign force had been crushed. He thanked President Sadat of Egypt and King Khalid of Saudi Arabia for their support during the brief rebellion. According to Numeiry, 80 per cent of the rebels were mercenaries from other countries. Ismail Fahmy, the Egyptian foreign minister, later revealed that the 1500 Sudanese troops stationed in Egypt had been immediately flown in Egyptian aircraft to Khartoum. President Sadat declared that the Libyan-backed coup attempt had been irresponsible and a crime against not only Sudan, but also the whole Arab nation, and was willing to meet any request from Numeiry for assistance. Some 16 000 Egyptian troops appeared in Sudan almost overnight. The details of the Saudi assistance were not made public.

The following day Numeiry's complaint to the UN Security Council was published in Khartoum. It stated that Sudan had been the target of an act of banditry, designed by Libya to create chaos and effect the overthrow of the legally constituted government, and that Libya had provided arms, ammunition and transport for about 1000 mercenaries, some of whom had been trained by Libyan instructors. A Sudanese protest against armed aggression was also sent to the Arab League. The Sudanese ambassador was recalled from Tripoli, all Libyan diplomats were ordered to leave Sudan within 24 hours, air links between the two countries were suspended, all joint economic projects were halted, Libyan aircraft were banned from Sudanese air space, no Libyans were allowed to enter Sudan and all road traffic was stopped at frontier posts. The severance seemed to be complete. Numeiry also declared a state of emergency in order to facilitate arrests and searches. It was announced that 300 people had been killed and another 300 wounded in the fighting, and that the dead included several loyal senior officers.

Meanwhile the authorities in Khartoum continued to arrest suspected rebels, house-to-house searches were intensified and the curfew was extended. On the 11th amended casualty figures were issued, it being claimed that over 700 rebels had been killed in savage fighting and 300 arrested. Among those arrested were over 60 politicians, including Ali Mohammed Husseini, a member of the Muslim Brotherhood who, had the coup succeeded, was designated to become the premier, and a new political bureau would have been headed by Sadik Mahdi, the former leader of the dissolved Umma Party. Amongst those arrested was (retired) Brigadier Mohammed Nur Saad. The government claimed that not a single Sudanese soldier on active service had participated in the rebellion.

Why the plot failed

Brigadier Nur Saad made a complete confession, stating that the plot to take over power in Khartoum by force had failed for three reasons: the absence of promised reinforcements from Libya; the absence of any public support from the Sudanese masses, which somehow the plotters had expected; and the failure of the plotters to identify themselves to the public as the radio broadcasting staff at Omdurman had fled before any rebel broadcasts could be made. Numeiry said in an interview published in Cairo on 6 July 1976 that the clear aim of the invaders had been to change the Sudanese government, and that the mercenaries had come from Chad, Ethiopia, Libya, Mali and Zanzibar, some being subsequently put before the press.

Sadik Mahdi, the prime mover in the attempted rebellion, issued a statement in Paris on 10 July in which he claimed it had not been a foreign invasion but a popular insurrection, which would have been successful had it not been for the intervention by President Sadat. He alleged that the Numeiry regime had lost all its ideological justification and would eventually be overthrown by a popular uprising. On 12 July the Sudanese newspaper *Al Sahafa* contained photographs of several former Sudanese political figures who were 'wanted' by the government, including Sadik Mahdi and three former ministers. On the 11th one cabinet minister, Mansur Khalid, personal adviser to Numeiry, said that the Sudanese government had known for three years that training camps for anti-Sudanese forces existed in south-eastern Libya, and that Numeiry had made representations about them, but that that Colonel Gaddafi had insisted they were there simply to train troops to fight against Israel.

Gaddafi alleged that Sadik Mahdi (if successful) would have established a union between Sudan and Libya as an expression of his thanks. It was also disclosed that three months previously the Sudanese troops at Katum in western Sudan had intercepted 230 armed men entering the country from Libya, and that during the night of 1–2 July the police had arrested over 50 members of the Muslim Brotherhood. Numeiry placed the country's press under control of the SSU, and a purge was carried out amongst working journalists to decide who should be transferred to other work. Special courts were established to try over 90 defendants. Over 70 were found guilty and sentenced to death, most of whom were executed on 4 August. Another court tried over 20 defendants, 17 of whom were found guilty and were executed on the 5th. A further 200 were still awaiting trial.

During the course of these trials details of the plot were exposed. It appears that plans for the coup had first been discussed at a meeting in London in March 1976, attended by Sadik Mahdi and Hussein Sharif Hindi (leader of the National Unionist Party). Brigadier Nur Saad admitted to training 1000 men in camps in Libya and Ethiopia. It had been planned that, if the coup was successful, the newly formed National Front, led by Sadik Mahdi, would rule for a year, during which time all who had helped and supported the Numeiry regime would be liquidated. This would have been followed by a referendum to decide whether the National Front would continue in power.

The Sudanese government assessed the value of destroyed or damaged aircraft, vehicles and military equipment as over $150 million, and its MiG spares as $8 million. It was confirmed that 97 Sudanese soldiers had been killed or were missing. The suggestion by Numeiry that the Soviet Union had also been involved in the plot was denied in Moscow (*Pravda*).

Sadik Mahdi admits responsibility

Sadik Mahdi gave a press conference on 4 August 1976 in London, at which he admitted that he had been responsible for the attempted coup. He said that it had been considered the only way to get rid of Numeiry, and claimed that the exercise had been supported by several Arab countries, including Libya, but that all who had taken part were Sudanese. The Sudanese minister of information protested to Britain for allowing publicity to be given to Mahdi's press conference.

The Sudanese government then established a special court to try, *in absentia*, Sadik Mahdi and Hussein Sharif Hindi 'for waging war against Sudan, with the help of a foreign power'. In due course both were found guilty. Numeiry reshuffled his cabinet, but said he would make changes to the SSU at its second congress, due in January 1977.

Defence agreements

The previous month President Numeiry had visited Egypt to sign a joint defence agreement with that country, in the interests of Arab solidarity. The agreement would remain in force for 25 years, and each country would regard an attack against one of them as being an attack against both. There was to be a Common Defence Council, to meet alternately in Cairo and Khartoum, and also periodic meetings of the joint chiefs of staff. An undisclosed clause was that Egypt would station 12 000 troops in Sudan until the security situation improved. In a TV interview in Cairo, Numeiry insisted that the Soviets had supported Gaddafi in the attempt to remove him from power. Then the two presidents moved on to Jeddah at the invitation of King Khalid, where another Arab solidarity statement was issued. In New York, at the UN HQ, the Arab group persuaded Sudan to withdraw the complaint it had made against Libya to the Security Council.

Unrest in the south

Meanwhile during the first part of 1976 there was serious unrest in the south, arising out of widespread discontent with the slowness of economic development in the region, and agitation and mischief-making by southern politicians. The situation was largely concealed from the outside world, and indeed from the majority of northern Sudanese.

On 28 February Abel Alier, head of the regional administration, reported to the Southern Regional Assembly that an army unit at Wau, which included former Anya-Nya members in its ranks, had deserted the previous week after killing three senior officers. The integration of former Anya-Nya into the regular army was proceeding as well as could be expected, but there was occasional friction, some acts of indiscipline and murmuring of discontent.

In March Abel Alier reported that several southern political leaders had been arrested, including Joseph Oduko, Benjamin Bol (deputy speaker of the Regional Assembly) and Izbone Mendiri (leader of the Anya-Nya negotiating team in 1972), and that others had fled the country, mainly to Ethiopia. Relations between Sudan and Ethiopia were poor at this juncture. Alier stated the following month that his authorities had crushed a conspiracy to instigate a military rebellion in the south, confirming that three members of the Regional Assembly had been arrested for implication in the plot and would soon be brought to trial. It was believed that there were up to 40 000 Sudanese refugees living in four camps in the Ethiopian province of Gambela, although this was denied by the Khartoum government. It was also noted that some restless southern politicians were showing considerable interest in the army in the south.

The southern air force mutiny

The next major plot in the south occurred in February 1977. On the 3rd Abel Alier announced that 12 Sudanese air force officers had been arrested after taking part in an attempt to seize the airport at Juba the previous day. By the 6th the total under arrest had risen to 30. It was revealed that the plot had been led by Philip Abbas Ghaboash (a former member the Sudanese Assembly), who was remembered for his opposition to Sudanese aid to Egypt in the 1967 Arab–Israeli War and was currently said to be living in Israel. Confessions from arrested suspects indicated that the aim of the plot had been to rouse a military rebellion, and to establish a separate state in southern Sudan. Alier claimed that the conspiracy had been manipulated by 'foreign hands', meaning Israeli ones, and boasted that he had crushed the rebellion within three hours.

9
Fluctuating Friendships

On 1 January 1977 President Numeiry accused the Ethiopian government of giving support to anti-Numeiry National Front personnel established in camps just inside Ethiopia near the Sudanese border, which had been visited by Sadik Mahdi in December 1976. One of the Eritrean groups opposing the central government, based in the vicinity of Humera, a town near the Sudanese border, had on several occasions attacked these camps, capturing members of the National Front and handing them over to the Khartoum government. Numeiry boasted that he was capable of repelling any attacks from Ethiopia and could enlist the support of the 140 000 (his figure) Eritrean refugees who had entered Sudan during the previous 14 years. If necessary he would provide a proportion of the latter with arms and ammunition. The Sudanese government also covertly assisted international journalists to enter, and exit, the civil war zones in Ethiopia.

Changing Ethiopian leadership

Ethiopia was undergoing violent changes of leadership. During the latter part of Haile Selassie's reign, Ethiopia was one the USA's 'base rights' countries, where in exchange for a considerable amount of military aid and credits it maintained, amongst other things, a huge communications base at Kagnew, near Asmara in Eritrea (then federated to Ethiopia). This was a huge 'listening station', run by the US army and part of a worldwide network codenamed USM-4, covering Egypt, the Arabian peninsula, the Gulf and parts of North Africa.

Addis Ababa, the Ethiopian capital, was the HQ of the Organisation of African Unity, which had been largely formed by Emperor Haile Selassie, who had hoped to influence African affairs through its auspices.

Early in 1974, unrest within the Ethiopian armed forces increased, beginning with the demand by troops for more pay and followed by mutinies and the arrest of government officials by the armed forces. A Supreme Military Council was established to bargain with the civilian government. On 12 September 1974 a provisional military government, headed by General Aman Andom, assumed power after deposing Emperor Haile Selassie, who was kept in detention until he died on 27 August 1975.

A provisional Military Administrative Council was formed, known as the Dergue (meaning 'committee' in Amharic). The council welcomed Soviet help as Western aid had suddenly ceased, and Western influence declined. During 1975 and 1976 the Dergue was faced not only with large-scale rebellion in its annexed province of Eritrea, but also demands for autonomy by other provinces, and soon 10 of the 14 provinces were in active revolt. There were continuous quarrels and purges within the Dergue, but in February 1976 Colonel Mengistu Haile Mariam emerged as the victor, becoming president and head of state in February 1977. That month Ethiopian troops clashed with Somalis in Ogaden Province, which resulted in Cuban troops entering this theatre of operations.

Sudan–Egyptian–Syrian agreement

Egyptian–Syrian relations had been strained for some time, but reconciliation was achieved with Saudi help by the Riyadh Agreement of October 1976, when the two countries formed a Unified Political Command. This was extended to include Sudan during a tripartite summit in Khartoum, a joint declaration being made on 28 February 1977. The object was to give support to President Numeiry in the face of his external and internal difficulties, and to contain any possible further extension of Libyan influence into the south-eastern Sahara area. Libya was becoming friendly with the Ethiopian Dergue, and Sudan and Egypt suspected that Colonel Gaddafi was trying to isolate Sudan. The Egypt–Sudan Defence Agreement of July 1976 was activated, both countries recalled their ambassadors from Sudan and Numeiry ordered the suspension of all flights between Sudan and Ethiopia.

A presidential election was held in April 1977, in which Numeiry was the sole candidate. He obtained 99.1 per cent of the votes, and so was duly re-elected for a second six-year term. His position thus fortified, the following month he and a ministerial team visited France in the hope of obtaining French arms, admitting that the Soviets were no longer supplying him and that he was forced to look elsewhere. He let it be known that Saudi Arabia might be financing his arms purchases. Numeiry spoke of Sudan's expanses of undeveloped fertile land and eulogised on his pet vision of Sudan becoming the granary of the Arab world and Africa. He also spoke of Sudan's unexploited mineral resources. Numeiry expressed regret that Colonel Mengistu, the Ethiopian head of state, had become deeply involved with the Soviet Union, and stated that he was on the side of secessionist Eritrea. Several economic and development agreements, including one relating to arms supplies, were signed in Paris, and a French military training team soon arrived in Khartoum.

Sudan ejects the Soviets

While Numeiry was still in Paris, it was announced in Khartoum on 18 May 1977 that the Soviet contingent of experts and their families (147 personnel) had left Sudan by air as the government had cancelled their work contracts, and the office attached to the Soviet embassy that had dealt with Soviet work permits since 1970 was closed. The government said that the Soviets had been given prior notice, but it was later alleged that the evacuation had been effected because of the non-supply of spare parts, without which much of the Soviet military equipment in the country was becoming useless.

On his return to Khartoum, Numeiry expelled some 30 Soviet diplomats, causing Moscow to recall the Soviet ambassador. The Soviets denied that the diplomats had been expelled and claimed that they had been recalled because of Numeiry's anti-Soviet attitude. In an interview published in Beirut on 1 June 1977 Numeiry declared that the Soviet policy in the Middle East and Africa had failed completely, but that the Soviets were continuing to supply arms to Ethiopia in the hope that that country would become involved in war with Eritrea, emphasising that if this were to happen, Sudan would side with Eritrea. The expulsion of the Soviets from Sudan was welcomed by China, and Numeiry paid an official visit to that country on 6 June to make capital of this, trading on Soviet–Chinese hostility.

Sudan and Ethiopia

Relations between Ethiopia and Sudan deteriorated further and at the second congress of the SSU in February 1977 a statement was issued urging a peaceful solution to the Eritrean problem, reaffirming Sudanese support for Eritrean's right to self-determination, and condemning the Dergue's acts of violence and the alleged assassination of innocent people. On the 24th Omar Ismail, the Sudanese commissioner for refugees, said that about 200 000 people had fled from Ethiopia into Sudan, some 40 000 of them being Eritreans, for whom his government was providing schools and employment.

On 6 April Numeiry denounced the presence of 'foreign troops' in Ethiopia (meaning Soviets and Cubans), alleging they had been introduced to massacre Eritreans and others in opposition to the Dergue. In reply Colonel Mengistu accused the Sudanese government of giving aid and shelter to Ethiopian and Eritrean resistance groups. He also protested to the OAU that Sudanese troops had helped resistance forces to seize two border towns in Ethiopia, named as Tesseni and Metemma. The Sudanese foreign minister, Mansur Khaled, visited Europe in search of help to support the 250 000 refugees who were wholly dependent on the goodwill of the Sudanese people, both Christian (Ethiopian) and Muslim (Eritrean).

The National Reconciliation Agreement

Although Numeiry had so far survived his power struggle with Sadik Mahdi, he came to realise that it was absorbing too much national energy and stultifying the economic development of the country. Numeiry decided it was time to make peace with his enemy, and as an opener he secretly met Mahdi at Port Sudan in early July 1977 to listen to his demands. Broadly in order to create a suitable climate for fruitful negotiation towards national reconciliation, Numeiry offered a general amnesty to Mahdi, his National Front organisation and his Ansar followers, who had been engaged in armed opposition against Numeiry. Mahdi additionally demanded the restoration of civil rights and political liberties, but did not want a multiparty state.

In an interview in *Le Monde* a few days later, Mahdi admitted to being the leader of the National Front and stated that he had sent President Numeiry a list of seven conditions to serve as a basis for negotiation. Mahdi too had realised that his armed struggle with Numeiry was ruining his country, and being basically a patriot he wanted reconciliation, and for Sudan to become a prosperous, forward-looking country. One of the main conditions was that Sudanese support for Eritrean resistance fighters be removed in order to avoid the destabilisation of the whole of the Horn of Africa. Two others were to have friendly but equidistant relations with the USA and the USSR, so that the latter would resume its arms supply and thus diversify Sudan's sources of supply; and to maintain the sovereignty and economic development of Sudan on socialist lines. An agreement was reached.

Meanwhile Numeiry had been preparing the ground, and in July some 900 Sudanese political detainees were released, followed by a government statement that Sudan no longer held any political prisoners. Numeiry issued a decree granting a general amnesty to all Sudanese for any political offences they had committed on or after 25 May 1969 (the day he had come to power) inside or outside Sudan, or any illegal act under the security laws, provided that they agreed to abide by the constitution, to work for the principle of national unity and, for those abroad, to return to Sudan. A list was published on 13 August of persons to whom full amnesty would apply, including Sadik Mahdi and Hussein Sharif Hindi. Mahdi returned to Sudan on 28 September 1977 after seven years in exile. The following month the government announced an amnesty for about 100 Sudanese who had been arrested in connection with the attempted coup in Juba in February 1977, and also several Libyans accused of being involved in the attempted coup of July 1976.

A formal National Reconciliation Agreement was signed in London on 12 April 1978 between representatives of the Sudanese government and Sadik Mahdi, on behalf of himself and his National Front organisation, to enable political exiles to return to Sudan and take part in political life. This agreement included the dissolution of the National Front (which did not include any communists), which was required to close its training camps and hand over all its weapons to the Sudanese National Army. All returning exiles were required to accept the 1973 constitution. There would be freedom for the Ansar to practice its own form of Islam, and the government would repeal all repressive legislation against it. Lastly, wholehearted support was required to solve the southern problem, on the lines of the 1972 autonomy agreement, which was running into difficulties.

Sadik Mahdi left Sudan in December 1977 to contact his widely deployed supporters. He returned to Khartoum on 24 February 1978 and announced that he had succeeded in persuading them to accept Numeiry's conditions. Numeiry then appointed several of his former enemies to official positions, and in mid March he appointed several more of them to the Central Committee of the ruling Sudanese Socialist Union. In an election for the Southern Regional People's Assembly several ministers lost their seats, so Numeiry appointed General Lagu as president of its Higher Council.

Numeiry reshuffled his cabinet, dismissing several ministers and taking over the defence portfolio himself. Hassan Turabi, leader of the Muslim Brotherhood, was brought in as foreign minister. In July, Philip Abbas Ghaboash, leader of the United Sudanese National Liberation

Front, which Ghaboash had established to enable active opposition to Numeiry, announced from exile in Nairobi that he had disbanded his organisation as he no longer doubted Numeiry's good intentions, and was duly reconciled. Sadik Mahdi became a member of the Central Committee of the SSU. Diplomatic relations with the Soviet Union were restored in May 1978.

Due to Sudan's support of the Eritrean secessionists its relations with the Ethiopian Dergue were bad, but a reconciliation was effected in December 1977 at an OAU conference, and the following month Sudan repatriated 240 members of an Ethiopian military unit that had withdrawn into Sudan to avoid being surrounded by Eritrean rebels. Numeiry promised not to support dissident movements in the Horn of Africa, and air links between the two countries were resumed.

In an attempt to improve relations with Libya, with which links had been severed after the Libyan-backed attempted coup in Khartoum in July 1976, a Sudanese ministerial delegation visited Tripoli in February 1978 for talks, which resulted in a joint statement that the two governments had reached agreement on several issues. It was decided to reopen the respective embassies in Tripoli and Khartoum, and to restore air links between the two countries. The Sudanese stressed that the Egypt–Sudan Defence Agreement of 1976 was a purely defensive one, and Sudan and Libya agreed not to enter into pacts against each other. At that time the Libyan government was supporting resistance groups in Chad and the Horn of Africa, and Sudan indicated that it would look the other way.

Arms from the USA

Sudan was busy tearing down hostile barriers, softening aggressive attitudes and trying to develop good relations with one and all in this suspicious, uneasy part of the world, where alliances were quickly made and just as quickly broken for diverse and devious reasons. Diplomatic relations with the USA (severed in 1973, when US Ambassador Cleo Noel had been murdered by BSO terrorists) were resumed, but remained cool. However in April 1978 the USA indicated that it would be willing to sell Sudan twelve modern F-3 fighter aircraft, being the first sale of modern aircraft to Sudan. The expulsion of the Soviets from Sudan had pleased the US Ford administration, causing it to decide that Sudan was eligible for arms purchases.

Previously (May 1977) the US Defense Department had obtained permission from the US Congress to sell Sudan six Lockheed C-130 transport planes, with spare parts and support services, and a US military mission was sent to Sudan, which started a flow of American arms to that country. Numeiry stated that all the Soviet weaponry held by his armed forces (then about 60 000 strong) was either out of date or inactive owing to a lack of spare parts, none having been supplied by the Soviets for some time. The Americans responded, and Numeiry began to rearm his security forces.

Economic difficuties

The year 1978 was a bad one for Sudan, which was beset by a heavy debt burden, a high import bill, high inflation and low devaluation. The situation grew worse towards the end of July, when the country was hit by torrential rain storms that flooded huge expanses of land, devastating half the cotton-growing area and making over half a million people homeless. Numeiry appealed for aid, and some Arab and Western countries made relief contributions.

Numeiry broke off diplomatic relations with Iraq because the latter had failed to deliver oil to Sudan, even though it had been paid for in advance, but he also accused the Iraqi ruling Baath Party of harbouring Sudanese exiles hostile to him, and in particular one Hussein Sharif Hindi, who had refused to accept the National Reconciliation Agreement. It was reported that crude oil was being supplied by Saudi Arabia and processed at the small refinery at Port Sudan.

The Jonglei canal project

A major talking point in Sudan in 1978 was the Jonglei Canal project on the eastern edge of the Sudd, a vast papyrus swamp flanking and choking kink in the White Nile and acting as a major obstacle to north–south river communication between Juba and Khartoum. The canal would start in the region of Bor and extend northwards to Malakal. There were only three narrow and unreliable courses through the Sudd, kept open for local navigation by primitive cutting machines mounted on small craft. The journey from Juba to Khartoum could take up to a month by road and river, depending on the season. All-weather roads were scarce in Sudan, and although plans were in hand to improve the existing ones and build others, progress was slow. A deep, wide canal through the eastern part of the Sudd would shortenen the journey from Juba to Khartoum by several days, but it would require 25 per cent of the White Nile waters, all of which were already spoken for by Sudan and Egypt under the Aswan agreement.

Originally the government had toyed with the additional idea of turning the Sudd into arable land (influenced by the granary vision), which provoked a rumour that it planned to bring in 2.5 million Egyptian settlers into the Sudd area. This caused riots in Juba and the idea had to be dropped. (Environmental critics had also said it would change the climate, while others claimed it would prevent the automatic replenishment of the aquifers and wells in the region and so extend the desert. There was no evidence of this as the annual rainfall in the Sudd averaged over 800 millimetres.) To please the powerful Dinkas, there would be special cattle crossing places in the canal, with sloping access and exits. Work on the canal began and was due for completion by 1984. Apart from speeding up north–south travel, it was hoped that the canal would considerably increase the volume of goods and passengers and prove a popular link between the Arab north and the animist/Christian south.

In pastoral areas there were occasional outbreaks of cattle rustling, with hereditary enemies raiding each other's herds. This sometimes developed into large-scale fights, although there were usually comparatively few casualties as the tribesmen possessed only primitive weapons. However there was one notable exception. In the summer of 1977 a Baggara raiding party attacked a Dinka encampment (both being nomadic cattle herding tribes) and over 400 Dinkas were killed before order was restored. The unique factor here was the possession of automatic weapons by the Baggara, who were from Kordofan Province and had allegedly been armed by Sadik Mahdi's supporters to destabilise the area.

Anti-Numeiry plots and student riots

Meanwhile the Khartoum regime continued to be haunted by plots and rumours of plots by anti-Numeiry factions. On 7 April 1979 it was announced that the armed forces had taken (unspecified) measures to prevent the use of recently imported arms by groups plotting against the security of the country. On 24 May Numeiry promoted himself to the rank of field marshal and made further leadership changes, dismissing eight ministers, one being Hassan Turabi, former leader of the Muslim Brotherhood. In July, Abu Kassem Ibrahim, the first vice president and secretary general of the SSU, was quietly dismissed. No reason was given, but it was said that while Numeiry was away at an OAU conference Ibrahim had taken measures contrary to the government's austerity policy, in particular granting tax exemptions to certain low-paid workers and promising pay increases to railway workers. Ibrahim reportedly moved to Saudi Arabia. Numeiry, who was ever reluctant to delegate and liked to give out any good news personally, took over as secretary general of the SSU.

Student riots broke out in Khartoum on 7 August 1979. The riots caused considerable damage and destruction, and were blamed by the government on remnants of banned political organisations that were continuing to plot and conspire against Numeiry. The immediate cause of the student unrest, and also of a coincidental strike by railway workers demanding a wage increase, was the rising cost of staple foods and fuel, but in a memorandum addressed to the president the students also called for freedom of the press, the liquidation of the SSU and the replacement of the government with what was described as a Ministry of Public Welfare. The situation grew uglier as anti-Numeiry factions joined in and the demonstrations spread to other major cities.

Help had come early from Egypt, and a few days before the student unrest had burst into violence Egyptian troops had quietly arrived in Sudan and dispersed to strategic points in Khartoum, Omdurman, Juba and elsewhere. It was officially denied that there were Egyptian troops in Sudan, but it was later admitted that Egyptian soldiers had killed ten demonstrators and injured others. The Sudanese army was placed on alert on the 9th, and during this period of widespread rioting and political uncertainty the new chief of staff, General Ali Malik assured Numeiry that the army was solidly behind him, and undertook to crush any traitors or plotters.

Meanwhile Numeiry had been making changes to the leadership structure of the SSU by reducing the size of its Central Committee. Among the southerners removed were Joseph Oduho, Lawrence Wol-Wol and Clement Mboro. Numeiry announced these changes on 18 August, and at the same time said that he was reducing the price of meat and fuel, and that the price of bread and cereals was to be controlled. This brought the rioting to an end, but Numeiry continued to make leadership changes, which were often prefaced by government announcements of alleged anti-Numeiry plots.

Numeiry's dedecentralisation plan

At the third congress of the SSU in January 1980 Numeiry outlined his decentralisation plan, which involved the reorganisation of the administration of the country (less the south) into five regional bodies, each of which would have a great deal of autonomy, with its own governor and regional assembly and responsible for its own budget. Economic chaos was bearing down on the country, wages in factories and on government projects were usually in arrears, there was a fuel shortage, trains ran erratically, the main roads badly needed repair, and tribal sheikhs and chiefs were discontent with SSU demands. Numeiry had been influenced by the southern autonomy model, which in the main had brought peace for some eight years; he was under the illusion that the southern administration was operating much better than it actually was. The main national ministries, including defence, finance, foreign affairs and planning, would remain under central control. The official reason for the move towards decentralisation was to 'give power back to the people'.

In the south in February, General Lagu, president of the Higher Execut-ive Council, stepped down following allegations of unconstitutional conduct and the misappropriation of funds. Unofficially Lagu's fall from grace was blamed on his feud with the powerful Dinka political clique. In May the Regional People's Assembly voted in Abel Alier, the former president, to take Lagu's place.

In May an assassination attempt on President Numeiry and some of his ministers resulted in the arrest and trial of a number of members of banned political groups. It was alleged this failed coup had been organ-ised by Hussein Sharif Hindi, former leader of the Democratic Unionist Party, still operating from Iraq. Previously it had been reported in the Beirut press that the DUP and the Sudanese Communist Party had merged in October 1979 to form the Sudanese Democratic Front (SDF).

During the course of 1980 several members of banned organisations who had returned to Sudan hoping for the best were arrested, tried and imprisoned, as were a few back-sliders who had initially accepted the reconciliation agreement but then reneged in some way. On occasion the SDF tended to embroider its claims, alleging on one occasion that SDF members had wounded Numeiry in an assassination attempt, but this was firmly denied by SUNA, the Sudan News Agency.

Cattle raiding persists

There was disorder in the rural area around Kapoeta in the south during June 1980, stemming from cattle raiding between tribes, especially the Taposa and Murle, whose livestock had been badly affected by the East African drought, which had extended into Sudan. The disorder was made more serious by the fact that tribesmen had been able to purchase weapons and ammunition from Ugandan soldiers loyal to former Pres-ident Amin during their withdrawal across part of Sudan. Technically, the Sudanese border with Uganda had been closed to normal traffic since

April 1979, when Amin was overthrown, but had been reopened on 10 January 1980.

The Bahar plot

On 16 March 1981 SUNA reported that the previous week the government had foiled a military plot led by a retired army officer, Brigadier Saad Bahar, who had allegedly been aided by certain foreign forces, taken to mean Syria and the Soviet Union. Bahar and several other suspects had been arrested. In a speech, Numeiry maintained that the Soviet intention was to infiltrate the Gulf region and Africa though such countries as Libya, and that in the face of such wanton Soviet encroachment, Sudan was prepared to offer military facilities to the USA. His suggestion was that the USA should construct three large military airfields for the Sudanese armed forces that could be used jointly in an emergency. Numeiry added that he did not mind the USA acquiring military bases in other regional states, provided it did not interfere in domestic politics. He said he would continue to purge anti-regime, corrupt and incompetent elements, and on 20 May announced that over 30 officers had been compulsorily retired, as had a large number of civil servants, thought to number over 2000.

Arab League schism

On 24–5 May 1981 President Sadat of Egypt paid a state visit to Sudan. Inviting Sadat was considered to be a bold gesture on the part of Numeiry. Since the inception of the Arab League the members had been united in their enmity towards Israel, and this had become an article of faith for them. Then in November 1977 Sadat had made his historic trip to Jerusalem to meet with Israeli Prime Minister Menachem Begin, to the horror and dismay of Arab League members, and indeed the whole Arab nation. This meeting had led to a second, American-organised, meeting between these two leaders and the US president – the Camp David Summit – in September the following year, followed in March 1979 by the signing of the Egyptian–Israeli Peace Treaty in Washington. The talks and treaty shattered Arab unity on the issue and President Sadat became the pariah of the Arab League, with several Arab states severing diplomatic relations with Egypt.

Sudan was the first Muslim country to welcome the Egyptian ruler since his historic trip to Jerusalem. Although there had been some hiccups between Sudan and Egypt, diplomatic relations had never been severed, not even after the signing of the Egyptian–Israeli Peace Treaty. Sadat's visit to Sudan signified full restoration of the close political links that had existed between the two countries since 1974, perhaps exemplified by the joint congress of the Egyptian–Sudanese People's Assemblies, held in Cairo in October 1977. Although this had been little more than a talking shop, it had had a significant impact on their unity of purpose.

A communique issued during Sadat's visit to Khartoum stated that the two leaders wished to offer military facilities to the USA. Furthermore Sadat announced that Egypt had presented Sudan with a tract of land on the Mediterranean coast, west of Alexandria, for the construction of a port, Sudan's only major maritime trading outlet being Port Sudan on the Red Sea. Subsequently, in July, Numeiry paid a return state visit to Egypt, being the first Arab ruler to do so since the signing of the Egyptian–Israeli Peace Treaty.

President Sadat was assassinated in Cairo on 6 November 1981, during a ceremonial parade marking the anniversary of the 1973 Arab–Israeli War.

Railway strike

The continual increase in the price of food and fuel was at the root of the nationwide strike launched in early June 1981 by some 43 000 members of the Sudan Railway Workers Union and navigation workers. The strikers were demanding a wage rise, but on the 14th the SSU condemned the strike as being politically motivated, declaring that it was a conspiracy directed from abroad. Numeiry ordered his security forces to arrest strikers who did not return to work, warning them they would lose their jobs if they did not do so. He described the strike as high treason, and accused the strikers of being saboteurs working for Moscow. The government banned the trade unions involved in the strike from all political activity, and the leader of the Sudan Railways Workers Union, Abbas Khidir, was deprived of his seat in the National People's Assembly. A further decree on the 21st invoked the death penalty for strike organisers and life imprisonment for strikers. A wholesale wave of union leadership arrests followed, which slowly brought the strike to an end. On 6 July the charges against union leaders were suspended, and they were released the following day. Numeiry had stood up to organised trade union power and defeated it by strong-arm tactics.

Chad involvement

Following Libya's military intervention in adjacent Chad, Sudan's relations with that country once again began to deteriorate sharply. In

December 1980 Numeiry condemned Libya's intervention as adventurism in the service of Soviet expansion, and on 24 March 1981 the Sudanese government formally proposed that Libya should be expelled from the Arab League on the ground that it had foreign bases on its territory. A few days later Numeiry called for international action by neighbouring states to overthrow Colonel Gaddafi.

Numeiry alleged that the Soviets were constructing a military base at Qarat Bishi in Chad, about 80 miles west of the Chad–Sudan border, and that Libyan occupying troops were carrying out acts of sabotage in the border region. The Sudanese government was concerned that they would stir up unrest in the adjacent Sudanese province of Darfur, where an estimated two million Chadian refugees and nomads were living. Just previously, in January 1981, Numeiry had run into difficulty over Darfur Province, having appointed a non-Darfuri as governor, which caused protest riots in El Fasher, the provincial capital, in which several lives were lost. Numeiry backed down and a Darfuri was appointed governor of the province, where the population was poor and deprived, even by Sudanese standards, and ripe for subversion.

Radio Tripoli in Libya, in its propaganda war against Sudan, made frequent reference to the activities and claimed successes against the Khartoum government of two Sudanese opposition groups operating in Libya, and perhaps also western parts of Sudan. One was the Sudanese Socialist People's Front, which called for the overthrow of Numeiry on the ground that he was turning Sudan into a province of Egypt, and the other was the People's Armed Forces for the Salvation of the Homeland (PASH), which alleged that the Numeiry regime was isolated from the people and that Numeiry was turning Sudan into a US military base. Both groups had been recently formed and were believed to be subsidised and manipulated by the Libyan government.

The Arab League's consideration of the Sudanese proposal to expel Libya was inconclusive and relations between Sudan and Libya deteriorated further. On 25 June the Sudanese government ordered the Libyan ambassador and his diplomatic staff to leave the country within 48 hours, and recalled the Sudanese ambassador and his staff from Tripoli. During the same period there was an explosion at the Chadian embassy in Khartoum. A guard at the embassy was handed a briefcase containing a bomb, which then exploded, killing the guard and injuring two other people. The culprit was arrested and admitted to being bribed by Libyans. Hissene Habre, the Chadian leader who had been defeated in the Chadian civil war in December 1980 by Goukouni Oueddei, with Libyan assistance, had been due to visit the embassy that day. In January 1981 the governments of Chad and Libya had announced their decision to work for full unity between their two countries, but the Chadian ambassador in Khartoum and his staff had rejected this decision and remained in place, with Sudanese permission.

Sudan's relations with Libya deteriorated further in October, when Libya deported over 90 Sudanese for refusing to join PASH, which now claimed to have branches in Sudan, probably in Darfur Province. The following month, in a letter to the UN Security Council, the Sudanese government rejected Libya's protest that Sudan was planning, in conjunction with Egypt, to attack it.

The cleansing of Khartoum

Khartoum was becoming packed to overflowing with people from elsewhere in Sudan and diverse immigrant groups, to such an extent that Numeiry, haunted by memories of mob-influenced street battles for power, decided to take action to reduce this risk. Beginning on 12 September 1980 the Khartoum police mounted a series of daily dragnet operations in different parts of the city, arresting all who could not give a good account of themselves. The latter were classified as either aliens or vagrants, and included criminals, the rural unemployed, refugees and other undesirables, who were bundled off to a holding camp at Sofa on the outskirts of the city to be processed. It was thought that Sudan contained some half a million refugees from Chad, Eritrea and Uganda, most gravitating towards Khartoum, as had an equal number of Sudanese looking for work. According to the authorities this invasion of Khartoum not only posed a security threat, but also encouraged black market dealings and placed a heavy burden on food supplies, transport, health facilities and other services. The shanty towns that sprang up like mushrooms near Khartoum and other cities were bulldozed to the ground as fast as they were erected.

These sweeps continued rigorously for some weeks, and the ordinary citizens of Khartoum had to carry their ID cards with them at all times lest they too were caught up in the dragnet, which did happen on occasion. The camp at Sofa was said to have a constant population of around 15 000 people waiting to be processed, for as fast as cases were disposed of fresh batches were brought in. Unemployed Sudanese were sent back to their home provinces, foreign immigrants and undesirables were deported, political refugees were moved away to distant camps and criminals were prosecuted. Soon the authorities stated that city crime had been reduced by 90 per cent. Numeiry regarded these dragnet operations as fine tooth combs to detect and deter subversives.

The latent oil industry

Oil-exploration activities in the 1970s had produced some modest rewards. Out of the 17 wells drilled by October 1980 (*Financial Times*) five were producing a total of about 18 000 barrels a day and it was hoped there would soon be sufficient to satisfy Sudan's domestic requirement. In August 1981 it was decided to build an oil refinery near Kosti, on the Nile River and close to the railway system, a few miles from Aba Island, and to construct a 340-mile pipeline between the refinery and the oil wells in the south. This caused some dissent as southern politicians thought that the refinery should be located closer to the wells in the south, where there was concern about deteriorating economic conditions. The refinery would provide local employment and produce oil revenues at a time when up to four million southerners were reportedly threatened by famine. There was some argument in government circles over the priority that should be accorded to the oil industry, as over emphasising its importance might lead to funds being diverted away from agricultural projects, which were given top priority due to the granary vision. Recent cotton crops had been satisfactory, and Sudan was finding that it could sell more cotton than it could grow, so the government wanted to expand this area of production.

Dissolution of the National People's Assembly

On 5 October 1981 Numeiry dissolved both the National People's Assembly and the Southern Regional Assembly, announcing that elections for these two bodies would be held within 60 days and six months respectively. He stated that this was intended to facilitate the decentralisation of government powers. The National People's Assembly would be reduced from 366 seats to 151 as many of its powers would be devolved to the five new regional assemblies. In the south, he appointed General Abdullah Rassas (a southern Muslim) as interim president of the Higher Executive Council, in place of Abel Alier, who still remained a national vice president.

The Alier government had brought peace and a measure of development to the south, but there was a feeling that if he had acted more firmly and speedily there might have been a greater administrative improvement, several of his ministers being lax. Alier, as a Dinka, had also disagreed with Joseph Lagu, who, when president of the Southern Higher Executive Council, had proposed to create a small independent administrative subarea, to be carved out from the southern tip of Equatoria Province, which would have relieved the general administrative blockage in that corner of the south. Furthermore, Alier's transport policy could be faulted by his failure to purchase more river launches, which would have improved communications between north and south. In small towns and large villages Arab traders with good a business acumen had established themselves as a minor trading network. This had helped to hold the southern economy together and did not seem to be resented locally.

Alier may also have been lax in improving the south' export drive. The south had the potential to produce exportable agricultural riches – its fertile land, watered by semi-tropical rains being able to produce tea, coffee, vegetables and exotic fruits – but the absence of an adequate transportation system prevented the realisation of this potential. As part of the East African hinterland, Juba's natural point of export access to the sea was Mombasa in Kenya, over four days away by truck, although the journey time would be slightly reduced when the projected all-weather road was completed. Mombasa had huge dock and shipping facilities, and was a regional maritime centre. Port Sudan, on the other hand, and the journey had lesser port facilities from Juba by truck to Port Sudan took about a month.

10
The Sharia Law Experience

Nineteen eighty two began with more student-led disturbances, sparked off by an announcement that sugar subsidies were to be abolished, resulting in a huge price rise for the people. Stones were thrown at passers-by and the People's Market in south Khartoum was set on fire. The demonstrations gathered ferocity, and when the mobs were joined by older school children on 5 January, all schools in the Khartoum area were closed. The police were unable to break up a rowdy protest march by some 5000 demonstrators, after which universities throughout the country were closed as the rioting spread to other cities, including Juba and Wau in the south, Port Sudan in the east, Merowe and Atbara in the north and Wad Medani, Kosti, Rufaa, El Manaqil and El Huda in central Sudan. Several people died at the hands of the police, and a number were injured. In Wau, rioters burned down the SSU office, causing the police to open fire.

Death of Hindi

On 12 January 1982 the death was announced of Hussein Sharif Hindi, leader of the Democratic Unionist Party. He had died from natural causes, reportedly in Saudi Arabia (SUNA), but in Athens according to Radio Tripoli. He had been the last remaining top Sudanese politician to refuse to accept the National Reconciliation Agreement, and had been in exile since Numeiry came to power in 1969, allegedly being the instigator of several plots against him. His funeral was held in Khartoum and was attended by over 10 000 mourners, despite an attempt by the authorities to play it down. His death was good news for Numeiry.

The SSU

In mid January Numeiry virtually disbanded the ruling SSU by dissolving most of its committees, which of late had been roundly criticised by politicians and senior military officers for being ineffective. He appointed a 217-member committee to try to make it more democratic, at least that was his story. On the 23rd he dismissed General Abdul Hamid Khalil (the first vice president, commander-in-chief of the army and secretary general of the SSU) and appointed Colonel Awad Malik as secretary general of the SSU. He then abolished the SSU Central Committee and its subcommittees, forming a Popular Committee of 41 members, chaired by himself, to reorganise the SSU. Khalil had obviously accumulated too much power, but he had also been voicing complaints muttered by senior and middle-grade military officers. In the Sudanese army system, medium-grade and senior officers served for just one fixed period in a particular rank, after which they were either promoted or retired. Although Numeiry had carried out a minor purge, dismissing over 20 senior officers, many officers had been able to extend their period of service, and the consequent senior and middle-rank promotion blockage was causing discontent.

Saudi Arabia, although still promising to send a certain amount of free crude oil to Sudan and continuing to give other aid, had become rather cool towards Numeiry. It was suspected that the Saudis had thought that Numeiry would not be able to weather the January disorders and rioting, and would be forced to hand over power to Sadik Mahdi, which would have been a step towards turning Sudan into an Islamic state, a move favoured by the Saudis and for which a Sudanese Islamic group in the National People's Assembly had been pressing since 1964. It was thought that the sudden flight of Khalil to Saudi Arabia might have been due to his involvement in an Islamic plot to this end. Once again Numeiry survived.

In an interview in *Middle East*, Hassan Turabi, leader of the Muslim Brotherhood and now Sudan's attorney general, admitted that an Islamic movement in the country was 'mission creeping' towards the introduction of Sharia law (the set of doctrines that intended to regulate the lives of all followers of the Islam), but that there was no organised Islamic presence as such in the army. He said that the Ansar movement was currently secular, but was in the process of Islamisation.

The Council for the Unity of South Sudan

Next President Numeiry announced that a referendum would be held in the south on the decentralisation issue, but only in Equatoria Province.

This was immediately seen by certain southern politicians as a plan to divide the south, causing a protest group to be formed: the Council for the Unity of South Sudan (CUSS), which protested to Numeiry that such a move was contrary to the 1972 autonomy agreement. Numeiry demanded that the CUSS leadership be arrested and taken to Khartoum. On 4 January in Khartoum about 20 southern politicians were charged with forming an illegal political organisation. They included former southern ministers and two former speakers of the Southern Region People's Assembly, which had been dissolved on 5 October 1981 but as yet no date had been set for new elections.

General Abdullah Rassas, interim president of the Higher Executive Council of the southern region, stated that the CUSS was illegal and against the constitution, that it had received financial and moral support from abroad, particularly Libya, and that it was not just a party structure but a whole government. In a speech Numeiry said that the CUSS leadership consisted of Clement Mboro (chairman), Samuel Aru Bol (deputy chairman), Joseph Oduhu (secretary), Michael Wol (foreign affairs) and Martin Magi (assistant secretary). On the face of it this was a powerful group of top southern politicians. The CUSS accused Numeiry of supporting the southern movement led by Joseph Lagu, which wanted to divide the south.

Lagu wanted Sudan to have a federal structure like that of Nigeria, and reasoned that decentralisation of the south, after being reorganised into its three original provinces, would reduce northern fears that the south intended to secede one day. Also, decentralisation in the south would make it equal in status to the other five regions elsewhere in Sudan. Few Arab northerners thought that black southerners were their equal – socially or in any other way. Lagu had roused the old traditional antagonism between the large Nilotic Dinka tribe and the Bantus, who included the Madi (Lagu's tribe). It was true that northern politicians paid little heed to the south, and often muttered that since the 1972 agreement there had been little in the south but quarrels between personalities and tribes, and that southerners themselves seemed little interested in their own development. Numeiry had not been to the south for months, and a scheduled visit to Juba University in December 1981 had been cancelled at the last minute. For their part, northerners admitted that there was a lack of interest in development in their rural areas.

Radio Tripoli continued its propaganda war against Sudan, reporting that the subversive Sudanese Socialist Popular Front had issued a rallying call to all personnel in the Sudanese armed forces and the police 'to consolidate themselves with the masses into one Front', to destroy the Khartoum regime of terrorism, domination and treason, and to establish the authority of the masses. The Sudanese hit back in the same medium, and a few days later SUNA, quoting reliable sources, gave details of an alleged attempted coup in Benghazi, in Libya, where there had been heavy fighting between anti-Gaddafi groups and Libyan troops, and also involving East German, Soviet, Cuban and Syrian soldiers. The truth of this report was denied completely by the Libyan authorities.

New Southern Regional People's Assembly

Elections were held for the Fourth People's Assembly of the Southern Region in April 1982, and the results were announced the following month. At the heart of the elections was the 'unity or division' issue; that is, whether the southern region should continue as a single autonomous part of Sudan, or whether it should be reorganised into its three original provinces and brought within Numeiry's decentralisation plan. Although all candidates were vetted by the SSU, some stood for complete unity, some were for the decentralisation plan and others wanted a compromise solution.

The unity group – led by Abel Alier, the quiet, patient, Dinka lawyer who had served as president of the HEC – advocated a policy called 'Change Two' (C-2), a name derived from the 'Wind of Change Alliance', a group that had successfully opposed Alier's re-election to the presidency of the HEC in 1978 and whose leadership included Clement Mboro and Samuel Aru Bol, the latter having been an unsuccessful candidate in the 1980 election.

It had been intended that the interim Rassas administration would organise a referendum on the future of the south, as according to the 1972 agreement a two-thirds majority was required for any such alteration. In February Numeiry had postponed the referendum until the new HEC had been installed, which had caused a campaign of civil disobedience and strike action to develop in Eastern and Western Equatoria. In the national elections in December 1981, ten out of 29 southerners elected to the National People's Assembly had been 'divisionists', a much used expression during this period.

On 23 June 1982 the new Southern Region People's Assembly elected Joseph Tombura, a divisionist allied with the moderate C-2 group, as president of the HEC, and Numeiry also appointed him as secretary of the regional SSU. The HEC coalition, approved by Numeiry, took the sobriquet 'Change Three' (C-3), under which the southern region would continue to be a single autonomous area pending the holding of a referendum at a date yet to be fixed. At the end of May, Tombura had been elected leader of the 'Greater Equatoria' divisionist group in the People's Assembly – General Lagu had called on his followers to elect assembly leaders on the basis of the three original provinces.

Thus there were three competing groups in the southern People's Assembly: Unity (Alier), Divisionist (Lagu) and C-2 (Bol), with the C-2 group supporting Tombura, thus forming the C-3 group. Tombura, aged 53 and a member of the Zande tribe, had joined the Southern Front in 1958. He had been elected to the National Constituent Assembly in May 1968, and in the third southern People's Assembly had served under Joseph Lagu as a minister. He was elected to the fourth Assembly as a representative of Western Equatoria. After the election Alier was dismissed as second vice president of Sudan, being replaced by Lagu

Egypt–Sudan Charter of Integration

On 12 October 1982 in Khartoum, President Numeiry of Sudan and President Hosni Mubarak of Egypt signed a Charter of Integration, to last initially for a ten-year trial period, which provided for political and economic integration and close coordination in foreign policy, security and development. There was to be a Higher Council for Integration, chaired by the two national presidents; a Nile Valley Parliament, comprising 30 Assembly members from each country; and a joint fund that would be open to contributions. A joint fund might attract Arab money that would not be given to Sudan alone because of past financial mismanagement, or to Egypt, which had made peace with Israel. This superseded a similar charter signed in 1985. The first session of the Nile Valley Parliament was held in October 1982 and the first meeting of the Higher Council of Integration met in February 1983, when it was decided to adopt a common currency, exchange agricultural experts and remove trade barriers. But this proved to be little more than empty rhetoric.

In November 1982 there was another devaluation of the Sudanese pound, and the following month an economic conference was held in Khartoum, attended by international economic and financial experts. Sudan had failed to meet the interest payments on its external debts and lacked a solid foreign income. The conference recommended that restrictions be imposed on new development projects for the next few years to enable work to continue on existing ones.

A nervous strategical twitch

There was a minor scare in February 1983 when Egypt accused the USA of overreacting to a Libyan threat to attack Sudan, causing the Americans to send four AWACS (airborne warning and control systems) to Egypt and to station a US aircraft carrier off the Libyan coast. The Egyptian government had told the USA that Gaddafi's troops were massing near the Sudanese frontier, and that Libyan combat aircraft were violating Sudanese air space. An international crisis appeared to loom, but then the USA – realising that the threat, if there was one, was minimal – backed away and declared that the military deployment had simply been a routine training exercise. Egypt had probably hoped to involve the USA more closely in its quarrel with Libya. Chad became the focus of Sudanese and Egyptian attention, seeing themselves as bastions against Libyan expansion in that country.

SSU reorganisation

The fourth congress of the SSU, held in February 1983, decided that Numeiry should continue as president of Sudan. Prior to this he had can-celled the SSU's internal elections and dismissed several senior officials from their positions. The new appointments had included one woman, Mary Bassiouni (a southerner and senior SSU official), who became the minister for internal affairs. On 24 May Numeiry was sworn in for his third term as national president, claiming to have gained 99.6 per cent of the vote.

Reorganisation in the south

In June 1983 Numeiry announced that the south would revert to its original three provinces and be brought into his decentralisation scheme. There would be eight separate political–administrative regions in the country, each with its own People's Assembly and regional gov-ernment, which would operate for an initial 18 months. The southern referendum was again postponed. Previously there had been disturb-ances in the south between northern Arab traders and black southerners, and on one occasion at Aryat, several Arab traders were killed in a clash with local tribesmen.

The re-emergence of the Anya-Nya

Early in 1983 in the south, a group calling itself the Any-Nya-2 began carrying out attacks against police stations and army posts, and was reputedly receiving help from southern army officers. The government's policy of rotating northern and southern army units in the south ended in February, when the southern battalion at Bor refused to leave at the end of its tour of duty and move to a northern garrison, threatening to fire on the northern soldiers sent to relieve them. This rebellion was led by Major Carabino Kuanyin and is said to have marked the commencement of Sudan's 'second civil war'. The situation resolved itself when the southern soldiers deserted en masse, many to join the Anya-Nya-2, or one of the other armed groups hostile to the northern government and usually wanting an independent south. Friction between northern and southern units grew, a state of emergency was declared throughout the armed forces, and reinforcements were sent south from Khartoum. Censorship suppressed the details of the developing situation.

In March, during the course of an intensified security operation in the south, two leading divisionists were arrested: Dahl Acuil (vice president of the southern People's Assembly) and Mathew Ubur (its speaker). The censorship curtain was lifted slightly in mid May to reveal details of the Bor mutiny, which had developed into full-scale battle between northern and southern soldiers, and in which '78 loyal soldiers had been killed'. The government blamed foreign *influence* meaning Libyans, but they were far more likely to have been Ethiopian. The southern opposition was now fuelled by a belief that decentralisation was contrary to the 1972 agreement. The following month Numeiry appointed the first governors of the three southern provinces: Lawrence Wol-Wol (Bahr el-Ghazal province), Joseph Tombura (Equatoria) and Daniel Kout Mathews (Upper Nile).

The Islamic card

On 8 September 1983 Sharia law came into effect in Sudan. The penal code was amended to conform to Koranic precepts, and offences such as theft, adultery, murder and certain other crimes would henceforth be judged and punished according to Sharia law. Alcohol and gambling were forbidden. Numeiry had chosen the Islamic card not necessarily because of religious conviction, but more as a means of diverting people's attention away from the disastrous economic situation and political instability. He changed his military uniform for the jellabah and turban of the good Muslim, and his presidential role for that of an imam. One of his first steps was ceremoniously to drop a bottle of beer into the Nile, after which a mass of dignitaries poured varying quantities of alcohol into the river for the benefit of TV cameras.

When first announcing the judicial reform, Numeiry had accused members of the judiciary of being corrupt, lazy and drunken. Now over 40 judges were dismissed, large numbers of lawyers resigned, and Hassan Turabi, attorney general and leader of the Muslim Brotherhood, was moved sideways in the cabinet. Courts were established to try Un-Islamic offences and mete out judgement, and a Court of Appeal was set up. Some 13 000 prisoners were released on the ground that they had been convicted under the old penal code.

More than half of the some 20 million Sudanese welcomed the introduction of Sharia law, many feeling that Islamic penalties would reduce the rapidly mounting crime rate. Some 40 per cent of the people (a nominal figure cited at the time by international critics) were against it, including 'moderate' Muslims and the some five million southerners, who were mainly animists and had a Christian education. Non-Muslims were supposed to be exempt from Islamic penalties, but Sharia law was initially applied to one and all.

Somewhat unexpectedly, Sadik Mahdi, leader of a claimed three million Ansars, made a speech sharply criticising Numeiry for introducing Sharia law at a time of such economic insecurity. He was immediately arrested, together with several other prominent Muslim critics. Mahdi had just formally accepted the leadership of the Ansar sect, which carried with it the title of imam, but Numeiry had already taken that title for himself and did not want there to be two rival imams in Sudan.

The Western media and certain Arab and Muslim countries criticised Sudan's adoption of Sharia law, largely because Islamic punishments were being conducted in public, and would soon be carried out in a purpose-built stadium in Khartoum. Criticism also came from Saudi Arabia, presumably because it was highlighting a system of religious government, unpopular by Western values, that had caused it to become a virtually closed country. An Italian was flogged for being in possession of alcohol, a Sudanese man convicted of theft was publicly hanged, and a regional minister convicted of being drunk at an official reception was sentenced to 40 lashes and flogged in public, his excuse that he had been on medication having been rejected.

One of the first snags to the exercise of Sharia law was that the state-employed Sudanese doctors (some 2000 of them), who had previously been on strike because of low pay, refused to be involved in key punishment amputation, so amputations had to be carried out by 'trained' prison staff. The first five men sentenced to amputation for their Islamic crime, bled to death for lack of professional medical attention. For more than one Islamic crime a person could be sentenced to a 'cross-limb amputation', that is, severance of the right hand and the left foot. It was said that the leader of the Muslim Brotherhood fainted when watching a cross-limb amputation, and *Amnesty International* reported that in Khartoum between September 1983 and August 1984, there were '58 sentences of public amputation, including 12 "cross limb"' ones.

SPLM–SPLA

Meanwhile in early March 1984 Joseph Oduhu, who was building up the Sudan People's Liberation Movement and establishing an office in London, declared that the aim of the SPLM was to overthrow Numeiry and install in his stead a People's Democratic Socialist Government. With the Cold War still in progress, Oduhu made clear that this government would not be Marxist–Leninist. The aims of the SPLM were similar to those of the CUSS, mainly opposition to the Khartoum government's breach of the 1972 agreement, to which was now added resistance to imposition of Sharia law in the south. The economic complaint was that southern natural assets, including water, grain, timber, minerals and oil, were being stolen by the north. At a press conference the following month Oduhu said there was no possibility of negotiating with Numeiry, and that he would cooperate with any group to get rid of him, boasting that his SPLM had over 64 000 members. He also confirmed that Anya-Nya-2 was the military arm of the SPLM and had control over all the armed opposition groups in the south.

However Oduhu's claims were rather dubious as by this time the undoubted leader of what came to be known as the SPLA (Sudan People's Liberation Army) was Colonel John Garang, who had been active for some months. One of his first exploits had been in July 1983, when five foreign relief workers had been kidnapped and held hostage, a ransom, clothing and international publicity being demanded in return for their safe release. It was suspected that these demands had been partly or wholly met, as the captives were released that month.

In early November nine foreign employees of the French consortium CCI (Compagnie de Construction Internationale), working on the Jonglei Canal project in the Kongor area, were seized and held hostage. On the 16th President Numeiry, who was on a state visit to France, stated at a press conference in Paris that the SPLA, led by John Garang, was responsible for the abduction of the workers, and accused Libya and Ethiopia of supporting it. The SPLA demanded the cessation of work on both the Jonglei Canal and the (now extended) oil pipeline to Port Sudan. The French subsequently announced they would stop work on the canal, even though the nine hostages had been freed after intervention by the Sudanese army.

The following month the town of Nasir in Upper Nile Province was besieged by Anya-Nya-2 fighters, who claimed that about 20 soldiers had been killed when the relief helicopters in which they were travelling were shot down. The government denied the loss of any helicopters, but claimed to have killed over 400 guerrillas when breaking the two-week siege. In January 1984 it was reported that large numbers of tribesmen in the Akabo area had fled into Ethiopia to avoid being involved in clashes between government troops and guerrillas.

On 2 February three foreign workers were killed and several injured in an SPLA attack on the Bentiu oil-exploration base, guerrillas claiming that Chevron company aircraft were being used by the army to monitor their movements. Work on the oil pipeline was halted, as was work on drilling projects. On the 10th the SPLA claimed responsibility for an attack on Sobat (40 miles north of Malakal), in which six foreign workers were captured and an Australian pilot killed. Three days later the SPLA claimed responsibility for an attack on a Nile river steamer and a convoy of barges. At first the government denied that this incident had occurred, but later admitted that 150 of the 800 passengers had been killed, and some 400 were still missing. A surviving navigation official later alleged that almost 2000 people had been travelling on these vessels, and that up to 1500 had either been killed in the attack, died as a result of fires on the boats, or drowned. After this incident river and rail transport into the south was halted. John Garang claimed that three of the main aims of the SPLA had been accomplished: work on both the Jonglei Canal and the oil pipeline to Port Sudan had been halted, and river and rail movement between north and south had been severely disrupted.

Air raid on Omdurman

A not yet fully explained incident occurred on 14 March 1984, when a single Libyan aircraft (a Tupolev-22 bomber) made an attack on Omdurman, damaging the government-owned radio station and killing five people. Sudanese armed forces were placed on full alert and the Sudan–Egypt Defence Agreement of 1976 was invoked. Both countries blamed Libya for this serious act of aggression, but the Libyan government denied any involvement and alleged that the incident had been carried out by 'revolutionary elements' of the Sudanese air force. On the 18th the USA sent two AWACS surveillance aircraft and other defence equipment to Egypt, and Egyptian troops were airlifted into Sudan. On the 27th the UN Security Council heard a Sudanese complaint against Libya for the air attack, and Libya's counter-complaint that the USA was arming states adjacent to Libya. Libya claimed that the USA had promised weaponry to Sudan, but this was denied by the Americans. The UN was indecisive.

The Sudanese government stated that the Libyan plane (supplied by the Soviets) had flown from the Al Kufrah air base in southern Libya, and returned to the same base after the raid on Omdurman. Joseph Oduhu said that the raid had been organised secretly by the Sudanese government as a pretext to invoke the defence treaty. Others thought it might have been an impromptu response by some Libyan airmen to a hostile speech made by Numeiry against Gaddafi. No one seemed to be exactly sure.

In April Numeiry proclaimed a state of emergency, asserting that enemies of the government were active both within Sudan and abroad, and the state of emergency was necessary to achieve maximum stability and security and prevent the spread of corruption. Impromptu strikes continued, embracing public-sector clerks, accountants, engineers and municipal workers. In the south there was strong opposition to the imposition of Sharia law. The army and police were given extra powers to arrest and detain people, enter private houses, make searches and open personal mail.

Ethiopia

Relations between Sudan and Ethiopia deteriorated during 1983, with each side accusing the other of harbouring and supporting each other's armed opposition movements. On 20 November the Sudanese armed forces were placed on full alert, as it was suspected that Ethiopia was assembling an invasion force with the intention of attacking the Sudanese town of Kurmuk. Ethiopia denied this, and alleged that Sudan was only making such accusations in order to distract attention from its own internal problems. Numeiry was in the USA at the time, having discussions with President Reagan on security and economic matters.

Sudan also blamed the Ethiopian government for negligence when an attack was made on the Sudanese consulate in the town of Gambela in south-west Ethiopia on 4 February 1984, when three Sudanese consular staff were killed. Due to Egyptian mediation the hostile press campaign these two countries were waging against each other ceased, and in March an arrangement was made for the Sudanese and Ethiopian foreign ministers to meet in Nairobi. However the meeting was abruptly cancelled when Ethiopia alleged that the USA was air-lifting arms to Sudan for use against Ethiopia. The Ethiopian government claimed that since the fresh upsurge of civil war in the south, about 120 000 southern Sudanese had taken refuge in Ethiopia.

Debate on the constitution

Pressure by southern members of the National People's Assembly caused Numeiry to postpone the Assembly debate scheduled for 11 July to amend the 1973 constitution, which would affect some 123 of the 225 clauses and make Islam the sole basis of legislation. The amendments would make non-Muslims subject to Islamic law, only Muslims would be eligible to stand for the presidency, the president would assume the title of imam and his tenure of office would be for life. These proposals were opposed by General Lagu (second vice president) and Abel Alier (minister of construction and public works), and a petition for more time to consider them was approved by a majority of members.

More alleged plots

In late July a number of people were arrested and charged with plotting to kill President Numeiry and General Omar Mohammed Tayib (first vice president), and to blow up the American and French embassies in Khartoum. Those arrested were said to belong to the Libyan-sponsored Sudanese People's Socialist Front, led by Mohammed Kafi Gibriel, who was reported to be a former paratrooper in the Sudanese army. In October another batch of arrests were made in connection with another plot against Numeiry. Many of those arrested were military personnel, and among the non-military detainees was Phillip Abbas Ghaboush, a southern politician. Some of the accused confessed to receiving money from Libya and to involvement in a planned attack on Ethiopia, to be mounted from Sudan. On 7 January 1985, the first day of the trial of around 200 suspects accused of plotting against Numeiry, the president suddenly announced a pardon for all, including Ghaboush, and they were instantly released. No reason was given.

Previously, in a speech on 29 September 1984, Numeiry had announced the lifting of the state of emergency, which had been in force since June 1983, and had also declared that he would rescind his decree on dividing the south into three regions, if that was what the people wanted. He had also suspended the Islamic courts set up in 1983, and appointed several new judges.

The Falasha airlift

In October 1984 Sudan became involved in a secret CIA–Israeli–Ethio-pian project known as Operation Moses. The aim was to fly some 25 000 Falashas (Ethiopians of ancient Jewish origin who had lived for some 2000 years in Gondar and Tigre Provinces) from refugee camps in Sudan to Israel. The Ethiopian government did not want to be openly involved, and the Falashas would be allowed to flee Ethiopia as famine refugees into Sudan. The Sudanese were persuaded to cooperate by George Bush (then US vice president), who visited Khartoum. Numeiry agreed to go along with the plan, provided it was kept secret, and handed the task over to the US Central Intelligence Agency (CIA), which worked in conjunction with the Sudanese state security service. The US State Department and the air force seem also to have been involved in this project. In theory the Falashas were to be flown to non-Israeli destina-tions, but in fact were flown directly to Israel.

Secrecy was broken in January 1985 when the operation was sus-pended by Sudan after protests from Arab League countries. Ethiopia professed ignorance and accused Sudan of illegally trafficking in Ethio-pians. In turn Sudan accused Ethiopia of trading Falashas for Israeli military equipment. Numeiry probably received more than $60 million as a personal payment, while his armed forces received some helicopters and other items of modern weaponry from the USA. The European air-line that had provided the aircraft for the operation was boycotted by Arab League states for some years. When the airlift was halted, some 800 Falashas were stranded in a Sudanese camp, but were eventually flown to Israel in March.

Guerrilla activity in the south

Meanwhile in the south, the SPLA, led by Colonel John Garang, con-tinued to attack army posts and government installations, but an army offensive in July 1984 forced the guerrillas to withdraw from their south-eastern stronghold near Pochala, not far from the Ethiopian border. The Ethiopian government was still allegedly supplying arms to and training the SPLA, while Numeiry continued to supply and support armed anti-government resistance forces in Tigre and Eritrea in Ethiopia. The SPLA claimed several more successes in the Nasir and Pochala areas, but gov-ernment troops soon claimed they had regained all lost territory.

In August the SPLA claimed that on the 27th an SPLA contingent, led by Gordon Kong, had killed 274 soldiers in an ambush of a steamer on the River Sobat (a tributary of the Nile), but the government would only admit that a small passenger steamer had been ambushed and four soldiers wounded. In September, four foreign priests were captured and held hostage near Bentiu until a ransom was paid. In October a government detachment – on its way to Bentiu to protect oil installations that had been lying idle since the CCI suspended operations – was attacked by SPLA guerrillas, who claimed to have killed 64 soldiers for the loss of only one man. These are examples of the types of claim periodically made by both sides, the accuracy of which is not possible to check, partly due to government censorship. Both sides tended to exaggerate – most events were probably founded on fact, but inaccurately related to suit the cause.

In December a delegation from the Wahdah subprovince, led by the local commissioner, Charles Knat Chatim, left Bentiu to negotiate with local SPLA leaders. A few days later an SPLA broadcast claimed that Chatim and his delegation had defected to the SPLA. However almost immediately the governor of Upper Nile province insisted that they had been kidnapped.

It was known that about this time Numeiry was trying to open negotiations with Garang, and on one occasion had used the offices of a well-known international businessmen, Tiny Rowland, to offer Garang the position of second vice president if he would desert the SPLA and go and work with him in Khartoum. Garang had refused, saying he was not fighting a war simply to become a Sudanese vice president.

In January 1985 four CCI employees were kidnapped by the SPLA at Sobat, but were soon ransomed. Negotiations in such cases were now carried out directly between the SPLA and the CCI. It was rumoured that large ransoms, perhaps up to $1 million, were sometimes paid, and that the CCI had also handed over radio equipment and other technical items to the captors. The SPLA stated that all hostages were released on humanitarian grounds, but it also wanted something in return. Some hostages were released into the care of the Ethiopian government, which annoyed Numeiry as it deprived him of political capital. That month the SPLA advised foreign workers in the south to leave the country for their own safety.

A government spokesman claimed that the army had killed over 600 rebels in the Terakeka area near Juba, but other reports indicated that members of the local Mandari tribe had been responsible, as they blamed the SPLA for stealing their cattle. The government also claimed to have destroyed a rebel camp (location unnamed), and on the 22nd Radio SPLA announced that the troops garrisoned at Bor had again mutinied, killing their commanding officer, and that almost 200 southern soldiers, police and officials had defected to the SPLA. All this was very difficult to verify.

A peace committee

On 3 March 1985 Numeiry announced that the army would unilaterally implement a ceasefire in the south, and would henceforth only engage in self-defensive action. He also repeated his previous offer of an amnesty to opposition forces. However the same day Radio SPLA announced that government troops had launched a renewed attack on SPLA positions. The ceasefire declaration was made on the day prior to the arrival in Sudan of George Bush (then US vice president) and was designed to show the USA, now a major donor to Sudan, that Numeiry was really trying to end the war in the south.

Nonetheless on the 13th Numeiry announced the formation of a 30-member peace committee, chaired by Khatim Khalifa, a former prime minister. Its task was to bring about a dialogue with the SPLA in order to establish peace and reconciliation. A few days later the SPLA claimed to have overrun the army garrison at Mongala near Juba, but the government contradicted this, stating that the rebels had been repulsed after suffering heavy losses.

11
The Transitional Military Council

On 8 January 1985, 76-year-old Mahmoud Taha and four other members of the Republican Brothers were convicted of heresy, opposing the application of Islamic law, endangering public safety, inciting opposition to the government and re-establishing a banned political party (the SSU was still the only permitted political party in the country). All were convicted, but given a stay of execution to recant their beliefs. Taha refused, and was hanged on the 18th.

A well-respected thinker and Islamic scholar, Mahmoud Taha had founded the Republican Party in 1945. He had advocated independence for Sudan, and had spent periods in prison for his political stance. During his incarceration he had revised the Sharia, developing a controversial interpretation that had brought hostility from Muslim fundamentalists and the Muslim Brotherhood. He had founded the Republican Brothers, a non-violent group that advocated a modern interpretation of Islam. Taha and some 50 of its members had been arrested in June 1983, after criticising the government for encouraging conflict through its policies on Islamisation. Released in December 1984, without being charged, they had soon been rearrested for distributing pamphlets expressing opposition to Sharia law. Taha's death caused alarm amongst Islamic intellectuals.

Numeiry ordered that all the movement's literature be collected and publicly burned. The other four members arrested with Taha were freed on the 19th, after they had publicly confessed to deviating from the true path of Islam, and had denounced Taha as a heretic.

In June 1984 four members of the Baathist Party (which had Syrian affiliations) had been arrested, and in February 1985 they were sentenced to terms of imprisonment and 80 lashes each for distributing anti-government leaflets. Meanwhile Sadik Mahdi, leader of the Ansar sect, imprisoned in September 1983 for criticising the introduction of Sharia law, had been released with a group of his supporters in December 1984.

Purge of the Muslim Brotherhood

In a nationwide broadcast on 10 March 1985, President Numeiry accused an unnamed religious sect of plotting to overthrow his government by infiltrating the political, social and economic structure of Sudanese society, and of creating an armed militia to foment unrest. This sect was the influential Muslim Brotherhood. At the sametime he announced the dismissal from government posts of several leading figures of the movement, including Hassan Turabi, who had been the presidential advisor on legal affairs until September 1983. Turabi was also deprived of the leadership of the SSU. Also dismissed were Ali Osman Taha, speaker of the National People's Assembly, and several leading judges.

In the following weeks more than 200 Muslim Brotherhood members were arrested, ostensibly to forestall the launching of an alleged coup. Numeiry also accused the Muslim Brotherhood of monopolising strategic commodities, particularly sorghum and groundnuts, which had led to shortages and high prices, and of infiltrating Islamic Banks and teaching university students how to riot. The previous February, after two days of rioting between members of the Muslim Brotherhood and rival factions, Khartoum University had been closed indefinitely, and later Numeiry banned all student political activity.

The declining economy

The economic situation in Sudan had declined in 1984 and continued to do so in 1985. There was a severe drought during this period and an influx of refugees from adjacent drought-stricken countries. The economic costs of this were compounded by a huge foreign debt, reputed to be some $8 billion. With some $60 million immediately required for debt repayments and the suspension of the economic recovery package financed jointly by the World Bank and certain Western countries, most major projects came to a standstill. Numeiry's introduction during 1984 of Islamic taxation and banking systems had also had a detrimental effect on the economy. Under Islamic law the charging of interest was prohibited, and bank loans had to be negotiated on a profit-sharing basis, which meant that hard currency tended to trickle abroad.

In short Sudan, a country with great agricultural potential, was now suffering from the combined effects of natural calamity, years of poor

planning and bad management. The Sudanese pound was again deval-
ued in February 1985. Shortages of bread and fuel were reported the
following month, then petrol rationing was introduced, and lack of
transport and electricity power cuts forced many schools to close. The
prices of petrol, bread and sugar were increased considerably.

Over 60 per cent of the prime arable land in Sudan was owned by
merchants, retired army officers and the judiciary, and was farmed for
profit in an unsustainable way, meaning that the land had become
exhausted and the crop yield had declined. Most of the grain produced
was exported to Chad and Central Africa. In the years 1981–4 the rains
had not come up to the minimum expectation, and the harvest of 1983
had been very poor. In the agriculturists' quest for additional arable land,
nomads and seminomads were forced out from fertile grazing areas,
which caused many scuffles and security forces had to intervene, with
consequent casualties. Due to the death of cattle in the drought, many
tribesmen suddenly had no income at all, and as an attempt to channel
them into agricultural work on the major schemes proved unsuccessful,
they had to be put into camps and fed by the government By mid 1985
there were over 100 000 poverty-stricken tribesmen in almost 50 temporary camps, the government not knowing quite what to do with them.
The World Health Organisation (WHO) reported that the Hadendawa
tribe in the Red Sea hills was facing extinction.

A general strike

On 26 March 1985, students at Omdurman Islamic University, a stronghold of the Muslim Brotherhood, staged an anti-government demonstration, causing the authorities to close the university. A similar
demonstration took place the following day in Khartoum largely student-led but including unemployed people and other discontented
groups. Anti-USA, anti-IMF and anti-World Bank slogans were displayed,
while banks and shops were attacked and some set on fire. On the 28th
the American embassy was stoned, and a government spokesman stated
that over 1000 people had been arrested. The following day the offices of
the SSU were broken into and ransacked by the mob. By this time rowdy
anti-government demonstrations had flared up in other cities, including
Port Sudan, where several people had reportedly been killed due to police
action.

On the 30th a large number of people, described by the authorities as
'saboteurs', were taken out of Khartoum in army vehicles, and troops
were positioned at strategic points. The following day doctors, led by

Dr Khalid Yagi, went on strike, protesting at the brutality of the security forces and claiming that the police were using electrified truncheons and guns to control the mobs. An official government statement accused the Muslim Brotherhood of instigating the riots and demonstrations, and special tribunals were established to try offenders. A pro-Numeiry rally on 2 April attracted up to 3000 supporters, but the following day a peaceful anti-government demonstration led by striking doctors attracted over 20 000.

The general strike proper began on the 4th, initiated by the militant doctors and receiving mass support from professional organisations, bank staff, engineers, communications workers, university staff and trade unions. These groups merged into what became known as the Alliance of Professional Organisations and Trade Unions (NAS), led by Khalid Yagi. The old Sudanese flag, used before Numeiry came to power, was much in evidence.

The army takes over

On the evening of 6 April 1985, the army announced in a national broadcast that it had assumed control of the country. General Swar el Dahab, commander-in-chief of the armed forces, declared that this action had been necessary to stem the flow of blood, and he asserted that the army would stand on the side of the people. A state of emergency was declared, the constitution was suspended and the president was dismissed, as were all his staff, advisers, ministers and regional governors. The SSU and the National and Regional People's Assemblies were dissolved. President Numeiry (who had left the country on 27 March on a private visit to the USA) was banned from returning to Sudan, and Khartoum airport was closed. The army stated that civilian authority would be restored to the people after an interim period, later fixed at one year.

The new military leadership ordered an end to the general strike, threatening that its continuation would be treated as treason, punishable by death, but met the strikers' demands in part on the 7th, when the General Command of the Armed Forces announced the release of political prisoners, the arrest of leading politicians and the dissolution of the State Security Service (which was eventually replaced by the National Security Service).

The general strike had continued on the day of the coup and the following day as the strike leaders (NAS) were trying to persuade the army to hand the country over to civilian rule straight away, but it ended on the 8th with the production of the Charter of the Alliance for

National Salvation, which was a summary of demands and proposals, signed by strike leaders (but not by the army). The proposals included a guarantee of basic human rights, regional self-government for the south, development of the country's natural resources, a non-aligned foreign policy, the decentralisation of government, the abolition of all Numeiry's institutions and a new constitution, to be ratified democratically at the end of the transitional period.

The Military Transitional Council

The initial meetings between military and civilian leaders were inconclusive, and so on the 9th General Dahab formed a Military Transitional Council (TMC) to undertake the head of state function, which he chaired. Dahab, a career officer, born in Omdurman in 1935 and a member of the Khatmia sect, had undergone military training in Jordan and the USA after joining the army, and had briefly been a military attaché in Uganda. As he was related to one of the instigators of the abortive communist coup of 1971, he had been banished to serve in the south for some years, but had eventually regained Numeiry's confidence and returned to Khartoum, convinced that the war in the south was unwinnable. He had eventually became commander of operations in 1983. On 16 March 1985 he had been appointed as minister of defence and commander-in-chief of the armed forces, just before Numeiry had left Sudan on his trip to the USA.

Interim Council of Ministers

After consultations between the army leadership and civilian representatives a 15-member interim Council of Ministers was appointed on 22 April 1985. It had a civilian premier. Gizouli Dafalla, and a southerner, Samuel Aru Bol, as deputy premier. Doctor Dafalla was leader of the medical association and had played a leading part in the doctors' strikes leading up to the coup, and in the subsequent negotiations with the military leaders. Samuel Aru Bol (a Dinka and former vice president of the HEC of the southern region, who had been arrested in January 1982 for involvement in forming the illegal CUSS) was made provisional leader of the newly formed Southern Sudanese Political Association. Other appointments were made, but Oliver Batally Bino (a southerner and former national minister under Numeiry), who had been appointed minister of public services and Labour, was dismissed after being found in possession of drugs at Jedda airport. One other person missing from the interim cabinet was Colonel John Garang, leader of the SPLA, who was told that a cabinet place was being kept open for him, which many hoped he would accept. But Garang chose to wait in the south to see what happened before throwing in his lot with the new military junta.

Three days after the Khartoum coup the SPLA announced a seven-day ceasefire and called upon the Sudanese military leaders to hand over power to a civilian government, suspicious that a military clique in the Numeiry mould would continue the former president's southern policies. On 26 April General Dahab announced an amnesty for political offences and a unilateral ceasefire in the south by the armed forces, apart from defensive action. On 25 May a seven-member regional cabinet, representing the three southern regions, was appointed. The military governors of the three regions (to be known as administrative regions) were to remain in office. General Dahab also announced the reimplementation of the 1972 agreement, which had united the three southern provinces into the autonomous southern region.

A new subversive political party, the Sudanese Movement for Revolutionary Committees, was established on 15 May. Led by Abdullah Zakaria Idris, the party was pro-Libyan in outlook and based its ideology on Colonel Gaddafi's 'Green Book'.

Abolition of the Islamic Courts

In mid May 1985 it was announced that the Islamic courts (suspended in 1984) were to be abolished. Although Sharia law would remain in force for the time being, there would be a re-examination of its more severe applications. The new attorney general, Omar Abad al-Ati, announced that all laws enacted during the previous regime were suspended, and that all the members of that regime, including Numeiry, would be put on trial. Numeiry was stripped of his rank of field marshal and pronounced a deserter from the Sudanese armed forces.

New foreign policy

General Dahab held meetings with representatives of Sudan's traditional allies and donors, including the USA, Egypt and Saudi Arabia, and pledged to maintain good relations with them. The USA took this to mean that the new Sudanese leadership was going to be pro-Western, although early statements indicated it would pursue a non-aligned policy, which took a knock when General Dahab made friendly overtures to the Soviet Union.

Dahab also made friendly overtures to Libya, sending a high-level delegation to meet Colonel Gaddafi, whereupon diplomatic relations between the two countries (broken off in June 1981) were resumed. Gaddafi had been the first foreign leader to recognise the Dahab regime and a Libyan delegation soon visited Khartoum, where it was announced that Libya had ceased to support the SPLA and would urge the southern Sudanese rebel movement to cooperate with the new Sudanese regime. Gaddafi visited Khartoum on 18 May 1985, the first foreign leader to do so since the coup, and subsequently Libyan aircraft were used to airlift food and equipment into famine-stricken areas of southern Sudan.

It was also reported that the Sudanese authorities had ceased to harbour the anti-Gaddafi National Front for the Salvation of Libya and banned its radio broadcasts into Libya from Sudan. Previously, Numeiry had claimed that Gaddafi had offered him large sums of money to conclude an integration pact with Libya and denounce the US-sponsored Camp David Agreement and the peace treaty between Egypt and Israel. Dafalla, the Sudanese premier, stated that all accords with Egypt signed by Numeiry were abrogated. Previously, in February 1985, Egypt had withdrawn the Egyptian anti-aircraft defence unit that had been stationed in Khartoum since the March 1984 attack on Omdurman. A defence agreement between Sudan and Libya was signed on 9 July, under which Libya would provide logistical training and assistance in naval and air defence. Brigadier Osman Abdullah Mohammed, the Sudanese defence minister, stated that this agreement was not a strategic alliance, and that Libya did not intend to interfere in Sudan's internal affairs or foreign policy.

President Hosni Mubarak of Egypt visited Sudan on 17 June at the invitation of General Dahab. No formal request had yet been made for the extradition of Numeiry, who had been granted political sanctuary in Egypt, Mubarak citing Egypt's traditional customs as his excuse (political sanctuary was included in the Egyptian constitution). Relations between the two presidents remained cool, but both realised that their interests were linked, and accordingly they must work together.

A Sudanese delegation had visited Colonel Mengistu Haile Mariam in Ethiopia on 25 April to discuss the matter of continuing Ethiopian support for the Sudanese, and Sudanese assistance to Ethiopian subversive groups. There were an estimated 700 000 Tigrean and Eritrean refugees in Sudan: no one seemed to know exactly how many. The main border crossing into Sudan for Tigrean refugees was closed on that day by the Sudanese, and the Ethiopian government complained that Ethiopian refugees in the Wad Kowli camp in Sudan had been refused donated food aid. A later visit by a higher-level Sudanese delegation reportedly improved relations. It was agreed to raise the diplomatic status of their respective representatives to ambassadorial level, and that neither country would interfere in the other's internal affairs.

The economy: still in decline

Sudan remained in the grip of severe drought, especially in the south and west, and in April 1985 General Dahab appealed to foreign donors for additional food aid, saying that the current pledges were insufficient to prevent a major disaster and some five million people faced starvation. Food reserves from the 1984 harvest, which had been poor due to inadequate rainfall, would be exhausted by July 1985. UN aid officials confirmed that over eight-million people would starve if food aid did not arrive by June 1985, when seasonal rainfall would prevent access to many remote areas. After June, Sudan would be totally dependent on imported food. Large numbers of tribal peoples were still leaving their home areas in search of water and pasture for their cattle. In addition there were over 1.5 million war and famine refugees, and soil erosion was forcing farmers to buy food they would otherwise have grown. In mid April there were food riots in Kosti, and police had to use teargas to disperse a crowd that was trying to gain entry to a grain depot.

Not all these misfortunes were due to natural disaster. For example the Gezira irrigation scheme – the largest and most important of such schemes, situated in the basin between the White Nile and Blue Nile and producing vital export crops such as cotton, groundnuts, wheat and sorghum – was failing to meet its targets due to the lowering of the Blue Nile waters in recent years. Planners and engineers had failed to compensate for the reduction in the amount of river water available.

In May 1985 the Sudanese government managed to secure a rescheduling of the debt repayments that had been due the previous year and a rescheduling of the basic debts for the current year. The new military leadership dissolved the National Oil Company, which had been established in October 1984 as a joint venture between the government of Sudan and a Saudi Arabian company owned by Adnan Khashoggi, a Saudi entrepreneur, who was given monopoly over all natural resources that were not already being privately exploited. This was considered to be a warning to Western oil exploration companies operating in southern Sudan – whose activities had been voluntarily suspended because of the danger their employees faced from guerrilla attacks – that their interests would be jeopardised if they did not resume work.

Guerrilla activity in the south

Meanwhile, the SPLA, long bogged down in hostility with Anya-Nya-2, which was itself struggling to avoid being brought under SPLA command, extended its activities into Equatoria Province, which had been relatively free from guerrilla activity for some months. In January 1985 it attacked a government post at Teraka, near Juba. The next month it raided a barracks at Lafon, and in the following weeks made two separate attacks on government outposts at Owiny Ki-Bul, the former Anya-Nya GHQ, now a strong government base.

Over one third of the Khartoum government's expenditure, perhaps much more, was taken up with the war in the south, and many thought that Numeiry's offers to Garang had always been too little and too late. Although Garang had strong left-wing views, his opposition to Numeiry brought him respect in the north, and many northerners would not have objected to him being made first vice president of a united Sudan. Garang believed that the USA was trying to set up military bases in Sudan, alleging it already had a small one near Port Sudan.

On 14 May the Council of Ministers declared the south a disaster area, and appealed to Garang to adhere to his ceasefire agreement in order to allow supplies into the region. Garang claimed there had been fairly good harvests in the south in the previous two years, and that the Khartoum declaration was simply a tactic to enable military equipment and troops to enter the south in the guise of providing humanitarian aid. Brigadier Mohammed, the defence minister, denied this allegation, saying that 80 people a day were dying of starvation in the south.

Attempts to build up stockpiles of food in western Sudan before the onset of the rainy season in June were hampered by the inadequacies of the railway system and the Sudanese bureaucracy. Some Western countries tried to deliver food and other international aid direct to the people in need by truck, barge and aircraft in order to circumvent the government's policy of regarding all food aid accepted centrally as economic aid to the country as a whole, rather than going directly to the starving. Muddle reigned smothering good intentions.

A left-wing plot

In June 1985 eleven senior army officers were dismissed from the service for plotting against the Transitional Military Council. The plotters were allegedly led by Brigadier Mohammed Salih Hussein and Brigadier Osman Abdullah Mahmoud, who were arrested just as they were about to board an army helicopter at the army GHQ in Khartoum to fly to Omdurman to make a nationwide radio broadcast to activate their coup. Their intention had been to abolish Sharia law and kill certain political leaders who had served under President Numeiry. Most of the eleven were members of the Baath Party, the others were communists. Little more was heard of them thereafter.

Terrorism

In July 1985 Sudan decided not to participate in joint military exercises involving the USA and certain Arab countries (Exercise Bright Star). The nominal excuse for this was that the Transitional Military Council was too preoccupied with domestic affairs, but the Americans saw it as a distinct sign of Sudan's new non-aligned policy, and was accordingly displeased. This displeasure was compounded by the fact that Sudan had come to a military agreement with Libya, then almost in direct confrontation with the USA. General Dahab made smooth assurances to the contrary. In November the USA warned its citizens to avoid Khartoum because of the presence of known international terrorists in that city, highlighting the presence of the pro-Libyan Sudanese Movement of Revolutionary Committees, which had ideological affiliations with the Libyan regime, and the fact that the Libyan government had opened a diplomatic office in Khartoum.

Southern activity

In May the SPLA launched a looting raid on the village of El-Gardoud in southern Kordofan Provinces, just outside its customary operational area. The guerrillas stole over 4000 cattle, and looted and set fire to shops and houses. In the fighting over 16 people were killed and many were injured. The following month the SPLA made two separate attacks on river steamers and barges, now almost the only remaining means of north–south transport. It also shelled the town of Bor, killing the garrison commander. Media enquiries revealed that the Sudanese army did not always inform the next-of-kin of soldiers killed in action, which made it difficult to assess the military casualties accurately.

A muddled mutiny

Shooting broke out on 26 September 1985 in army barracks at Khartoum and Omdurman. This was at first thought to be a mutiny by southern troops in the regular army protesting against the conduct of the war in the south. Two people were killed in the shooting, several were wounded, and a number of southern soldiers fled from the barracks. Order was restored by loyal paratroops. By the 28th a night curfew had been imposed and over 160 people had been arrested in Khartoum, Khartoum North and Omdurman, including army officers and soldiers. It was announced that several people would face trial for plotting to assume power.

On the 30th the defence minister, General Osman Abdullah Mohammed, stated the three ringleaders were Colonel John Garang (leader of the SPLA), Yusef Kuwa (a Nubian intellectual), Yacoub Ismail (a member of the Sudanese Revolutionary Forces, a newly formed dissident movement) and Philip Abbas Ghaboash (a Nubian and leader of the Sudan National Party). Had the first part of the plot been successful, it was said the three would have flown in from Ethiopia to Omdurman to head the insurrection. The logic of this explanation was doubtful.

It was reported that the coup had failed because the conspirators had opened fire too soon and alerted the paratroops. Another report stated that a number of northern soldiers, due to be posted to southern garrisons the following day, had been involved. Premier Dafalla called the incident an 'ethnic plot' that had been designed to assassinate members of the Transitional Military Council, the cabinet and several prominent politicians. At the time leaflets issued by the African Organisation for the Liberation of Blacks were circulating in Khartoum and Omdurman. The SPLA denied all knowledge of the plot, and said that at the time it had been launching attacks against government garrisons at Bor and Nasir. Discontented soldiers and blacks, and perhaps fringe elements of the SPLA, had been involved in this disorganised coup attempt, in which there had been no clear leadership.

The attempted coup proved to be a turning point for the Transitional Military Council. It had played on northern fears about southern subversion, tending to exaggerate its seriousness, and allowed advocates of a military solution to the southern problem to call the shots. But there was little the army – weak in number, weaponry and motivation – could do, particularly as it lacked adequate aerial capability. The council also forgot that the majority of southerners were against the war,

A war of attrition

On 10 October 1985 the SPLA declared a two-week ceasefire, only days after it had bombarded government troops in Upper Nile Province. The following month it was alleged that the SPLA had killed the leader of

Anya-Nya-2, William Abdullah Chuol, at the village of Pangan in the same province. The SPLA benefited from this, as many of the now leaderless Anya-Nya-2 flocked to join it. Unlike Garang, Chuol had been willing to talk to the Khartoum authorities, and on one occasion had met and talked with the governor of Upper Nile Province. Before the end of its ceasefire period the SPLA attacked another river steamer, its weak explanation being that the steamer had been a suspicious moving target, and therefore a legitimate one. In November the SPLA lunched a major offensive in Equatoria Province, moving successfully into new territory. The cost of the war in the south was reaching almost a $1 million a day, and it was suspected that Garang was deliberately fighting a war of attrition to bleed dry the Transitional Military Council, which he thought would soon fall.

The SPLA was in direct contact with international firms engaged in massive projects in southern Sudan, extorting blackmail money to ensure that their huge and very valuable stocks of construction plant would not be attacked and destroyed, and to ensure that no work was done on the projects. Total, the French oil exploration company, had accordingly shut down its operations in Upper Nile Province, as had American-owned Chevron after the February 1985 attack, and its Rib Kona base camp was stocked with millions of dollars worth of abandoned equipment. Christian-educated southern leaders appreciated the value of a Western education, and part of the blackmail demands were sometimes scholarships for southern students in Western universities.

In December 1985 the Sudanese minister of the interior, General Abbas Medani, announced that several members of the extreme Islamic Jihad organisation had been arrested in Khartoum after distributing leaflets threatening assassinations. To please the USA, several members of this group were expelled from Sudan. US aid to Sudan (in the Middle East, second only to US aid to Egypt) had continued after the fall of Numeiry, but the whiff of terrorism and friendliness with Libya caused this to come to a temporary halt.

A treason trial

The trial of General Omar Mohammed Tayib, former first vice president and head of the now defunct State Security Service, began in Khartoum on 9 October 1985. He was charged with treason as a result of his involvement in the airlift of the Falashas to Israel in 1984, as technically Sudan had still been at war with Israel. Tayib was accused of accepting a bribe of $2 million from the US CIA in exchange for Sudanese cooperation. The trial was broadcast live, and allegations of American involvement increased the tension between Sudan and the USA. Tayib was eventually found guilty of a number of charges, including allowing US military aircraft to operate secretly in Sudan, ordering state security operatives to work for a foreign power and breaking the anti-Israeli embargo. Three international refugee resettlement agencies were expelled from Sudan, following evidence given at the Tayib trial that implicated them in Operation Moses. On 15 December 1985 the country changed its name to The Republic of Sudan.

General Election

In April 1986, at the end of the agreed one-year transitional rule by the military government, a multiparty general election was held, the first since April–May 1968. More than 40 parties contested the election, including several of the parties banned by Numeiry. Most, however, had been formed since his fall. Polling in part of the south was postponed indefinitely because of the civil war, in which Colonel Garang was demanding a secular government. A high turnout of voters in most areas was reported, and the election was generally well conducted. The only incident of note was the death of a Sudanese African People's Congress candidate in an ambush between Juba and Nimule. Some 264 deputies were elected to the new, 301-seat Constituent Assembly.

The three parties with the most sizeable number of seats were the Umma Party (UP), led by Sadik Mahdi, with 99 seats, the Democratic Unionist Party (DUP), led by Osman Mirghani, with 63 seats, and the National Islamic Front (NIF), led by Hassan Turabi, with 51 seats (although Turabi himself lost his Khartoum seat). When the Constituent Assembly met on 6 May, General Dahab formally ceded power to the civilian government and a five-member Supreme Council, to be the collective head of state, was sworn in. Twenty-seven southern deputies and all eight of the Sudanese National Party deputies walked out because they thought that southern interests were under-represented in the cabinet. The NIF, which wished to retain Sharia law, was not represented in the cabinet. The SPLM, the political wing of the SPLA, had refused an invitation to participate in the new government, and indeed Colonel Garang had rejected the whole election process, intensifying his guerrilla activities in the south in an attempt to disrupt it. He now condemned the Constituent Assembly as unrepresentative because elections had not been held in parts of the south.

The Mahdi government

Sadik Mahdi, as leader of the Umma Party, became premier and announced his government on 15 May 1986. Southern deputies had demanded six cabinet seats, but received only four, this being due the importance of the now joint Sudanese–Egyptian Jonglei Canal project, whose progress had been halted by guerrilla activity. Mahdi stated that new laws would be drawn up to replace the Sharia ones, that the military agreements made with Libya and Egypt would be revised, and that preparations were being made for a national constituential conference.

The war in the south intensifies

Meanwhile in the south there was an upsurge in the civil war in the months following the Transitional Military Council's accession to power, with the SPLA succeeding in extending its control northwards and westwards. The Council failed to bring about a negotiated solution, despite announcing a ceasefire and offering an amnesty to southern troops to persuade them to lay down their arms. The Ethiopian government, in the absence of good relations with the newly installed Council, continued to provide tactical and logistical support for the SPLA, but Libya, which had previously supported it, ceased to do so after Numeiry's downfall and instead helped the new Sudanese government to fight against its rebels.

After the death of William Abdullah Chuol the Anya-Nya-2 seemed to lose its energy and influence, leaving Colonel John Garang as the dominant leader of the revolt in the south. In August 1985 Garang indicated that he would be willing to negotiate with the Transitional Military Council, and sent a messenger to the garrison commander at Nasir with details of his conditions, the government offering safe conduct for the envoy. However on 19 September the Council issued a statement accusing the SPLA of escalating the war, and criticising the fact that the envoy had arrived at Nasir 'with a fully armed regiment which refused to vacate the area'.

During this month the SPLA intensified its campaigns in Upper Nile, South Kordofan and Blue Nile Provinces, carrying out extensive shelling of the towns of Bor and Nasir. In Khartoum, an anti-SPLA demonstration was organised by the NIF in protest against its new offensive, but permission to hold it was refused, causing scuffles to occur on the 21st between SPLA supporters and members of the Muslim Brotherhood.

Garang's list of conditions that would have to be met before peace talks could begin included the dissolution of the Transitional Military Council, the lifting of the state of emergency (imposed in April 1985), the removal of Sharia law, and abrogation of all accords with Egypt and Libya. Garang also demanded the formation of a new government, to contain representatives of all political forces and the two combatant armies.

On 30 September the SPLA launched a mortar attack on Malakal (the capital of Upper Nile Province, which garrisoned about 5000 government troops) and placed the town under siege. On 19 October the SPLA announced a two-week unilateral ceasefire to facilitate the start of the peace negotiations, and Garang called for a national conference to discuss the southern problem.

In late October, Brigadier Mohammed (minister of defence) accused the SPLA of violating its own ceasefire by attacking a Nile steamer and killing a number government troops. This was mistakenly thought by the government to indicate that Garang was not fully in charge of his guerrilla fighters. In December the SPLA was also accused of massacring over 60 villagers at Yirol as its guerrilla units progressed northwards towards Rumbek, which was besieged in January 1986 and captured in early March. Just previously a government counteroffensive had cleared the strategic Bor to Juba road, which for many months had been impassable to government troops, and lifted the three-month siege of Nasir. By the end of 1985 the SPLA was in control of the entire southern region, apart from a few towns, and effectively isolated it from the rest of the country, severing most road and river transport links. The SPLA claimed that it had killed 425 government troops during 1985, compared with 160 in 1984.

On 13–15 March 1986 government forces attacked the guerrilla's positions at Rumbek, using two Soviet-made Tupolev-22 bombers, secured from Libya under the terms of the military protocol signed in July 1985 and reportedly flown by Sudanese pilots serving in the Libyan air force. A number of people were killed in these air attacks. In May, government forces claimed to have recovered Rumbek, and on the 18th a government helicopter was shot down by the SPLA, killing the governor of Lakes Province, the Bishop of Wau, three senior army officers and a charity worker. The Sudanese army now had several helicopters, some on loan from Libya.

The Koka Dam declaration

On 20 March 1986 a meeting took place in the Ethiopian town of Koka between the SPLA and representatives of the Alliance of Professional Organisations and Trade Unions (NAS), which had been instrumental in organising the politically motivated strikes that had helped bring down the Numeiry regime, but was not affiliated to any particular political party. Khalid Yagi, leader of the NAS, had been asked by Premier Sadik Mahdi to organise the national constitutional conference suggested by Colonel Garang, and had already met Garang in Ethiopia to discuss the matter with him. Garang again presented a list of his demands and proposals, which became known as the Koka Dam Declaration. A date for the proposed conference was set, but then postponed, and other fruitless SPLA–NAS meetings subsequently took place in Ethiopia. The Mahdi government also tried to negotiate with the SLPA, but the continued existence of Sharia law stifled progress. Eventually the premier and Garang met on 31 July in Ethiopia, but nothing was achieved apart from their announcement at separate press conferences that they would keep in touch with each other.

When advancing towards Juba in June, the SPLA attacked the town of Terakeka, some 40 miles from Juba. Its main objective was the capture of Juba airport. Mahdi's first visit to the south since becoming premier had to be postponed until the following month, due to the unstable security position. He did make it on 13 July, but did not stay for long. Juba airport was closed on the 17th due to the approach of SPLA forces, which also caused thousands of people to flee from the town into the countryside. The airport reopened on 30 July. The closure had severely affected the distribution of famine relief to the south, especially as Garang had refused to allow convoys of UN trucks from Kenya into the areas of southern Sudan where fighting was in progress. A UN spokesman stated that the combined effects of drought and civil war had made southern Sudan one of the most severely affected famine areas in Africa. Sudan resorted to barter deals to try to dispose of unsold stocks of cotton to Western Germany, Romania and the Soviet Union, with over 600 000 bales of the 1985 crop still standing in warehouses.

12
Premier Sadik Mahdi

The prospect of an end to the civil war in the south dimmed on 16 August 1986 when the SPLA, led by Colonel John Garang, shot down a Sudan Air civil airliner soon after it had taken off from Malakal on a scheduled flight, all 60 people on board being killed. On the 19th Premier Sadik Mahdi declared that the proposed peace talks, which had been initiated by the SPLM and included a planned meeting between himself and Garang, were suspended.

Garang now headed both the political arm (the SPLM) and the military arm (the SPLA) of the main resistance force in the south. The failure of the SPLA to extend its boundaries beyond southern Sudan was attributed to the efforts of the Anya-Nya-2 movement during 1985–6. Formerly an anti-government southern secessionist grouping, the Anya-Nya-2 were now acting as a pro-government militia in armed opposition to the SPLA. Ideological differences and fierce power struggles – frequently based on tribal rivalry – for the leadership of the southern rebellion had culminated in the emergence of the SPLM–SPLA as the principal opposition movement. The leader of the Anya-Nya-2 was now Major Gordon Kong, a former supporter of Colonel Garang, who had been active in the original Anya-Nya during the previous civil war.

The SPLA had warned that it would shoot down all aircraft entering its airspace, having earlier revoked the permission it had given to the Red Cross to carry out relief work in the south. The Red Cross had begun a major airlift of relief supplies from Entebbe (Uganda) to Wau, the major food distribution point for famine-affected areas in the south. SPLA guerrillas had been placed on full alert and ordered to shoot at all aircraft in their airspace 'without exception'. After the Malakal incident, all air links between Sudan and the south were suspended.

This SPLA action was a response to a visit paid by the Sudanese premier to Libya on the 8th, when it was believed that plans had been made for the Sudanese army, backed by Libyan combat aircraft, to launch a major attack on the SPLA in the south. This would have coincided with the much advertised, Red Cross-organised, international food airlift under the terms of the Sudanese–Libyan Defence Agreement of 1985.

The civil war began to escalate and the SPLA fighters were ordered to attack government garrisons in the south, and to ambush and destroy hostile river, road and air traffic. On the 19th Radio SPLA, operating from Ethiopia, warned civilians to abandon the major southern towns of Wau, Malakal, Juba and Bentiu, as it was about to lay siege to them. It later claimed to have bombarded Wau, although this was denied by the government.

International relief efforts

The control and distribution of food aid in the south became a weapon of war for both the government and the guerrillas. The SPLA, claiming to have effective control of the whole of the southern countryside, urged international aid agencies working in Sudan to channel their food and emergency aid through its own organisation, the Sudan Relief and Reha-bilitation Association (SRRA), arguing that as it controlled over 95 per cent of the south, 95 per cent of the aid should go to it and only 5 per cent to the Khartoum government. The international aid agencies wanted to distribute the food and other aid themselves to ensure that it reached those who needed it most. For its part, the Sudanese govern-ment had an army in the south to feed.

The SPLA wanted to get its hands on any international food aid avail-able, having up to 20 000 unpaid volunteers who were having to live off the land. The result was that little got through the battle areas, and the impact of the war was such that whole communities in the south were abandoning their homes – their their cattle and agricultural produce having been stolen – and pouring into the towns to escape the fighting. Previously the UN had launched Operation Rainbow, which for many months had successfully flown in food and medical aid, but had been terminated when the airliner was shot down at Malakal. A few agencies still tried to get aid through to the south in barges, but this was only a trickle.

By mid September 1986 serious food shortages were reported in Wau, the town's population having increased from some 60 000 to about 100 000 within a year as people fled to the town to escape the fighting and drought. There had been a number of deaths from malnutrition, and the UN estimated that between two and three million people in the southern region were in danger of starvation. The Sudanese frontier with Uganda had been closed by President Yoweri Museveni earlier in the year in protest at the Khartoum government's sheltering of pro-Obote dissidents, and the international aid convoys from Entebbe had ceased. The airport at Wau remained shut, and provisions had to be brought in by road, heavily guarded by government troops.

The guerrilla war continues

The rainy season ended in October and the guerrillas became more active, having consolidated their positions in Eastern Equatoria, particularly in the Boma plateau region near the Ethiopian border, and in Upper Nile Province as far as the Red Sea. The SPLA, which had camps in Ethiopia, had consolidated its positions in Eastern Upper Nile, as far north as Renk, and extended its area of control in Bahr el-Ghazal Province, disrupting access to Wau by road and air. However the SPLA had failed to gain ground in Western Equatoria, or to make any serious inroads into northern or western Sudan.

The government occasionally succeeded in jamming SPLA broadcasts, and also toyed with issuing black propaganda of its own, falsely announcing, for example, that Colonel Garang had been killed by his deputy, Colonel Korobino Kuanyin. Premier Sadik Mahdi continued his efforts to convene the proposed national constitutional conference, but when thwarted declared that the SPLA was hostage to Ethiopia, criticising the government of that country for remaining friendly with Garang even though Sudan had returned to democratic rule.

US–Sudanese relations improve

In October 1986 Premier Sadik Mahdi visited the USA and secured the release of a certain amount of economic aid, which had been suspended because of Sudan's failure to meet its debt repayments. It was also agreed that the American diplomatic staff – who had been withdrawn after the (allegedly) Libyan-backed anti-US attack in March 1973 – would return to Khartoum, thus restoring diplomatic relations between the two countries to almost normal. The USA's stated reason for the relaxation of its position was the departure from Khartoum of a number of Libyans associated with international terrorism. Sudanese–Libyan relations were wearing a bit thin, but Sudanese–American ones were improving.

Transitional Administrative Council for the South

On 31 January 1987 a Council for the South was formed, to be the interim administrative body until a constitutional conference could be held. It included the representatives of six southern-based political parties and the governors of the three regions in the south. The chairman was Mathew Ubur. The minister for peace and unity, Dr Khalid Yagi, who was responsible for seeking a solution to the conflict in the south, and organising the national constitutional conference, resigned for reasons of ill-health and was not replaced.

Large numbers of people were moving to Khartoum in search of work and security, particularly migrants from western Sudan but also groups of refugees of different nationalities. On the political scene, decentralisation was becoming a national issue, encouraging the revival of former regional groups such as the Darfur Development Front, the Nuba Mountain Front, the Beja Congress in eastern Sudan, and the Sudan National Party, all of which were gaining popularity.

Another difficulty was that the civil war in Chad was spilling over into Sudan, with contesting factions crossing and recrossing the western Sudanese border, and indeed occupying sections of Darfur Province. There were reports from Darfur of foreign troops killing, pillaging and terrorising the people, and it was alleged that over 3000 members of the Fur tribe had already been killed. The unrest was blamed on tribal animosity between Arabs and non-Arabs, which escalated with the creation by the Umma Party of armed Arab militias, nominally to protect themselves and their cattle against the SPLA. These included the Dinkas and Neurs of the Upper Nile, the Baggaras in Darfur, the Mundaris in Equatoria and the Ferit in Bahr el-Ghazal. Cattle raids and fights that had formerly been settled with spears could now be determined more decisively with automatic weapons. Slave trading was not unknown, and the issue was raised in the National Assembly of 450 Dinka women and children from the Aweil district being captured and sold in the markets of Kordofan and Darfur.

Internally the premier was having trouble with the powerful Sudan Railways Trade Union, the railway network having been divided into five autonomous zones. The trade union was still led by Abbas Khidir, who had previously been sentenced to death for leading a strike. The railways were being deliberately neglected and allowed to deteriorate, as united and prosperous they posed a powerful political threat to the Khartoum government. On the second anniversary of Mahdi's returns to power, Colonel Gaddafi presented him with four Soviet-built MiG-23s, each fully equipped with bombs, at a time when the Sudanese air force probably only had two C-130 transport planes, about half a dozen Chinese-made MiG-19s and about a dozen helicopters.

December 1986 had been a rousing month for the SPLA, and it claimed to have inflicted hundreds of casualties when it ambushed four Nile river steamers at Lul on the White Nile, just north of Malakal, and also to have killed over 70 government troops in fighting at Mongala, near Juba. On the government side, it was later admitted that in fighting at Kosti it had been necessary to execute 22 rebels as there had been no means of evacuating them. It also announced that the 23-month siege of Bor had been lifted.

In March 1987 the SPLA claimed that, after ten days of fighting it had captured the town of Pibor, which had been garrisoned by government troops. Garang described the operation as having successfully defeated the government's 'dry season' campaign. Other incidents highlighted by the SPLA included the sinking of a Nile steamer on 10 March; the shooting down of a commercial aircraft near Malakal on 5 May, killing 13 people; and the shooting down of a Hercules transport aircraft, carrying government troops, on 11 May near Wau airport. In April the SPLA rejected the government's offer of a ceasefire pending the resumption of peace negotiations, demanding that the state of emergency, in force since April 1985, should be lifted in conjunction with the implementation of any ceasefire.

The Mahdi regime continued Numeiry's policy of arming Arab tribes to encourage tribal warfare, with the ultimate aim of weakening the SPLA. This was extended to the Messitiya Arabs, and the Meurki near the Ethiopian border, their value being their knowledge of the local terrain and guerrilla tactics, which the army lacked. In one clash between the Dinkas (from whom the SPLA drew its major support) and the Arab Rezigat tribe in the El Daein region of Darfur, it was alleged that up to 1000 Dinkas were killed, and that the local police gave tacit support to the Arabs. A few days previously the Dinkas had inflicted a defeat on the Rezigat tribesmen.

The new Mahdi government

In May 1987 the chairman of the Supreme Council, Ahmad Mirghani, dissolved the Council of Ministers and asked Sadik Mahdi to form a new government, which he did, retaining the premiership and the defence portfolio. This was done in an attempt to bring an end to the dissension within the Council of Ministers between the Umma Party and the

Democratic Unionist Party, the latter being weakened by internal power struggles. The continued existence of the 'September Laws', as the Sharia laws had become known, rankled many, but Mahdi, with his Ansar following and heritage, was hesitant about becoming the man who abolished Sharia law in Sudan. The new Council of Ministers, announced on 3 June, was another uneasy coalition, with the Sharia law problems still to be resolved.

The Sudanese Nationalist Party, along with other southern parties that comprised the 'African bloc', led by Philip Abbas Ghaboush, maintained their boycott of the Constituent Assembly. Ghaboush, who supported the so-called Koka Dam Declaration, had been arrested and accused of illegal acquisition of wealth.

Sudanese relations with Libya had cooled over the presence of Libyan troops in western Darfur near the border with Chad, with Sudan being used as a springboard for attacks onto Chadian territory. Premier Mahdi publicly condemned the Libyan presence and insisted that his government had ordered the departure of the troops, who had entered the Darfur region without permission in February. He said the force consisted of 700–1000 troops, with rocket launchers, anti-aircraft guns, light weapons and 400 vehicles. It was reported that the Libyan troops would withdraw under Sudanese supervision, but no date was specified.

Sudan's relations with Egypt were already cool as the extradition of former President Numeiry was still being contested in Egyptian courts, and the presence of the Libyan troops caused further friction as Egypt was in confrontation with Libya at the time. Sudan's relations with Ethiopia were also poor, the Ethiopian government complaining that Sudan was giving sanctuary and aid to its anti-government rebels, and in turn the Khartoum government alleged that Ethiopia was providing weapons and training camps for the SPLA. Previously, in December 1986, the Ethiopian air force had carried out bombing raids near the border on camps and villages that were harbouring Eritrean refugees and guerrillas, and it was reported that a number of civilians had been killed. Mahdi next visited Iran to reopen the Sudanese embassy in Tehran, which had been closed in 1982 when Numeiry had sided with Iraq in the Iran–Iraq War (1980–8). He returned to Khartoum with 15 Sudanese prisoners of war who had been captured by Iranians while fighting for Iraq.

Transitional charter

On 22 August 1987 the coalition government was suspended when the Democratic Unionist Party, which wanted to abolish the September

Laws, broke away and the National Islamic Movement, which wanted the September Laws to remain, joined the coalition. Agreement was not reached until 10 January 1988, when a transitional charter was signed by all Sudanese political parties but the SPLM. The charter was designed to see the country through until the proposed national constitutional conference was held. Sadik Mahdi was re-elected premier in April, but remained ambivalent about the September Laws. The six southern political parties, the so-called African Bloc, maintained contact with the SPLA, and even Mahdi showed some interest in reviving negotiations with Colonel Garang.

The Anya-Nya-2 splits

Evidence that the Any-Nya-2 had split into two factions came in September 1987, when one faction refused to sign an agreement to merge with the SPLA. The reasons for this were partly tribal, the objectors being from small tribes that feared an alliance with the Dinka-dominated SPLA, but others objected to Garang's strong left-wing views.

There had been a massacre in Wau in August, the details of which were disputed. Radio SPLA reported that on the 11th the governor of Bahr el-Ghazal Province had rounded up civilians in the town, and that at least 450 people had been killed in the course of two days. The Khartoum government initially denied the incident, but later admitted it, insisting the actual toll was much smaller. It was also alleged the governor had divided the town into two sectors, one exclusively for the Dinkas, who were sympathetic to the SPLA. Some Western reports indicated that the massacre had been committed by Arab militiamen in response to SPLA activities against them. At this juncture the Western media was interested in following up revelations made in a booklet entitled *The Daein Massacre and Slavery in the South*, written by Dr Abdullah Mahmoud, a southern academic.

In an interview broadcast on Radio SPLA on 28 September, Colonel Garang admitted that government forces remained in control of towns in the south that had military garrisons, specifically mentioning Juba, Torit and Bor, but boasted that the soldiers could not move more than five kilometers from them, and that the SPLA had reached to within 5–10 kilometers of all the garrisons in the war zone. Garang insisted that 'We are in full control of the countryside', but the Sudanese GHQ claimed that the 'rebels were contained militarily', although it admitted that the SPLA had taken control of the town of Jokan near the Ethiopian border in May. The army attributed the SPLA's success to heavy mortar bombardment of the town and the support given by 'white mercenaries and Ethiopian troops', but claimed that it had killed 560 rebels in the fighting. The government also admitted to the loss of the 196-strong garrison at Nasir, claiming to have killed 170 rebels.

In November the SPLA took the border town of Kurmuk in Blue Nile Province after three days of fighting. The Sudanese government protested officially to Ethiopia that Ethiopians had participated in the attack, shelling Sudanese troops from Ethiopian territory. This was denied, but it was probably quite true. The government recaptured Kurmuk on 22 December. The Sudanese army, now technically the 'People's Armed Forces', constantly alleged that the SPLA was receiving military aid from East Germany and Cuba, though Garang's left-wing contacts.

Previously, in July, a British nurse and three US aid workers had been captured by the SPLA during fighting between government troops and guerrillas at Mundri near Juba. After seven weeks they had been released unharmed at Pibor. Radio SPLA made propaganda out of the situation, saying that they had been guests not captives, and that their release had been the result of a personal appeal by former US President Jimmy Carter, saying they would welcome his continued humanitarian work behind SPLA lines. Three Jesuit priests were also briefly held captive.

In January 1988 an emergency airlift of food to Juba began. On 26 January the SPLA claimed to have captured Nasir, and in February it went on to capture Lira on the 15th and Torit on the 26th. Radio SPLA hailed the victory at Torit as the greatest in the war so far.

The USA now joined in the negotiations (some of which were held in Washington) at the behest of the international relief agencies, which were being hopelessly handicapped by the war. It was suggested that a broad-based government be formed and the DUP–SPLA agreement accepted. The General Command of the People's Armed forces also put pressure on the premier, who in March rearranged his coalition. King Fahd of Saudi Arabia, who made it clear that while he favoured Sadik Mahdi he had no intention of becoming involved in a conflict between Arabs and Africans, urged Mahdi to take more positive action, warning him that both Iran and the USA had candidates for the premiership in mind if he did not shake off his lethargy.

National Unity government

On 14 May 1988 Mahdi formed a new National Unity government, which was really a new coalition. The September Laws remained a bone of contention and arguments continued until 4 October, when the Constituent Assembly was adjourned. Unsuccessful attempts were were made to resolve the civil war in the south, where the raging famine brought allegations that government troops were using scorched earth tactics.

Terrorism

On the same day as the National Unity government was sworn in (15 May), a timebomb was planted in the Acropole Hotel in Khartoum and an attack was made by gunmen on the British Sudan Club. Seven lives were lost, five of them British. Initially there was confusion about the identity of the culprits, it being assumed that the underground Muslim Brothers had conducted the attacks in order to intimidate Mahdi. The government rushed to avow that neither the PLO nor the SPLA were responsible, and later stated that three Arabs with Lebanese passports had been arrested. Their identities were not revealed, but they were believed to be members of the cells of the Arab Fedayeen, a Beirut-based terrorist group linked to the pro-Iranian Hezbollah group, which warned the Sudanese government that there would be repercussions if any of the suspects were ill-treated. This organisation had first come to public notice the previous month during negotiations for the release of hostages on board a hijacked Kuwaiti airliner. The group had threatened that if any Shia prisoners in Kuwait were harmed, Western hostages being held in Lebanon would be executed.

As the summer of 1988 ended, so did the drought, only to be replaced by heavy rains that caused catastrophic flooding. Partly due to the end of the drought, but mainly to the good work done by the UN and other agencies in delivering food aid in the face of extreme adversity, the long-predicted biblical loss of life was averted.

During September and October the SPLA captured the three garrison towns of Katiri, Keyala and Ikotos in Eastern Equatoria Province, and the garrison at Farajok near the Ugandan frontier. The DUP, led by Osman Mirghani and wanting a ceasefire, broke away from the Khartoum government coalition and made a separate agreement with Colonel Garang, to take effect after ratification by the government, but this failed on the Sharia law issue. In January 1989 the premier reshuffled his cabinet.

SPLA ceasefire

On 1 May 1989 Colonel John Garang announced a unilateral, one-month ceasefire, provided government troops did not exploit it by moving away from garrison towns or re-plenishing their arms supply. Once again the Sharia law problem got in the way, but Garang extended his deadline. Meanwhile he had been contacting Western statesmen, and had had a meeting in Torit with a US congressional delegation led by former President Jimmy Carter. Coincidal with the negotiations there had been a resurgence of intertribal fighting in the Darfur region, near the border with Chad, reports indicating that hundreds of people had been killed and many villages destroyed by fire.

Sadik Mahdi deposed

The civilian government of Premier Sadik Mahdi was overthrown in a bloodless military coup on 30 June 1989 by a group of army officers led by Brigadier Omar Hassan al-Bashir. The group called themselves the National Movement for Correcting the Situation. (Previously, on the 18th, the government claimed to have foiled a planned coup and several officers had been arrested.) Bashir, who promoted himself to the rank of general, stated that his regime was neither left-wing nor right-wing, nor did it represent any tribal or ethnic interest. Journalists speculated that the British and Egyptian governments had been involved. Bashir suspended the constitution, abolished the Constituent Assembly and all political institutions, banned strikes and trade unions, and imposed media censorship. Bashir, born in Shendi, was a paratrooper, had served with the Sudanese contingent in the Arab–Israeli War of 1973, and had recently been commanding troops in the south.

Command Council of the Revolution

General Bashir established the Command Council of the Revolution of National Salvation and set up four commissions to run the country, ruling out any early return to multiparty democracy. He avowed to crack down hard on embezzlement and corruption, and declared that the death penalty would be imposed on anyone hoarding foreign currency. He sent a delegation to Ethiopia to meet the SPLA and offered an amnesty if they would lay down their arms. The offer was rejected, but both sides agreed to take part in a national constitutional conference. John Garang visited Washington and London, declaring his willingness to find a solution to the five-year war in the south, based on autonomy and a guarantee against full implementation of Sharia law. He appealed for foreign commercial investment in his region, and it was believed that the Lonrho Group, an international trading consortium, had paid his travel expenses.

Bashir forms a government

On 9 July 1989 General Bashir formed a cabinet, in which he became premier and defence minister. Some of the ministers were former civil servants who had headed departments, and others had contacts with the banned National Islamic Front. Bashir rejected the DUP-negotiated peace accord with the SPLA, and in an interview said he would accept southern secession as a solution to the conflict, although he afterwards denied this. He also suggested that he would seek unity agreements with both Egypt and Libya, which he knew would upset southerners. The SPLA ignored Bashir's offer to negotiate. He also proposed to introduce military conscription, and devote more resources to the army to enable it to prosecute the war in the south more successfully. Sadik Mahdi had been arrested, together with a group of his former officials, to be tried before a special military court for economic crimes. By this time the ceasefire in the south, the ending of the drought and renewed deliveries of international food and other aid had enabled certain local populations to reach a degree of self-sufficiency.

Government talks with the SPLA

On 1 December 1989, talks chaired by former President Jimmy Carter between the Khartoum government and the SPLA were held in in Nairobi, Kenya. Carter had previously held separate talks with General Bashir and Colonel Garang, but as the government had refused to compromise on the Sharia law issue they had soon broken down. On the 7th Colonel Mohammed Khalifa, a member of the Command Council, stated that Sharia law would be fully implemented, including punishments by amputation, which was understood by some as a tactic to jolt the south into declaring its secession, a course that Garang had earlier rejected. An Amnesty International report issued on 12 December roundly condemned Sudan, alleging that thousands of unarmed civilians had been executed over the past six years, that rebel prisoners had been routinely tortured and maltreated, and that tribal militias had killed tens of thousands of people, notably Dinkas. It also detailed atrocities committed by the SPLA.

13
The Bashir Regime

The talks on ending the civil war having broken-down in December 1989, fighting erupted again in the south in January 1990. The SPLA claimed several victories, including the capture of Kajo Kaji, a garrison town on the White Nile south of Juba, and the destruction of a relieving government armoured column. Kaya, a garrison town, fell on the 14th, and the SPLA claimed to have captured Yei on the 28th. During a brief local ceasefire, over 100 foreign workers were evacuated from besieged Juba, where food stocks were running low and reportedly troops were shooting civilians attempting to flee. The army rejected appeals by the SPLA for the some 300 000 civilians in Juba to be allowed to leave. At about the same time fighting broke out between the Arab Sabaha and African Shilluk tribes around Kosti, when large numbers of Shilluks who had fled their homes were working for local farmers. An argument over the length of the Christmas break was said to have triggered off the clashes, in which up to 600 people were later reported to have been killed.

Africa Watch allegations

The human rights organisation Africa Watch claimed on 18 March 1990 that Sudan was a human rights disaster area. It said that over 500 000 people had been killed in the civil war and resulting famine, with both the government and the SPLA using starvation as a weapon, and that thousands of women and children in the south had been sold into slavery. It noted that civil rights violations in the north had also increased dramatically since the June 1989 coup, that there had been purges in the judiciary, civil service and military, that trade unions were banned and that hundreds of political detainees had been tortured. Several Western journalists working in the country had been detained, and others deported.

The USA banned all economic and military aid to Sudan until it reverted to a democratic political system, but a cabinet reshuffle in April merely served to strengthen the fundamentalist element in the government. Bashir was becoming aggressive towards the south and calling for the elimination of dissidents. One of his pronouncements, often repeated, was 'It might be better if we let the south go.'

When Bashir came to power most people in Khartoum – having suffered the chaos, mismanagement and neglect that accompanied the Mahdi regime – were pleased, hoping for an improvement in social and economic matters and an end to the war in the south, but they were soon disillusioned. Central power seemed to strengthen and was distributed among three main bodies: Revolutionary Command Council, which included military officers who had carried out the coup; the government, comprising more than 20 ministers, many of whom were former senior civil servants; and the shadowy movement known as the Council of Defenders, consisting of over 40 members, mainly from the proscribed National Islamic Front (NIF), but also including some young officers. Many believed that the latter group was the real power centre, supporting and advising Bashir, who remained the dictator.

Hassan Turabi, leader of the NIF, was reputed to have masterminded the coup that brought Bashir, the NIF's prodigy, to power, knowing that he would never have made it through normal democratic processes. At this stage the NIF was split into two wings, a moderate one dominated by Turabi, who advocated a more gradual approach to Islamicisation, and a radical one led by Ali Osman and Mahdi Ibrahim. Sorbonne-educated Turabi, upon whom Bashir relied extensively, was the ideologue of the coup and regarded the war in the south as a religious one.

An alleged attempted coup

On 23 April 1990 the government announced that over 30 army and police officers had been executed for taking part in an attempted coup against the military government. It was alleged that they had tried to take over Radio Omdurman and Omdurman airport, but had been overpowered by loyal troops. Bashir blamed the thwarted coup on the 'alliance', meaning the signatories of the National Democratic Alliance Charter, drawn up in October 1989 by political parties, trade unions and professional associations; and also the SPLA. However journalists and diplomats suspected that the whole thing was a fiction, being simply an excuse to remove individuals whose loyalty was in doubt, especially as some of those executed had been held in detention before the alleged event This was the forerunner of other reported coup attempts, some of which were also thought to be fictitious.

During March and April, fighting in the south centred on the garrison towns of Yei and Rumbek, supply convoys to them being attacked by guerrillas and both sides claiming victories.

The Gulf crisis

On 2 August 1990, Iraqi armed forces occupied Kuwait, and the Crisis leading up to the Gulf War began. Sudan was one of the few Arab states to support Iraq, and was therefore regarded as a pariah by the USA and other Western and Arab countries that fought against that country during the war itself. Consequently all aid from those sources ceased, which added to Bashir's difficulties. Since coming to power, Bashir had developed close relations with Iraq, which had provided him with some conventional arms. He had visited Baghdad, reportedly in the hope of obtaining chemical warfare weapons, while Iraq was hoping for base facilities on Sudan's Red Sea coast, but nothing seemed to come of this. However the warm Sudan–Iraq relations did not prevent Bashir from carrying out a witch-hunt against members of the Iraqi Baathist Party in Sudan.

Siding with Iraq in the Gulf War caused a profound blow to the Sudanese economy as there were some 750 000 Sudanese workers in the Gulf states, over 75 000 of whom were in Kuwait and whose remittances home exceeded $750 million. Furthermore the Gulf had been major market for Sudanese livestock and cereals. Arab emergency assistance dried up, causing Bashir to be thought of not only as incompetent, but also as politically naive, especially when he claimed in a speech that 'We can eat what we grow, and wear what we can make.' He was also criticised for rejecting the DUP–SPLA peace accord as it was estimated that the war in the south was still costing $1 million a day.

As Sudan's isolation increased, owing to its open support for Iraq, internal unrest strengthened, with threats of strike action by railwaymen and other groups of workers. Added to this, the spectre of famine reappeared in the south and other parts of the country, and grain rationing had to be introduced in September.

The following month the government suddenly bulldozed the Hilat Shouk refugee shanty town near Khartoum (one of more than 20 such camps on the perimeter of the capital and sustained by relief agencies), its some 30 000 inhabitants being transported to another site some 60 miles away. The official excuse was that the inhabitants were responsible for the rising crime rate in Khartoum, but probably the real reason was fear that they would become involved in the anticipated food riots.

The continuing war in the south contributed to the general discontent, being such a heavy drain on the economy. General Bashir seemed to be influenced by Turabi, and to tolerate the NIF (although nominally political parties were forbidden), which wanted to retain the September Laws, and indeed strengthen them, which hampered the peace negotiations.

Regional reorganisation

On 8 February 1991 General Bashir, as chairman of the ruling Revolutionary Command Council, signed a decree dividing Sudan into nine states, subdivided into 66 provinces and 281 local government areas. The states were to be responsible for tax collection and local administration, with the central government retaining control over foreign policy, military affairs, trade and other key responsibilities. This was presented by the government as devolving power away from the centre, and a move towards resolving the war in the south by lessening the north–south division.

On 1 February Bashir had signed a decree on a revised penal code, similar to the previous one and still based on Sharia law. This came into effect on 22 March, but for the time being would not apply to the three southern states of Bahr el-Ghazal, Upper Nile and Equatoria. Bashir was trying to make Sharia law more acceptable, and punishments by amputation had not been imposed for some months. The SPLA rejected the new code, and continued to demand the abolition of Sharia law and the restoration of regional autonomy. A national conference on the political system was held in Khartoum at the end of April, when former Premier Sadik Mahdi was released from house arrest and amnesty was given to a number of other political detainees and exiles. There had been another reported coup attempt in April, followed by the now customary announcement that the military officers involved had been executed.

In the meantime the Sudanese government was criticised by international relief agencies for the maldistribution of food aid, little or none having reached the south, where the civil war dragged on. The government's response was to forbid UN aid aircraft to fly food into rebel areas. Provisional arrangements were made with both the Sudanese government and the SPLA for relief supplies to be taken to Juba by river barge. There would also be air drops to certain areas where Sudanese refugees were returning from Ethiopia, where the regime of Haile Mengistu Mariam had fallen in May 1991. Mariam's government had been supporting the SPLA because Sudan was assisting the Eritrean rebels, but now the SPLA elements in Ethiopia had to hurry back to Sudanese territory.

The National Democratic Federation

Political parties continued to be prohibited in Sudan (although the NIF seemed to be tolerated, but not acknowledged), so Sudanese opposition groups in exile gathered together in Cairo. The Egyptian government, whose relations with Sudan were now very poor, afforded them sanctuary and allowed them to engage in a degree of political activity. Egypt was also resisting Sudan's attempts to extradite Numeiry from Cairo, hoping he would return in victory to Khartoum one day. In May the Sudanese opposition in exile formed the National Democratic Federation (NDF), which consisted of banned Sudanese political parties (excluding the NIF), together with over 50 unions and syndicates, all hostile to Bashir. The driving force of the large and unwieldy NDF was the Sudanese Armed Forces Leadership (SAFL), which consisted of officers who had served in the Sudanese armed forces prior to the 1989 coup. The SAFL, led by General Fathy Ahmad Ali, a former head of the Sudanese armed forces, produced a plan, or rather a movement, to depose Bashir, which it called 'Ana al-Sudan' (I am Sudan). It was suspected that, prior to the change of government, Ethiopia had also been giving aid and support to anti-Bashir exiles in Cairo and Addis Ababa.

Much to the annoyance of the USA and other Western democracies, Bashir maintained good relations with Libya, which was lending him MiG-23 combat aircraft to bomb the SPLA in the south. The friendship was demonstrated at the celebrations to mark the second anniversary of Bashir's ascent to power, when Colonel Gaddafi was invited to join in the demolition of the infamous Kobar prison, whose some 1300 inmates, mostly political prisoners and detainees, had been released.

Colonel Mohammed Khalifah (an RCC member), in the hope of improving US–Sudanese relations, told senior American officials in Addis Ababa that negotiations on the south were imminent, although this was questionable. He also told a press gathering in Khartoum that over 800 members of the SPLA had recently surrendered while Garang was away lobbying in Washington.

On 23 August yet another coup attempt was announced, the fifth since Bashir came to power. A number of serving officers, leading figures of the banned Umma Party and the DUP, members of the Ana al-Sudan group and others had been detained although the government blamed it on 'foreign powers'. The defendants were brought to trial and condemned to death, but this time most of the sentences were commuted to imprisonment.

SPLA split

In late August 1991 a statement published in Nairobi indicated that there had been a revolt within the SPLA. Apparently three (of a said 13) field commanders – Riek Machar, Lam Akol and Gordon Kong – had taken over the leadership, supposedly because of what they saw as John Garang's dictatorial behaviour. However, apart from personality clashes, the real reason was differences of opinion over whether or not the south should secede from Sudan. The dissident group generally favoured a black independent state, while Garang and his loyalists still wanted a united secular Sudan. Garang's dream was for the south to secure equal status to the Muslim north, and for the country to open up to democracy proper. His constant claim was that he was fighting for the freedom of all Sudan.

There was some suggestion that the Khartoum government might now be willing to contemplate the secession of the south, eventually leading to some form of federation with the north. Negotiations were proposed, this time with the Nigerian government trying to mediate between the two SPLA sections, perhaps with the motive of luring the south into black Africa.

The main SPLA body, which mainly recruited Dinkas, became known as the Torit group, as it was based in that town, while the dissident elements, largely recruiting Nuers, were known as the Nasir group, after the town of that name. The Nasir group and the dissident leaders each had their own following. Clashes between the two factions began in late November, resulting in numerous casualties (including civilians) in and around the southern towns of Bor and Kongor, north of Juba. The war in the south took a nasty turn when both the Torit and the Nasir began to kill tribesmen who supported their adversaries. An Amnesty International report of 14 April alleged that during the initial fighting between the two groups, the Nuers had massacred over 2000 civilians (mainly Dinka tribesmen in the Bor area) as they moved southwards. It also alleged that human rights violations by both factions included the torture of political detainees in specially adapted buildings known as 'ghost houses'.

A ceasefire was negotiated in Nairobi on 27 November, but broke down on 2 December. Eventually, on the 12th, both factions ratified a 12-point peace plan, negotiated in Kenya with the mediation of the National Council of Churches. The Sudanese army criticised this Kenyan interference, complaining that it was trying to bring the two factions of the SPLA together so that it could persuade the whole of the south to secede.

Meanwhile the main body of the SPLA resumed its shelling of Juba, causing numerous casualties, and in the southern part of Darfur state it engaged in action against government forces. Meanwhile Sudanese war planes (borrowed from Libya) bombed SPLA-held villages. In the capital in December, a number of inhabitants of a refugee shanty town were killed while trying to prevent their homes from being demolished.

Also in December an Iranian delegation, led by President Rafsanjani, visited Sudan, a country he saw as advancing steadily towards full Islamicisation. Several agreements were concluded on oil deliveries, trade and technical assistance. Rafsanjani rejected press reports that Iranian Revolutionary Guards were training Sudanese troops in the desert, and denied that his country had been funding the purchase by Sudan of Chinese weaponry for the past two years.

National Transitional Assembly

In an Independence Day speech on 1 January 1992, General Bashir announced his intention to form a National Transitional Assembly as a step towards democracy. It would consist of 300 members, but Bashir gave no indication of when the elections for it might be held. However he did mention that the main obstacle to elections was the war in the south. He also announced a Peace and Development Foundation for the south. The following month comprehensive austerity measures and economic reforms were announced. This three-year 'economic salvation programme' was given a cautious welcome by the IMF, which had declared Sudan to be a non-cooperative member. The programme was to include some privatisation, including the sale of the national airline, telecommunictions and shipping.

Sudan managed to cling on to the membership of the IMF, despite being accused of hindering its own economic reform by blocking foreign aid, which to some extent was true. The IMF did not like Sudan's move towards Islamicisation, and perhaps hoped that further economic hardship might provoke a change of government to one more to the IMF's liking. Sudan, one of the world's poorest countries, had a per capita gross domestic product of about $100, made up in 1991 entirely of emergency aid. In February 1992 Sudan freed its pound from official control, and it duly fell in value by 60 per cent (*Financial Times*).

Yet another attempted coup was revealed when it was reported that some 40 Sudanese military officers had been arrested on 2 February. It seems the conspirators had planned to use two military helicopters to bomb the GHQ building during a joint meeting between senior army commanders and members of the RCC, who were discussing the implementation of austerity measures. This was followed by an anti-government 'sit in' protest on bridges between Khartoum and Omdurman by civil war veterans, supported by civil servants, and on the 9th there was a mass demonstration in Omdurman

Government offensives

In February and March 1992 the army mounted an offensive against the SPLA – with four columns fanning out from garrison towns in the south, including Juba and Malakal – while at the same time indicating that it was still prepared to participate in any peace talks the Nigerians could arrange. The SPLA had been considerably weakened by the defection of the Nasir group and the change of government in Ethiopia in May 1991, which meant it could no longer operate from bases in that country. Khartoum had re-established diplomatic relations with Addis Ababa, and on 9 March, in conjunction with Sudanese units, Ethiopian forces drove SPLA guerrillas from the border town of Pochala, where they had been ensconced since 1985, although this was officially denied. A few days later a joint Sudanese–Ethiopian action cleared the SPLA from the border town of Gambela. The Sudanese opposition National Democratic Alliance, based in Cairo, claimed that over 8000 Iranian soldiers were deployed in the south near Juba. This was denied, but it was probably founded on fact.

Nubian ethnic cleansing

An Africa Watch report of 10 December 1991 condemned the Sudanese government repression of the Nubian people, living mainly in south-eastern Kordofan Province. It described the process as a steady war of attrition in which the authorities were seeking to eliminate community leaders and the educated classes in Nuba. It also spoke of widespread killings and disappearances at the hands of government-backed militias, and efforts to Islamicise the Nubians. According to one source (SUNA) a jihad had been declared against them in southern Kordofan.

On humanitarian grounds the UN and USA urged the Khartoum government to stop the forcible relocation of the inhabitants of the shanty refugee camps on the outskirts of the capital, alleging that over 400 000 had been forcibly relocated already and their mud-brick dwellings razed to the ground. Foreign refugee migration to Sudan was increasing, consisting mainly of Chadians, Ethiopians and Malians, some elements of whom were getting out of hand.

The London-based Sudan Human Rights Organisation (SHRO) alleged that in the campaigns against the Nubians in 1992, government forces had killed over 6000 and wounded more than 2000, and that its ethnic cleansing operations had reduced the Nubian population from about one million to about 800 000. A massacre of the Nubian Kawaleb tribe was mentioned, but without precise details. The report mentioned that the government-armed Popular Defence Militia was selectively killing Nubian leaders. Although many Nubians identified themselves with the south both politically and racially, most resided in northern Sudan, mainly in the Nuba Mountain region.

The Haliab Triangle

Meanwhile in 1991 the disputed ownership of the Haliab Triangle, a small, barren piece of coastal territory on the Egyptian–Sudanese frontier and said to be rich in manganese, oil and minerals, was highlighted again when the Sudanese government alleged that Egyptian troops and prospectors had moved into the area. It was said that Egypt was negotiating deals with Germany and Japan for many tonnes of ferro-manganese bars, used in the manufacture of very high-grade steel. At about the same time Canada asked Sudan for concessions in the triangle, whereupon Egypt reasserted its claim over the territory, simultaneously accusing Sudan of sponsoring international terrorist operations, in conjunction with Iran, in North Africa and Egypt. In early 1992 Egyptian officials visited the Haliab Triangle, which had no maritime facilities or paved roads, and issued Egyptian birth and identity certificates to the Ababda and Beshareya tribes living there, while construction work began on a small port facility and a road network. The Sudanese government was helpless for the time being, and relations between the two countries deteriorated. In December 1992 the Sudanese government complained to the UN Security Council about the alleged Egyptian incursion. The incident was eventually resolved by negotiation with the help of Syria, Libya and the PLO.

Government successes in the south

After capturing Pochala, government forces quickly moved on to take the towns of Kongor and Bor, the main SPLA body now being concentrated in the towns of Torit and Kapoeta in the southern part of Equatoria Province. Bor, which had been under SPLA control since April 1989, fell on 4 April 1992 being seized by a 2000-man column, supported by artillery. Next came Yirol to the north east of Bor, which fell on the 11th, followed by Pibor on the 22nd and Mongalla (south of Bor) on the 25th, However another column, moving south-eastwards from Juba, was halted at Nbangala by the SPLA. The following month another government column, moving from Wau towards Tambura, was slowed to halt by the arrival of the rainy season. By way of excuse, Colonel Garang of the SPLA said that most of the government gains had been at the expense of the dissident Nasir group, still based in Nasir, Wau and Akobo.

Garang's tactic had been to besiege and isolate garrison towns, and then bombard them. This had brought successes, but caused devastation to the countryside, which in turn exacerbated the famine conditions. Boutros Boutros-Ghali, the UN secretary general, expressed concern that the fighting in the south was driving out the few remaining international aid agencies, causing the Khartoum government partially to lift its ban on aid flights to the region.

On 1 May the government claimed it had destroyed the largest rebel camp in Bahr el-Ghazal (the exact location was not given), killing over 500 rebels and seizing large quantities of arms and ammunition. On the 12th Garang's guerrillas were driven from Liria, east of Juba on the road to Torit, and Kapoeta fell to government forces on the 28th.

The previous month the government had announced that a number of serving and retired army officers had been arrested for plotting to overthrow the government. This time the blame was put on the NDA (based in Cairo), which wanted to restore Numeiry to power in Khartoum and had sought a meeting between Numeiry and Garang.

SPLA unification talks

Talks aimed at uniting the two factions of the SPLA opened on 26 May 1992 in Abuja, the Nigerian capital. The talks ware hosted by President Ibrahim Babangida (as chairman of the OAU) and both the Torit group and the Nasir group were represented. They had been reluctant to attend the talks together, and had only agreed to do so when Kenya said it would withdraw all material and moral support from both factions if they failed to comply. Neither group had been successful in trying to gain ceasefire preconditions, especially in the light of the government's recent successes in battle in the south. The talks ended on 5 June, when a joint communiqué announced that the two parties were committed to peaceful negotiation, but that was about all as they differed over the constitutional future of the south.

The Sudanese government now began to accuse Saudi Arabia of being the SPLA's main financial supporter and supplier of weaponry. This stemmed from the government's capture of an SPLA camp named as Kit (about 30 miles south-west of Torit), where a huge quantity of Saudi-manufactured military equipment had been found. This was officially denied by the Saudis.

The southern town of Torit, 50 miles from the Ugandan border and the main SPLA base since 1989, was evacuated by Colonel Garang, who moved his Torit group HQ to Kajo Kaji near the border, although he claimed that his guerrillas were now besieging the Torit government garrison.

Operation Lifeline Sudan relief flights to Juba were temporarily halted on 21 July because government troops had commandeered a UN aircraft and used it to transport troops and military equipment. This also caused the UN to move its HQ for the operation from Khartoum to Entebbe in Uganda. Operation Lifeline Sudan was resumed on 20 August, but without any SPLA guarantees. It was again halted on 7 September, but soon after resumed, only to be suspended on the 30th after the murder of a UN official and a Western journalist in the south.

Amnesty International alleged that government troops were committing atrocities in the Juba area, using civilians as human shields. During September, fighting again broke out between the two SPLA rival factions in the Malakal area. The Nasir group, led by Riek Machar, seized Malakal on 18 October, which was a severe loss to the government since the town was a major government base, with stocks of weaponry and ammunition. Some reports indicated that Anya-Nya-2, now a government-armed militia, had subsequently made an unsuccessful attempt to wrest Malakal from the Nasir group. Other reports noted the appearance of a new SPLA splinter group – the Forces of Unity, led by William Nyuon Bany – which was somehow also involved in the fighting around Malakal. A planned resumption of the Abuja talks was abandoned.

A large Iranian delegation visited Khartoum on 30 November for talks on strategic cooperation, resulting in the introduction of an Iranian aid programme, which included the construction of a large modern military centre in Khartoum. Rumours that Iranians were helping to train Sudanese troops were still rife, but continued to be denied. On 4 December the UN held a meeting in Nairobi, Kenya – attended by representatives of the Sudanese government and the Nasir and Torit groups – to discuss the distribution of relief supplies in the south.

In a speech, General Bashir denounced the allegations of human rights violations by his troops as baseless rumours. The UN General Assembly passed a resolution condemning Sudan following reports that at least 300 people had been executed in Juba. There were also reports of continued harassment of Nubians, and allegations that the Khartoum government was engaging in ethnic cleansing because of the Nubians' resistance to converting to Islam.

During January 1993 tension developed between General Bashir and Hassan Turabi, leader of the NIF, who so far had been working well together to advance the cause of an Islamic state. The situation came to a head when Turabi declared that the RCC should be abolished. This fracturing of relations between Islamic and military members of the government coincided with disturbances in several cities over food shortages and rising prices.

A ceasefire

During February 1993 President Museveni of Uganda mediated talks between a Sudanese government delegation and one representing the Torit group, led by Colonel Garang, both of which had agreed to resume the Abuja talks, which had been adjourned in July 1992. The Nasir faction, led by Riek Machar, met with other rebel groups in Nairobi, in an effort to unite them before the anticipated dry season offensive was launched by the government. The Nasir group and the Forces of Unity leaderships withdrew for further consultation to Kongor, where both were ambushed. This led to in-fighting and the death of several people including Joseph Oduhu, a veteran southern politician and accepted author of the original SPLA manifesto. At about this time large numbers of Sudanese refugees were flooding into Uganda, due to raids by government troops and the SPLA on each others' refugee camps There were also signs of the famine returning, and outbreaks of disease in some camps.

On 17 March Garang unilaterally declared a ceasefire. Previously the Transitional National Assembly had stated that it was trying to unite the SPLA, and was committed to peace. On the 19th the government declared its own ceasefire, and then the Nasir group did likewise. Garang then called for the establishment of 'safety zones' in the south and the Nuba Mountain area – where famine was reappearing – to enable UN relief supplies to be delivered. However on the 31st there was a clash at Kongor between the Torit group and the Forces of Unity faction, the latter accusing the former of killing displaced people and war victims, and of stealing UN relief supplies. The personnel of the UN's Operation Lifeline Sudan had already been withdrawn.

The SPLA-United

On 5 April 1993 the SPLA-United was formed by Riek Machar, consisting of the Nasir group, the Forces of Unity and the Bol faction, the latter led by Carabino Kuany Bol. The stated belief of the new group was that there could be no military solution to the conflict, and it asserted its commitment to a comprehensive peace settlement. Meanwhile Sadik Mahdi, the former premier, was arrested yet again after criticising the government in a speech.

The peace talks at Abuja between the Sudanese government and the Torit group came to nothing, but during a meeting held on 7–21 May in Nairobi the delegations from the Sudanese government and SPLA-United, both accepted the principle of a unified federal state. However there were differences over the implementation of Sharia law in the south, and other constitutional matters. On the 28th the Torit faction and SPLA-United signed a ceasefire agreement whereby they would withdraw their forces from the Ayod, Kongor, Wau and Yei landing strips by 5th June in order to allow emergency humanitarian aid to be delivered to the south.

On 5 August 1993 the government launched a major offensive against Colonel Garang's Torit group. Bomber aircraft were used to sever rebel supply routes and significant losses were inflicted. The offensive also led to the displacement of over 100 000 people from the southern border towns, most fleeing into Uganda and some into Zaire. When the inconclusive fighting died down at the end of the month, it was conceded that the Torit group still retained considerable firepower. By this time the UN aid agencies were again warning of the likelihood a dire famine.

Sudan: sponsoring international terrorism

On 19 August 1993 the US government placed Sudan on the list of states sponsoring international terrorism. The Sudanese government protested, accusing the USA of targeting Sudan because of its Islamic orientation, but as it had sided with Iraq during the Gulf War and was also friendly with Iran, it was already a pariah in American eyes. There were allegations in the US media of Sudanese involvement in the bombing of the World Trade Center in New York, and several of those indicted in connection with the incident were Sudanese nationals. Sudan, which was the seventh state to be put on the list (joining Iran, Iraq, Syria, Libya, Cuba and North Korea), immediately became ineligible for the receipt of all but humanitarian aid. For some time Egypt had been accusing Sudan of fomenting Islamic fundamentalism.

The US government stated that its decision to put Sudan on the list had been taken after an eight-month FBI investigation of Sudanese activities, which had concluded that Sudan's fundamentalist government had consistently provided sanctuary, safe passage and military training for at least five groups involved in international terrorism. Sudanese nationals had been arrested in the USA and charged with conspiring to foment urban terrorism in US territory. On 16 September former President Jimmy Carter declared that the decision had been motivated by American hostility towards Islam, for which he was praised by General Bashir.

Civilian government

On 19 October 1993 General Bashir announced a package of political reforms, preparatory to holding fresh presidential and general elections in 1994 and 1995 respectively. The following day the ruling Revolutionary Command Council was dissolved and Bashir became president and head of a new civilian government. Most of the former RCC ministers were to remain in their posts as civilian ministers for the time being. On the 29th the nationwide curfew, in force since June 1989, was lifted, Bashir announcing that Sudan had 'become safe'. However a rash of civil violence followed, the worst since 1989, mainly due to fuel shortages. There were rowdy disturbances in Khartoum, Omdurman and other cities. The government blamed the shortages on foreign oil companies that had not honoured their contracts, and on OPEC for withholding its oil until the anticipated price increases came into effect.

In November Bashir promised that elected provincial councils would be in place by June 1994, and that the elections would be free and open, hoping perhaps that a façade of democracy would ease his problems. His economic problems were immense, as he was operating in a void of poverty, crushed by international debt, ostracised by Western nations, saddled with Islamic laws and still had an unresolved civil war on his hands.

14
Negotiation and Hesitation

On 10 January 1994 John Garang of the SPLA Torit faction and Riek Machar of the SPLA-United met in Nairobi and agreed to participate in ceasefire talks with the foreign ministers of the seven member states of the Inter-Government Authority on Drought and Development (IGADD). The aim was to bring the SPLA factions into talks with the Sudanese government, but there was little progress. On the contrary, it was reported that President Bashir was reinforcing his army in the south with the intention of blocking off the SPLA supply routes from Kenya and Uganda. Indeed a major government offensive began early the following month, the beginning of the dry season, which seemed to be an all-out effort to defeat the SPLA once and for all.

Army columns, supported by bomber aircraft, advanced from the garrison towns of Wau, Torit and Juba with the intention of capturing Nimule and other SPLA-held towns on the Ugandan border. No details of the fighting were released to the media, but on 14 February the UN urgently appealed for extra aid to cover the needs of some 100 000 people displaced by the fighting. Refugee camps in Sudan became completely deserted as people fled into Uganda.

Another national redivision

Under the terms of a constitutional decree, President Bashir redivided the country into 26 states, rather than the nine proposed in his decree of February 1991, each state government to have executive and legislative powers. On 15 February 1994 he announced that the country was entering a unique constitutional phase. George Kongor Arop, a Dinka, was appointed as second vice president to put an end to the complaint that southerners were being excluded from senior government posts.

Following its decision in August 1993 to suspend Sudan's voting rights, the IMF (consisting of some 178 member countries) began proceedings to expel Sudan for its constant refusal to cooperate with the arrears strategy, it now being indebted to the tune of $1.7 billion. The economic situation of Sudan remained perilous.

In March, Madeleine Albright, the US permanent representative at the UN, visited Sudan and warned President Bashir that he would face continued international isolation unless he changed his attitude towards human rights and abandoned his support for international terrorism. She also privately told him that he would have to abandon Sharia law if he wanted American support. Her suggestions were rejected. This might have marked the commencement of the US decision to work for the removal of President Bashir from power and the start of a demonising campaign against him.

IGADD's continued its efforts to bring about a peace conference proved successful on 18 May, when the Sudanese government and the SPLA resumed their talks in Nairobi, two days after signing agreements to allow the unhindered passage of relief supplies to the south. The conference then adjourned, to meet again later to draft a declaration of principles. Vice President George Kongor Arop, who had opened the conference, stated that the period of autonomy between 1972 and 1983 had bred nothing but tribalism, which he contrasted with the government's new policy of power sharing. This was seen as an attempt to isolate the SPLA.

The arrest of Sadik Mahdi

On 20 June 1994 Sadik Mahdi, former premier and leader of the banned Umma Party, was arrested. It was alleged that he had been planning to carry out assassinations and destroy installations, and that he was in league with a foreign country, meaning Egypt. Several senior Umma Party members were also arrested.

The dispute over the Haliab Triangle still simmered on, with both Egypt and Sudan increasing their military presence. However the Sudanese government wanted to improve its relations with Egypt, hoping to use that country to help enhance its standing with the USA, and so the Haliab problem was given a low profile.

IGADD talks

The third round of the IGADD-sponsored talks in Nairobi took place between 18 and 28 July 1994 and resulted in the government declaring a unilateral ceasefire, to take effect on the 23rd. Both of the major SPLA factions initially rejected the possibility of a ceasefire, but on the 28th John Garang's Torit group ordered its forces to stop fighting – the SPLA-United remained active. On the 6th the UN World Food Programme warned that nearly four million displaced people in the region were facing starvation.

The fourth round of the IGADD talks took place in Nairobi on 5–9 September, but ended in deadlock over southern determination and the relationship between state and religion. Relations with Egypt continued to deteriorate over the Haliab problem, the Sudanese alleging that Egyptian troops in the triangle had attacked their Sudanese counterparts, kidnapping an officer. This was denied by Egypt. On 14 November President Bashir formally inaugurated the 96-member Supreme Council of Peace, which included some 40 southerners, saying it was an important step towards national reconciliation.

Terrorist stigma

The Khartoum government was embarrassed by the US accusation that it was aiding international terrorism, and wanted to be removed from the list of proscribed countries. There was no doubt that Khartoum was sheltering several terrorist leaders, one being the notorious Carlos the Jackal (Illich Ramirez Sanchez), who in the 1970s and 1980s had committed a string of high-profile terrorist exploits and eventually found sanctuary in Sudan. However Sudan was trying to improve its relations with France and Carlos was arrested in August 1994, but as there was no extradition treaty between Sudan and France he was drugged and 'kidnapped' by French intelligence agents and whisked off to France. There he stood trial, and to this day remains incarcerated in a French prison. This clandestine operation was masterminded by Hassan Turabi, and it is believed that a large sum of money changed hands.

Several other Western countries would no doubt have liked to have got their hands on Carlos – a prestige terrorist prize to grace their courts for a dramatic trial and enhance the reputation of their intelligence agencies – including the USA, which criticised France for dealing with a fundamentalist Islamic regime that was on the US list of proscribed states. A snide manifestation of envy perhaps, but France had long been engaged in rivalry with the USA for influence in northern and central Africa, involving themselves with newly emergent nations and their struggles, and had never really completely severed its contact with Sudan. It was a case of international one-upmanship. One journalist, Stephen Smith, writing for *Liberation*, went further and accused the French government of liaising with the Sudanese government and helping it with its struggle against the SPLA. He also alleged that the USA was providing the Sudanese government, via Uganda, with Stinger anti-aircraft missiles and intelligence about SPLA locations, gained by satellite pictures and other means. He further hinted that President Museveni of Uganda – who had publicly stated that an independent buffer state was needed against the spread of Islamic fundamentalism, meaning an independent south – thought that France should give him weaponry to pass on to the SPLA.

Bashir calls for a jihad

On 1 January 1995, in his Independence Day speech, President Bashir called for a jihad against unbelievers in Sudan, meaning the mainly Christian SPLA, promising to train one million people for the task (Sudan at this stage had a population of 26 million) and calling on citizens to join popular defence camps.

The following day the first stock exchange opened in Khartoum with 24 registered companies, it being hoped this would help attract foreign investment. There were some signs of the economy recovering due to the drastic reforms of the three-year Salvation Programme, but despite this there was an air of general economic gloom in the country.

Colonel Garang announced on 16 March 1995 that he had just launched an offensive in cooperation with the opposition NDA militias in the east, with whom he had formed the New Sudan Brigade. He stated that the new organisation intended to unite insurgent groups in order to oust the Bashir government, and called upon the Umma Party and the DUP to cooperate with it. This seemed to be an out-of-area venture by Garang.

The Southern Sudan Independence Movement

Wide divisions within the SPLA-United appeared at the beginning of 1995, and in March its former leader, Riek Machar, formed the congress of the Southern Sudan Independence Movement (SSIM) in London. The SPLA-United continued under the leadership of William Nyuon Bany and Carabino Kuany Bol. On 3 April Machar announced a cessation of hostilities by the SSIM, claiming he had been persuaded to do so by Jimmy Carter, but added that this was entirely dependent on the government controlling its armed forces, alleging that they had frequently violated previous ceasefires. In April, Russia, which had broken off relations with Sudan in 1971, resurrected its previous agreement to provide Sudan with technical equipment and train personnel.

On 27 March President Bashir announced a two-month ceasefire agreement with the SPLA to support the peace efforts made by Jimmy Carter, who had visited Sudan. This received a cautious welcome, and Colonel Garang asked IGADD to monitor it, alleging that the government had not always respected previous ceasefires. The government later announced a two-month extension of the ceasefire, and the SSIM followed suit.

Opposition conference

On 15 June 1995 a conference of Sudanese opposition parties took place in Asmara, the Eritrean capital, hosted by Eritrea's governing party, the People's Front for Democracy and Justice. It lasted a week and was attended by representatives of the Cairo-based NDA, the DUP, the Umma Party, SPLA elements, the Sudanese Communist Party, various trade union leaders and former military officers. It was accepted that religion should be separated from politics in Sudan, and in due course a referendum on secession from the republic should be held in the south. Although representatives of the SSIM had not been invited, the conference considered that it had successfully achieved a fusion between SPLA elements and the other main opposition parties. Bashir denounced the delegates as a gang of renegades.

Attempt to assassinate the Egyptian president

During a state visit to Ethiopia on 25 June 1995, President Mubarak of Egypt became the object of a failed assassination attempt when gunmen opened fire on the motorcade taking him from the airport to an OAU summit meeting. A mini gun battle erupted and Mubarak's car was hit several times. Two Ethiopian guards were killed and others were wounded. Mubarak said that it was unlikely that the Bashir government was involved, but pointed out that Bashir was giving sanctuary to Egyptian terrorists. Nor could he not rule out the involvement of the Sudanese fundamentalist NIF, which was widely believed to have an influence on President Bashir. Hassan Turabi, leader of the NIF, denied any connection, but the incident further blackened Sudan's reputation for involvement in international terrorism. Arrests were made by the Ethiopian police, and some suspects were killed in a later shootout. Suspicion eventually came to rest on Egyptian Islamic militants from the Gamaat

Islamiya and Al Jihad organisations, elements of which were allegedly sheltering in Khartoum.

On the 27th, Egyptian and Sudanese troops clashed briefly in the Haliab Triangle and two Sudanese soldiers were killed. The following day some 70 Sudanese police, who had been guarding frontier areas in the triangle, were ejected. In August President Bashir again reshuffled his cabinet to remove certain ministers who may have been involved in the attempt to kill President Mubarak in Ethiopia.

In 12–14 September there was a three-day riot in Khartoum, in which several people were killed and over 30 were injured. This was the most serious disturbance since Bashir came to power, enlivened by students protesting about the arrest of some of their number. The police reportedly used tear gas, tanks and live ammunition. Former President Numeiry, now a leading opposition figure in Cairo, described the demonstrations as a final warning to the Bashir government. The government blamed the banned Communist Party and foreign interference, meaning Eritrea and Ethiopia, its relations with those countries having deteriorated in recent months.

Ugandan threats

In April 1995 Uganda severed diplomatic relations with Sudan, alleging that the Sudanese government was supporting Ugandan rebels, a policy that seems to have continued until 29 October, when it was claimed by Radio Omdurman that a Ugandan army division, supported by tanks and artillery, had attacked Sudanese armed forces positioned in the Parajok and Magawe areas along the Ugandan border. The attack was described as a foreign conspiracy and a futile attempt to assist the SPLA, which was partially true.

At the beginning of September, Colonel Garang, leading his Torit group, the main body of the SPLA, launched a new offensive. On the 5th it claimed to have had seized Pagere, a village on the White Nile, and then other towns and villages in the vicinity. By the 9th it was advancing towards Juba, forcing government troops to retreat, destroying bridges and roads in their wake. The government claimed that some 7000 Ugandan and Tanzanian soldiers, supported by 30 Ugandan tanks, mortars and artillery, were cooperating with the SPLA in a major attack, but denied they were being successful.

President Bashir declared a general mobilisation on 7 November, calling on all the people to respond, and for the youth to enlist in the Jihad battalion to protect the faith and the country, meaning they should fight against the southern resistance groups, now aided by small detachments of foreign African troops. On 11 November SUNA claimed that government forces had inflicted a shattering defeat on the SPLA and its foreign allies. The governments of Uganda and Tanzania denied any involvement in the fighting, but the Sudanese government retained a blustering attitude. On the 24th the first vice president threatened that Sudanese troops would teach the foreign invaders a lesson they would not forget.

Meanwhile international aid agencies continued to lodge complaints against the Sudanese government. For example Gasper Biro, UN Special Envoy for Human Rights for the Sudan, reported an alarming increase in cases of abduction and rape, mainly by government armed forces, and that there had also been an increase in slavery, servitude and forced labour. He claimed to have evidence of children being abducted from the south and sold to wealthy families as servants or concubines, and that this traffic seemed to meet with the government's approval.

Ethiopian hostility

On 13 January 1996 the Sudanese foreign minister announced that he had complained to the UN Security Council about Ethiopian aggression in Sudanese territory. This coincided with the publication of a statement by the Sudanese GHQ condemning frequent Ethiopian acts of aggression in the south-eastern border area since 27 December 1995, and citing an incident that had taken place on 11 January 1996, when Ethiopian armed forces had attacked and occupied the Taya area, inside Sudan's borders. These accusations were denied by the Ethiopian government, which in turn accused Sudan of trying to divert international attention away from its involvement in the assassination attempt on the Egyptian president in Addis Ababa.

Newly independent Eritrea had severed diplomatic relations with Sudan in December 1994. Tension between the two countries increased when the opposition NDA held its congress in Asmara, and later President Issaisa Afewerki of Eritrea stated that he would support the Sudanese opposition without hesitation, and would provide military support, training and weapons.

On 30 January the UN Security Council unanimously adopted a resolution condemning Sudan's role in the assassination attempt against President Mubarak, and ordered Sudan immediately to hand over three Egyptian terrorists who were implicated in the incident and had sought sanctuary in Sudan. The following day all American diplomatic staff were withdrawn from Khartoum, supposedly because the USA lacked confidence in the Sudanese government's ability to protect them against extremist threats.

General elections

Non-party elections were held in Sudan from 6–17 March, the first presidential and legislative elections since the 1989 coup. President Bashir was returned to power with just over 75 per cent of the votes. Bashir claimed that the voter turnout had been over 70 per cent, while the opposition Voice of Sudan radio alleged there had been widespread vote-rigging. It had been announced on the 7th that a group of army officers had mounted a coup attempt at the start of the elections, organised by an (unnamed) officer who had served under President Numeiry.

Hassan Turabi, an elected deputy of the new 269-member Assembly, was unanimously elected its speaker on 1 April. The formation of a cabinet was postponed while the government waited to see whether the UN would impose sanctions on the country for failing to extradite the three wanted Egyptian terrorists to Ethiopia.

On 24 March a Sudan Airways airliner flying from Khartoum to Port Sudan and Jedda was hijacked by two men just after take-off. The pilot was forced to fly to Asmara in Eritrea, where the hijackers asked for political asylum. The Sudanese government requested their extradition, but was refused.

UN sanctions were imposed on Sudan on 26 April. The sanctions included a reduction in the size of diplomatic missions, limited movement abroad by members of the government and diplomatic staff, and the banning of international and regional conferences in the country, and would remain in force until the three wanted men were extradited. These measures, were in fact fairly mild, but they nonetheless angered the Sudanese.

Previously, on the 10th, a member of the Sudanese mission at the UN HQ in New York, Ahmad Yusuf, had been expelled for allegedly being engaged in terrorist and espionage activities in the USA. Ali Osman Taha, the Sudanese foreign minister, denied that the expulsion was linked to the 1993 bombing of the New York World Trade Center, when six people had been killed and more than 1000 injured.

A peace charter

On 10 April 1996 the government signed a peace charter with Riek Machar's SSIM and the SPLA-United, now led by Colonel Carabino

Kuanyin Bol. It seems that these two leaders had dropped their demand for southern independence, as the charter declared that the unity of Sudan would be preserved. It also provided for a referendum for south-erners to express their aspirations, by allowing them to retain the right of special legislation with regard to the implementation of Sharia law, although some conditions and terms were vaguely worded. Colonel Garang of the Torit group rejected the peace charter, criticising the government for its links with the SSIM and the SPLA-United. Some saw the peace charter as reinforcing Garang's claim to be the most influential SPLA representative, with whom the government must deal directly at some time.

President Bashir appointed a new government on 21 April. There were no opposition representatives, but it included the first woman minister in Sudanese history, Ihsan Abdullah al-Ghabshawi, who was given the health portfolio. He did not nominate a premier.

The NDA challenge

On 10 June 1996 the Cairo-based National Democratic Alliance called on the government of President Bashir to step down to avoid bloodshed, accusing Bashir of handing over power on behalf of the army to the National Islamic Front, a minority party that monopolised the govern-ment and was imposing its religious views on the country. It called for the government to hand over the reins of power to a transitional national government, which would convene a constitutional conference and organise democratic elections. On the 20th a further NDA statement threatened civil disobedience and political strikes if its demand was not met. Meanwhile the government introduced a series of austerity meas-ures in an effort to reduce government spending and curb inflation.

Osama Bin Laden

On 18 June 1996 it was confirmed that Osama Bin Laden, a Saudi Arabian businessman, alleged to have organised several terrorist incid-ents, and his group of 'Afghan Arabs' had left Sudan at the government's request. Bin Laden was reputed to have raised and armed large numbers of Arab volunteers for the Afghan jihad, and been living in Sudan with some of his former Afghani mujahedeen fighters since 1994, after being stripped of his Saudi citizenship for financing militant Islamic groups. Bin Laden was the leader of the Advisory and Reformation Committee, a group opposed to the Saudi royal family. In April, four men who had confessed to bombing a US military building in Riyadh, Saudi Arabia, in November 1995 claimed that Bin Laden had organised the attack. No details of Bin Laden's destination were given, but Arab media reported sightings of him in Afghanistan, Ethiopia and Somalia.

In August the UN Security Council voted to increase its sanctions against Sudan by imposing a ban on all international flights by Sudan Airways if it did not extradite the three Egyptians wanted for the attempted murder of President Mubarak. Little happened until 22 November, when the Security Council, hesitant about resisting American pressure, decided to postpone the ban for another 30 days, reportedly at the request of France and Russia. The UN secretary general sent an envoy to Khartoum to discuss the problem, but the Sudanese government still refused to extradite the three wanted men, saying it would prefer to resolve the matter directly with Egypt, this being taken to mean that it wanted to retain them as hostages available for exchange purposes.

September was notable for the so-called bread riots in Khartoum, in which protesters set fire to vehicles and attacked government buildings. The bread riots, which followed other riots on the 1st, in which two people had been killed, were prompted by the refusal of bakers to bake bread following the imposition of new government regulations on the price and size of a loaf. During the previous fortnight Khartoum had also suffered water shortages and power cuts.

In November it was revealed that the USA was intending to send military aid to Ethiopia, Eritrea and Uganda, three countries that supported the opposition NDA and had publicly called for the overthrow of Bashir. The USA seemed to be backing both sides, as it admitted it had sent military aid, worth some $20 million, to Sudan, claiming it was mainly surplus US military equipment and insisting it was non-lethal and defensive, such as radios, uniforms, boots and tents. On the 5th the Sudanese government suspended Red Cross operations with immediate effect, claiming that the organisation had deviated from neutrality and the basic principles of humanitarian work. It accused the Red Cross of transporting armed troops and ammunition on behalf of Colonel Garang of the Torit group. The year ended with the flight of Sadik Mahdi, the former premier and leader of the Umma Party, to Eritrea, claiming that Bashir was seeking to implicate him in armed resistance against the government.

Fighting in the south

In January 1997 there was a confused upsurge of fighting in the south, and Ethiopian officials reported an influx of Sudanese refugees to escape the war, famine, mass destruction of crops and livestock, and looting in the Blue Nile region. The UNHCR reported on the 11th that 4000 Sudanese refugees were being cared for in the Ethiopian town of Asosa, with another 15 000 waiting to cross the border.

The SPLA Torit group reportedly seized Kurmuk and Keissan just south of the Damazin hydroelectric power station, which supplied 80 per cent of Khartoum's power. An SPLA spokesman described this as the turning point in the 13-year war. President Bashir again called for a jihad against the enemies of Islam. These SPLA gains put the government troops under pressure, coinciding as they did with the threat posed by the Eritrean-based opposition group, the NDA, in the east to the road link between Khartoum and the Red Sea. The SPLA–NDA alliance had become more effective since the arrival of Sadik Mahdi in Eritrea. A government statement on the 11th admitted Eritrean troops were attacking Kurmuk and Keissan with artillery fire from across the border, and confirmed that Sudanese army reinforcements had been sent to Blue Nile Province.

On the 17th the army contradicted the SPLA's claim that it had captured Maban in Blue Nile Province, and also Garang's claim on the 21st that his forces had killed over 200 soldiers at Abu Shaneina, south of Samazin, and another 150 at Keili, further to the south. A confused and violent situation developed in the region, with foreign aid workers reporting that government forces were bombing and burning property. On the 26th Bashir stated that Sudanese military forces were attacking an SPLA base near the Ugandan border, causing President Yoweri Museveni to ask the OAU to declare that the fighting in the south was a colonial conflict, which would allow African countries to provide material support for the SPLA.

During January and February, while fighting continued in southern Sudan, several leading southern politicians and a number of alleged saboteurs were arrested in Khartoum, which prompted threats by the rebels that they would stir up trouble in the capital and take that city by force. There were offers of mediation from distinguished African and Arab leaders, but none were accepted. Eventually on 1 February, Abel Alier, the veteran southern political leader, proposed that a conference be held where the NIF, the NDA, the SPLA and other southern groups could discuss the south's future and analyse the possible choices, but there was no official response.

In mid March there was another burst of fighting in the south. Garang claimed to have seized the government-held towns of Kaya and Gumuli on the Ugandan border, and to be advancing on Yei. Reports from both sides spoke of exchanges of artillery fire across the frontier, and both made extravagant claims about casualities inflicted and prisoners taken. On the 14th Garang claimed to have captured Yei, and two days later Bashir claimed to have taken the garrison town of Chali, near the Ethiopian border, which was said to be held not only by Garang's SPLA, but also by detachments of the newly formed NDA militia, which were preparing to enter the fray and thrust northwards towards Khartoum. On the 25th Garang claimed that his guerrillas had gained control of the entire southern border, expelling government forces from White Nile and Equatoria Provinces, and announced the commencement of an NDA offensive in the east.

Fighting in the east

A statement issued in Asmara on 1 April 1997 indicated that the NDA militia had taken Akik on the Red Sea and was advancing northwards to Port Sudan. On the 4th it was claimed that Garang's armed forces had captured a strategic crossroads west of Juba, in the process destroying the 1000-strong force of government troops sent to counter them, and were now advancing towards Juba. Contrary claims were made by the government of great victories in counter-offensives in Blue Nile Province that had succeeded in preventing Ugandan troops from taking Juba. The Sudanese government lodged complaints against Eritrea and Uganda with the UN Security Council, but both countries denied any involvement.

There was heightened tension as SPLA factions and Eritrean and Ugandan detachments moved towards the Sudanese frontier region, it being thought that they were on the point of making a concerted push into the south to try to defeat the government armed forces in a decisive battle and bring about the collapse of the Khartoum government, but nothing happened. Various reasons were put forward for this, mostly political. The real reason was that the attacking forces were highly diverse, completely uncoordinated and logistically incapable of anything more than a skirmish. Meanwhile the government sat back and waited for the military opposition's unity of purpose to shatter, which it soon did. Hence both protagonists were waiting for the other to make the first move, but neither did.

New chapter of cooperation

On 21 April 1997 a peace agreement was signed between the six surviving factions that had broken away from the SPLA in 1991. The terms of the agreement included self-determination for the south, the suspension of Sharia law and amnesty for members of the six groups. The groups in question were named as the SSIM, the Bahr el-Ghazal group, the Bor group, the Equator Defence Force, the Independent Movement and the United Sudanese African Parties, of which active elements survived. Garang was dismissive about the agreement. On 10 May in Kenya, President Bashir had a meeting with President Yoweri Museveni of Uganda and they reportedly agreed to start a new chapter of cooperation. Museveni wanted to bring Garang into the discussions.

Despite the peace initiatives, throughout May the main rebel groups – Garang's Torit group and the NDA militias – continued to fight government forces in various parts of the country, the NDA not confining its efforts to the south. Garang claimed to have liberated Rumbek on the 1st, and on the 5th the NDA said it had destroyed a battalion of 600 men in the Red Sea state in eastern Sudan. The Sudanese defence minister refuted these claims, but on the 22nd it was admitted that fighting was in progress in Bahr el-Ghazal Province against the SPLA, and a few days later the loss of Rumbek was acknowledged.

In June tension rose between Sudan and Eritrea, causing Bashir (on the 7th) to order a 'maximum state of mobilisation' in the eastern region of Kassala and to close the border with Eritrea. A government spokesman accused the Eritrean government of plotting against Sudan following the reported arrest of a group of alleged Eritrean saboteurs inside Sudan.

NDA terrorism

It was reported on 11 June (*Al-Anaba*) that a Sudanese national, Adil Mahjub, who had hijacked a Sudan Airways aircraft en route to Egypt in 1994, had been arrested in Sudan, together with a number of others, and charged with planning to carry out a number of assassinations on the orders of the Eritrean president, Isayas Afewerki. Apparently Mahjub, after his trial in Egypt, had not been imprisoned as reported, but had been recruited by the Egyptians to help the Cairo-based NDA, now fighting the Sudanese government in the east. Radio Omdurman later reported that Mahjub had confessed to plotting to blow up the Sudanese National Assembly. Eritrean and Egyptian officials denied any involvement.

It was also reported that the Israeli defence minister had made a secret visit to the Eritrea–Sudan border, and it was suspected that Israel might be involved in a plan to invade Sudan as it favoured complete independence for the south. On the 15th Garang claimed that his faction had

captured Yirol, causing heavy casualties and thus preventing government reinforcements from reaching Juba.

On the 7th Eritrea protested to the UN Security Council that Sudan
was plotting to assassinate the Eritrean president. Details were given of
alleged terrorist activities carried out by the Sudanese, including the
assassination of Eritrean embassy staff in Khartoum. Bashir replied that
Eritrea was not seriously seeking to ease the tension or halt terrorist
activities carried out in Sudan.

On 9 July the Sudanese government accepted a declaration of peace
principles as the basis for discussion, although the IGADD peace initiative had been moribund since 1995. The principles included the separa-
tion of religion and state, and self-determination for the south. Garang
said he would not resume negotiations unless the principles were binding on the Sudanese government.

In August President Mandela of South Africa pushed himself forward
as a mediator. He wanted Garang to be brought into the negotiations and
offered to host direct peace talks between Bashir and Garang. In the
meantime Bashir appointed Riek Machar, leader of the SSIM, as chairman of the newly established Southern States Co-ordination Council.
This upset Garang as he wanted to be the sole representative of the
south. On 4 September Lam Akol, leader of the SPLA-United and once
active in Upper Nile Province, declared a ceasefire and travelled to Khartoum, accompanied by the chief of the Shilluk tribe, who had acted as
his mediator. Bashir and Garang met in Nairobi on the 22nd and agreed
to commence talks aimed at ending the civil war in the south. Talks
between representatives of the Sudanese government and the SPLM
eventually began in Nairobi on 29 October, hosted by the seven-nation
IGADD and brokered by President Mandela.

Meanwhile, on the 10th, Garang claimed that he had captured the
garrison town of Belinia in South Kordofan Province, in which the NDA
militia was probably involved. On the 18th he boasted of inflicting a
devastating defeat on government troops near Torit, forestalling a government offensive. As was customary, the government denied these
claims, but later partially admitted to their accuracy.

The IGADD peace talks in Nairobi were adjourned on 11 November
without making any progress. Garang blamed this on the Khartoum
government as it would not accept his proposal that Sudan be divided
into a two-state (north and south) confederation. Bashir was willing to
grant autonomy to the south, but not full statehood. Blame was also put
on the USA, which on 4 November had imposed harsh economic sanctions on Sudan and again accused the government of supporting inter-

national terrorism and having an abysmal record on human rights. Delegates at the Nairobi conference were reported as saying that the USA was interested only in overthrowing Bashir's regime and had done everything possible to cause the talks to fail. On the 19th Bashir confirmed that this was his opinion too. In seeming confirmation that the US objective was to remove Bashir from power, on 10 December 1997 US Secretary of State Madeleine Albright held a meeting in Kampala with representatives of the opposition NDA and Garang's SPLA element.

15
Stalemate

On 11 January 1998 the Sudanese State Radio reported that over 1000 SPLA rebels had surrendered to government forces at Maryal Bai in Bahr el-Ghazal Province, and subsequent reports indicated that for the next few days they were surrendering at the rate of over a 100 a day. However this seeming government advantage was cast in doubt on the 29th when the SPLA launched a major attack on Wau, where fighting continued around the airport and railway station. On the 31st the SPLA claimed to have captured Aweil and gained control over the Aweil–Wau corridor, which the government denied. The SPLA attack had been led by Colonel Carabino Kuany Bol, who subsequently turned his coat and went over to the government side. An SPLA spokesman stated that Bol's defection had been a carefully orchestrated trap. At this point Garang seemed to be regaining influence over some of the SPLA dissident factions.

Better news for the Khartoum government was that its relations with Egypt were improving, and a trade and security conference had been held in Cairo on 12–13 January between the foreign ministers of the two countries. As a result, Nile river traffic between Sudan and Egypt had recommenced on the 14th after a break of four years.

During February fighting continued around Wau. On the 12th a government helicopter carrying the first vice president (Zubeir Mohammed Saleh) and a dozen other senior government officials, who were on a tour of the battle zones, crashed near Nasir and all on board were killed. A debate developed over whether the crash had been due to bad weather, or whether the helicopter had been shot down by ground fire.

In early March Bashir again reshuffled his government, bringing into his administration Lam Akol, a southerner and former close associate of Garang who had defected in September 1997. On the 24th Bashir dissolved the Supreme Council of Peace, transferring its functions to the

Southern States Co-ordination Council, chaired by another SPLA defector, Riek Machar, its task being to further the IGADD-sponsored peace talks.

The UN-coordinated Operation Life-Line Sudan resumed deliveries of food aid to Bahr el-Ghazal Province – the fighting around Wau had caused a flood of homeless refugees, some of whom were said to be dying of hunger. Arguments then arose over the severity of the anticipated famine.

The government's military expansion plans were making a shaky start, as illustrated on 7 April when a group of over 250 conscripts attempted to escape from their camp near Khartoum – more than 50 drowned while trying to cross the river.

IGADD-sponsored peace talks were held in Nairobi on 4 May between the government and the SPLM, the political branch of the SPLA. It was agreed that an internationally supervised referendum should be held on self-determination for the south.

The Ugandan authorities freed 42 of 114 Sudanese government soldiers who had been captured on 9 April 1997 during a combined Ugandan–SPLA stand-off operation on the southern Sudanese border. The release was described as a goodwill gesture. In return the Sudanese government freed only two Ugandan soldiers, but perhaps they were all it was holding.

A new constitution

The Sudanese Election Commission announced on 24 June 1998 that 96.7 per cent of the voters in the nationwide referendum held the previous month had approved the new draft constitution. President Bashir signed it on 30 June, the ninth anniversary of his coup. He called on opposition politicians in exile to return, promising them a share of power, political freedom and civil rights in a broadly based citizenship. The new constitution replaced all previous presidential decrees.

Fighting was reported in several areas in the south in June, and on the 3rd the SPLA captured Ulu, a garrison town in Blue Nile Province, close to the Ethiopian border and fairly close to the Khawr Adar oilfields. In the west, clashes between Arab and non-Arab communities in West Darfur were followed by an exodus of some 10 000 refugees into adjacent Chad. In South Kordofan Province on the 9th, two Sudanese employees of the World Food Programme were killed and four others wounded when a UN aid convoy was attacked. The government blamed the SPLA.

A ceasefire

The SPLA declared a unilateral and unconditional three-month ceasefire in Bahr el-Ghazal Province, claiming that it was a humanitarian truce in response to the famine conditions. In return the government stated that it would observe a reciprocal ceasefire, but for one month only.

In July 1998 there was fighting in the newly formed state of Wadah (adjacent to Bahr el-Ghazal and the town of Bentiu) between two government-sponsored factions: the South Sudan Defence Force and the South Sudan United Movement. One source (*Al-Anbaa*) stated that some 70 000 civilians had been displaced in these clashes and a huge number of soldiers and civilians had been killed. In Khartoum there was a brief spate of bomb explosions that caused considerable damage, but no lives were lost. Although more than 300 people were arrested, the culprits were not detected.

The rains came at the end of July, breaking two years of drought in Bahr el-Ghazal Province and causing aid agencies to modify their famine predictions. In mid July the World Food Programme had estimated that some 2.6 million people in the south were in need of food assistance. On 3 August the government declared a unilateral ceasefire throughout the south to enable non-governmental relief agencies to issue supplies to people in the combat zones.

Cruise missiles strike Khartoum

On 7 August 1998 coordinated terrorist bomb attacks were carried out against the US embassies in Nairobi (Kenya) and Dar es Salaam (Tanzania). At least 253 people were killed in Nairobi, including 12 US citizens, and over 5000 others were injured. Ten people were killed in Dar es Salaam, none of whom were US citizens, and over 75 were injured. Considerable damage was caused to both embassies and adjacent buildings. Several national and international intelligence agents, particularly Americans, descended on the sites. It was soon announced that the Nairobi bombing was probably the work of two Saudi Arabians from the Martyr Khaled al-Said battalion, and that the suspected perpetrator of the Tanzanian one was an Egyptian from the Martyr Abdullah Azzam battalion. The mastermind was named as Osama Bin Laden, previously living in Khartoum but now believed to be based in Afghanistan. Several arrests were made.

American vengeance came on the 20th, when over 75 US cruise missiles were launched from US warships and a submarine, aimed at Bin

Laden's base camp in Afghanistan and the Shifta Pharmaceutical Indus-
tries plant just north-east of Khartoum. The US authorities claimed that
the latter was financed by Bin Laden and was manufacturing precursor
chemicals for VX nerve gas. The plant was very badly damaged and ten
people were injured. The Sudanese interior minister, General Abdul Rahman Hussein, denied that the plant was involved in the production of
chemical weapons, insisting that it only manufactured medical drugs.
The attack on the Shifta plant provoked deep anger in Khartoum, and
mobs vandalised the empty US embassy. The British embassy was also
mobbed, and Britain hastily withdrew its diplomatic staff from the city.
President Bashir denounced President Clinton as a war criminal.

Shortly after the attack the Sudanese government invited the UN to
search the Shifta site, but the offer was refused. The USA's stated reason
for the attack was that it had secretly taken soil samples near the Shifta
site and discovered the presence of a chemical called EMPTA, and that
the factory building was suitable for synthesising VX nerve gas. Several
experts doubted this for technical reasons, and Sudan, although on the
US list of nations aiding international terrorism, had not previously been
thought to have the capability of manufacturing the means of chemical
warfare.

To carry this saga through, a Sudanese government committee invest-
igated the factory and reported on 28 December that there was no
substance to the US claim that it had manufactured nerve gas, or any
other ingredient of chemical weapons. Later, another report was commissioned by the owner of the Khartoum factory, Salih Idris, with a view
to taking legal action against the US government. This investigation was
carried out by a New York-based firm and its findings were released on 5
February 1999. According to the report, the factory contained no chem-
ical-weapon manufacturing capacity, the factory had never belonged to
Osama Bin Laden, and Salih Idris had no links with Bin Laden or the
Iraqi government. Later, on 5 May, the US Treasury Department released
over $24 million that had been frozen in Idris's US bank accounts. A tacit
and grudging admission of his innocence, but no more.

Conscription problems

During October 1998 the Sudanese defence minister, General Ibrahim
Suleiman, appealed to the National Assembly for funds to recruit 50 000
volunteers to fight against the SPLA, the first batch of which, some 7000
men, had just been inducted for training. A plan was discussed for some
100 000 volunteers to be solicited from the civil service and private

business, and the minister of culture and information announced he would lead a brigade of them from his own department. However enthusiasm soon ebbed after this initial flush of jingoism.

Fighting broke out mid October in Eastern Equatoria over the 100-mile Torit to Juba road – the government claimed a great victory, and the SPLA admitted to a strategic withdrawal. It was claimed that a number of Chadian troops were fighting alongside SPLA factions in the Torit–Juba corridor, as were small detachments of Ethiopian and Eritrean troops, who were hostile towards each other at this moment and remained as separate groups near the southern border. The amount of devastation and number of casualties were such that the Red Cross appealed to the UN to intervene to avoid disaster.

Restoration of the multiparty system

The National Assembly voted on 23 November 1998 to reintroduce the multiparty system, thus formally ending the ban on political parties, trade unions and other groups. The new law would come into effect on 1 January 1999. On 21 December, Speaker Hassan Turabi resigned, but the National Assembly refused to accept his resignation, and he remained in office. The National Islamic Front had just formed a new 30-member leadership body, of which President Bashir was to be chairman and Turabi the secretary general. Turabi was meeting some opposition within the NIF over his policies, and his position as speaker gave him added prestige in the country.

Within the SPLA rivalry remained rampant, and at times was bitter. The previous month there had been an attack on Colonel Garang and his family in Nairobi, where several of the SPLA leaders and their families lived for safety. The culprits were identified as supporters of the SPLM, now headed by Colonel Carabino Kuany Bol. Garang escaped unhurt, and several arrests were made by the Kenyan authorities.

Political parties register

During January 1999, would-be political parties began to register under the new conditions, and on the 3rd the voting age was reduced from 18 to 17. The parties registering included the ruling National Islamic Front, the Muslim Brotherhood, the Sudanese National Party and the United Democratic Salvation Front, led by Riek Machar. Osman Mirghani of the former DUP stated he would not register his party yet as the process was too restrictive. Women were required to wear Islamic clothing and a head scarf.

In the south the government announced a further three-month extension to the ceasefire in Bahr el-Ghazal Province, but on the 28th, in a two-day battle at Buny in the Blue Nile region, it claimed to have killed over 150 SPLA personnel.

Bashir's statement

On 20 February 1999 President Bashir, speaking on Qatari State TV, said that his government would try to preserve the unity of the mainly Muslin north and the Christian and animist south, but that southern secession was better than continual civil war. Garang was no longer fighting for a united Sudan, and wide divisions of opinion were developing over where the south should begin and where it should end, influenced by the location of mineral and agricultural resources.

Asked by the UN to investigate evidence of the continued existence of slavery in Sudan, in March the government denied allegations that it was institutionalised in the country, but conceded that tribal kidnappings were a common feature of the civil war. On 1 March the Sudanese dinar replaced the pound as the official currency, its exchange rate being initially quoted at 196 dinars to US dollar.

A hostage situation

On 18 February 1999 two Swiss and three Sudanese working for the Red Cross were captured by the SPLA. Red Cross officials appealed to Garang to release them, but for a while nothing happened. The two Swiss were eventually released on 12 March, but there was no news of the Sudanese captives until 3 April, when it was reported that they been murdered, but that the SPLA would not release the bodies. On 19 April the Sudanese government stated that it was postponing the peace talks with the SPLA – due to take place in Nairobi on the 20th – until the matter was resolved. The previous week the government had offered a ceasefire throughout the south, subject to a reciprocal move by the SPLA, but the SPLA would only agree to extend the current ceasefire in Bahr el-Ghazal Province.

Numeiry returns

On 22 May 1999 former President Numeiry returned to Khartoum after 14 years' exile in Egypt. Opposition parties immediately called for his prosecution in connection with alleged massacres, and for the murder of the imam of the Ansar sect. Numeiry had already registered his political party, now called the Alliance of People's Working Forces, and he form- · ally met Bashir on the day of his return to Sudan. How Numeiry will fare in to the top leadership struggle in Khartoum remains to be seen – he had openly and loudly voiced his ambitions in this respect during his exile in Cairo.

The SPLA rejects a ceasefire

On 5 August 1999 President Bashir declared a two-month ceasefire throughout the areas of operation in the south, but this was instantly rejected by the SPLA, an official spokesman saying that the SPLA did not want a comprehensive ceasefire, only a selective humanitarian one, pointing out that the SPLA was already observing humanitarian cease-fires in Bahr el-Ghazal Province and parts of Upper Nile Province to facilitate the delivery of aid by international agencies. This flat refusal indicated that the general stalemate in the Sudanese civil war in the south was solidifying.

16
At the Crossroads

Sudan is stuck at a cross-road, unable to decided which of three main routes to take. In fact it has been bogged down there for some considerable time. Briefly, it can strive for a united republic in the full sense of that term, or it can grant the south federal status, or it can allow the south to become completely independent. Each of these three options has advantages for the Khartoum government, and each has its drawbacks, hence the hesitation. Compromise will only prolong the stalemate.

The first course would be the ideal solution for Sudan – the fusion of north and south – and President Bashir has gone some way towards this by creating local self-governing provinces in the hope of erasing the rigid north–south demographic division. First, however, the civil war in the south must be settled amicably, and southerners encouraged to think and work in national terms. Efforts should be made to exchange tribal attitudes and nepotism for broader democratic ideals. Much easier said than done, as true Western-style liberal democrats must also accept the principle of basic justice, the binding nature of multiparty election results, and individual freedoms. The keys to this will be education, economic development, trade, a steadily rising standard of living and a deep northern interest in the welfare of southerners.

The majority of southern politicians, aware that they are surrounded by predator states, could probably be persuaded to back this option, but for one major factor – Sharia law, which the Khartoum government wants to extend to the south. Sharia law does not cater for religious tolerance. President Bashir has been trying to dress the September Laws in more acceptable garb as his position is not strong enough to allow him to rule that they need not apply in the south. Neither he nor any other Sudanese Muslim leader wants to be associated with the abolition of Sharia law, or the secularisation of the country. This remains the major barrier to Sudanese unity. The pay and trappings of office are attractive to all politicians, compared with the hard, frugal life in the bush, and many southerners have been tempted by government offers to defect.

With heavy international debt and no real income, Sudan is virtually existing on foreign charity, and for some years successive governments have been overburdened by the civil war in the south, in which probably over 1.5 million people have perished (no one knows exactly how many) and which probably costs over a million dollars a day to run. The civil war continues in the south, where towns are dominated by troops and the countryside is at the mercy of local government militias (which occasionally change loyalties) tussling with resistance fighters, both ravaging the territory.

The civil war cannot be won by military means; the government realises this but will not admit the fact. A brief comparison of the respective armed forces shows the futility of hoping for a decisive military victory. The Sudanese army is comparatively small, numbering only about 94 000 (out of a population of about 31 million), of which some 20 000 are conscripts (IISS figures). This small force has to defend over one million square miles of territory, and cope with the war in the south, which embraces just over 250 000 square miles of forest and jungle-type terrain. The troops are inadequately armed and equipped for such a task.

The government forces face several opposition groups, the largest being the SPLA, which probably has up to 25 000 guerrilla fighters, armed with infantry weapons. The other main groups are the Sudan Alliance Forces, with over 500 men based along the Eritrean border; the Beja Congress Force, also with over 500 men and operating in the Eritrean border region; and the New Sudan Brigade, with a probable 400 armed men based in the Ethiopian frontier area. All are well versed in guerrilla warfare.

The Sudanese armed forces have about 50 combat aircraft, mostly of Soviet origin, and up to 50 helicopters, barely enough for reconnaissance and supply purposes and garrison duties. Their offensive capabilities are limited to bombing raids and the occasional short-term punitive operation. Barely a holding capability. The government cannot afford to modernise and increase its armed forces, and so it is finding it difficult just to stand still. As regards internal security, which essentially means the security of Khartoum, the government has 15 000-strong paramilitary force, backed by the National Islamic Front militia reserve. The latter consists of about 85 000 men and could be deployed in lightly armed battalions, each of about 1000 men: a rather fragile national military framework, within which new-fangled conscription is not working well.

Commonsense demands that the civil war be terminated immediately, but Sudanese national pride stands in the way, as does that of the SPLA and other resistance movements. And even if the Khartoum government could obtain sufficient funds to create a massive modern army with supporting modern aircraft, it would be unlikely to triumph over the opposition guerrilla forces in the vast areas of closed jungle in the south. It would simply be another Vietnam, with the southern forces attracting arms and sustenance from a wide variety of sources bent on troublemaking. The central government will only make peace on its own terms, and prolonged negotiations have simply moved the goal posts. Bashir remains determined to pursue the war, despite occasional remarks by rulers in their frustrated war weariness. Much of the mineral and agricultural wealth of Sudan is in the south, and its loss would be a huge economic blow to the poverty-stricken Khartoum government.

In addition the White Nile, its major tributaries and the Blue Nile flow through the south, which gives the government some international prestige and potential power that it would be loath to lose, especially in its negotiations with Egypt over the Nile waters, which are required for Sudan's economic development. Water is becoming one of the most vital catalysts for conflict in parts of the Middle East and Arab North Africa, and may become a greater catalyst than the disputed possession of land. The civil war is hampering the completion of the Jonglei Canal project, which will facilitate communications between north and south. It is also handicapping oil exploration and development in the south.

In late August 1999 it was announced that the first domestically produced oil had passed through the major (mostly underground) oil pipeline from the south to the refinery near Port Sudan. This is good news, and the new oil wealth may revitalise Sudan. The other good news for the government is that the SPLA seems unable to prevent the flow of oil – although the government has announced that oil revenues will be used to develop the south, few believe this, feeling that it will be spent on modern arms to allow the military to pursue the civil war with greater vigour and capability.

If its mineral and agricultural resources could be developed unhindered, a united Sudan could soon become a creditor nation, and as it has a foot in both the Arab north and black Africa there is no reason why it should not become an important market place astride two major trade routes. Sudan's dream of becoming Africa's granary could be realised. It is in Sudan's interest to remain united, and to pursue the civil war for prestige purposes alone would be foolish.

Autonomy or federalism

The second alternative is for the Khartoum government to grant autonomy to the south. The case against this is that it has been tried before and failed miserably. The south had autonomy between 1972 and 1983, during which it fell into chaos, being neglected by the Khartoum government and mismanaged by southern politicans. The government seems to be prepared to grant autonomy to the south on much the same lines as before, but this time it is the southerners who are objecting, feeling that the north would reap all the economic advantages and they would be left with only limited local administrative responsibility. The major decisions would still be made in Khartoum, and the north would be developed and take the major share of economic benefits and profits, while the south would again be neglected. Southerners had hoped that the oil refinery would be sited in the south rather than Kosti, as most of the oil wells are in the south, but boundary goalposts are being moved to the disadvantage of southerners.

Federalism is a further step towards independence, involving the transfer of more power. Many southerners would probably accept federalism as it would give them some control over their mineral and agricultural resources, and the associated profits. Defence could be a joint responsibility, and the southern traditions and character could be retained. However the Khartoum leadership is strongly against federalism, which it sees as a first step towards southern independence.

Southern independence

For some time the SPLA has been fighting for complete independence, but the main question is whether this would be viable. The south could have a common defence agreement with Sudan, which would take care of predator adjacent nations, but it would be landlocked and its export trade would depend on arrangements with adjacent states in respect of embargoes and blockades, but economically it could survive. The main drawback is that the south, now with a probable population of up to six-million spread over an area of some 250 000 square miles, is far from being united internally, as SPLA splits are compounding age-old tribal differences. One sees a vision of disunity, of the development of civil wars within civil wars, inflicting further damage on already devastated territory. An independent south would have difficulty attracting foreign investment as law and order are basic requirements for foreign investors, who steer clear of hostage-taking and guerrilla blackmail. The Jonglei Canal and oil exploration and exploitation ventures provide discouraging examples. The OAU would like to encourage such ventures, but would not be strong or influential enough to protect them.

Sudanese leadership problem

President Bashir, head of an Islamic fundamentalist military dictatorship, seems to be preparing his country for at least some form of democratic government. It may turn out to be an Islamic fundamentalist form of democracy, which would not commend itself to Western governments, who favour religious tolerance and multiparty political freedom. Sudan needs Western help to prosper. Bashir has become chairman of the National Islamic Front, and probably hopes to retain his leadership through possession of this post. But there are other Sudanese leaders who covet the role. One is Sadik Mahdi, the *de facto* leader of the Ansar sect; another is the recently returned former President Numeiry. This leads one to fear that the history of Sudan since independence may be about to repeat itself; that is, a succession of coups, periods of military dictatorship, and brief intervals of ineffective multiparty democracy.

Sudan remains on the US list of states assisting international terrorism, and would do well to cleanse its stables and eschew terrorism of any sort. In recent years Sudan has had alternating good and bad relations with neighbouring states, including Egypt, Libya, Ethiopia and Eritrea and Uganda, caused in the main by changes of regime and Sudan's sheltering of the refugees and opposition groups of these regimes. These states have alternately helped or hindered Sudan by supporting or attacking the SPLA. This vicious circle of harbouring or helping each other's political opponants and terrorists should be broken.

As a last note – if Sudan is to take its place in the new millennium amongst the world's mature and civilised nations it should put its house in order, clean up its act and pay some attention to its image. For example it should not only abandon all association with terrorists, international and otherwise, but also do something about the smear of slavery that is pinned on it, as revealed periodically, despite censorship, by the Western investigative press. According to *The Sunday Times*, government-supported militias are roaming the south, seizing women and children to become slaves. In an effort to counter slavery one

British humanitarian agency has even been buying slaves, mainly women and children, by the hundred in the slave markets of south-west Sudan and then freeing them, despite criticism by other agencies that this tends to lead to the seizure of even more people for financial gain.

Bibliography

Asher, Michael (1984) *By Camel through Sudan* (Harlow: Longman).

Collins, Robert (1963) *Shadow in the Grass: Britain in Southern Sudan 1918–56* (London: Yale University Press).

Daly, M. W. (1983) *Sudan* (Oxford: Clio Press).

Deng, Francis Mading (1982) *The Recollections of Baba Namir* (London: Ithaca Press).

Deng, Francis Mading (1995) *War of Vision* (Washington, DC: The Brookings Institution).

Gordon, Charles (1984) *Sudan at the Crossroads* (Wisbech: Menas Press).

Mahmoud, Fatima Babiker (1984) *The Sudanese Bourgoisie* (London: Zed Press).

Malwal, Bona (1981) *People and Power in Sudan* (London: Ithaca Press).

Mansour, Khalid (1984) *Nimairi and the Revolution of Dismay* (London: Routledge).

Prendergast, John (1997) *Crisis Response* (London: Pluto Press).

Ryle, John (1982) *Warriors of the White Nile* (London: Time-Life Books).

Thomas, Graham F. (1990) *Sudan: 1950–85: Death of a Dream* (London: Darf Publishers).

Thomas, Graham F. (1995) *Sudan: Conflict and Minorities* (London: Minorities Rights Group).

Index

Note: The following are not shown as they appear throughout the text – Africa(n)(s), ANAF, Anya-Nya, Khartoum, Sudan(ese).